RENEWALS: 691-4574

DATE DUE

MAY 10			
GAYLORD			PRINTED IN U.S.A.

HISTORY
AND
THEORY
AFTER THE FALL

HISTORY
AND
THEORY
AFTER THE FALL

An Essay on
Interpretation

FRED WEINSTEIN

The University of Chicago Press
Chicago and London

Fred Weinstein, professor and department chair in history at the
State University of New York at Stony Brook, is the author of
The Dynamics of Nazism and, with Gerald M. Platt, *The Wish to Be
Free* and *Psychoanalytic Sociology*.

The University of Chicago Press, Chicago 60637
The University of Chicago Press, Ltd., London
© 1990 by The University of Chicago
All rights reserved. Published 1990
. Printed in the United States of America

99 98 97 96 95 94 93 92 91 90   54321

Library of Congress Cataloging-in-Publication Data
Weinstein, Fred, 1931–
History and theory after the fall : an essay on interpretation /
Fred Weinstein.
p.   cm.
ISBN 0–226–88606–9 (alk. paper)
1. History——Philosophy. 2. Relativity 3. Historiography.
I. Title.
D16.9.W39   1990
901—dc20   89–20486
                                                  CIP

⊗ The paper used in this publication meets
the minimum requirements of the American National
Standard for Information Sciences—Permanence of
Paper for Printed Library Materials, ANSI Z39.48–1984.

To my family

Contents

Preface

The fate of history and theory has recently been the subject of intense discussion, not only in a large number of books, academic journals, and conferences, but, surprisingly, considering the abstract and even arcane content of the discussion, in journals of popular opinion. There, the argument prominently but unexpectedly featured for the instruction of a wider audience is that one historical interpretation of events is as good as another, that there is no way to discriminate better from worse interpretations by reference to evidence, and even that writers of fiction are better able to write interpretive histories than historians. As for social theory or the social sciences more broadly, there occurs a related claim that, in its most radical form, holds that it is pointless to continue to invest resources in these disciplines because they cannot solve the problems that they were intended to solve. A number of well-placed social scientists had already concluded on their own that there was trouble ahead because of the inability to account for the contradictory sources and effects of multiple interests and multiple perspectives. They did not need this other philosophical-linguistic critique, but they got it anyway.

All this may appear to be a familiar kind of struggle over turf, and it is in a way. But it is much more than that, too, principally because of the issues encompassed by the struggle, whose language will be used to describe and explain events, whose ideological standpoint or frame of reference will prevail, and who can make the best claim to the attention and respect of the audience. There is also an important political question about the effects of such a struggle. One answer to this question is that the relativism of the position described above is the true state of affairs, that people can learn to cope with the indefinite conflict that this state implies, and that the result will be the further democratization of culture. The opposed answer is that the relativism is not the true state of affairs and that, if it were, people would not be able to cope with conflict indefinitely. Rather, they would be impelled at some point to seek out authoritative leadership to bring under control a situation they perceive as chaotic. It is therefore important to persist in the acquisition of knowledge in a traditional sense, and there are good reasons for doing so.

I have tried in this book to address these complicated issues in a preliminary way, in terms of why history is so difficult to write in an interpretive sense and what happened in history to make it so. In fantasy, such an effort is of course greeted by the intended audience with nary a sign of tension or conflict. In practice, any articulated point of view will be too readily perceived by this heterogeneous audience not merely as mistaken but as transgressing. Fortunately, however, the practical outcome of such perception is still rather remote. More immediate and gratifying is the opportunity afforded by a preface to acknowledge the generous, thoughtful, and timely assistance of friends and colleagues, including especially Gerald M. Platt, who, unstinting as always, contributed greatly to the completion of this book, as well as Naomi Rosenthal and William R. Taylor, who also read the book and made many valuable suggestions from their respective (sociological and historical) points of view. I must also underscore here the advice, encouragement, and instruction offered over a long period of time by Mel Albin, Werner Angress, Karl Bottigheimer, David Burner, Dominick Cavallo, Ruth Cowan, Elizabeth Garber, Richard Kuisel, Ned Landsman, Herman Lebovics, Lawrence Levine, Gary Marker, Bruce Mazlish, Joel Rosenthal, Bernard Semmel, Charles Strozier, and John A. Williams.

Versions of portions of this book have appeared elsewhere. Material in the introduction and chapters 1 and 2 appeared originally in "The Problem of Subjectivity in History," in *History and Psychology,* ed. William McKinley Runyan (copyright © 1988 by Oxford University Press, Inc.); the material is used by arrangement with the publisher. Chapter 3 first appeared as "Transitional Objects, Transitional Phenomena, Transitional Space: A Commentary on Limits," in *Klio und Psyche,* ed. Thoms Kornbichler (in press), and is reprinted with friendly permission from Centaurus-Verlagsgesellschaft mbH, D-7801 Pfaffenweiler. Material in chapter 4 appeared earlier in "The Sociological Implications of Charismatic Leadership" (*Psychohistory Review,* vol. 10, no. 2 [1981]) and is reprinted with permission.

Introduction

The claim that historical interpretations are fictions, inventions, that they are always ideologically contaminated, intended to serve present needs, closure rather than truth, has become routine. On this view, the constructs that historians employ to interpret the significance of events are themselves no more than subjectively interested ways of talking about the social world, which is too heterogeneous, fragmented, and discontinuous to be reduced to such constructs. Hence, the aptness of Hayden White's conclusion (which appeared significantly in a journal of popular opinion) that "it is possible to tell several different stories about the past and there is no way, finally, to check them against the fact of the matter. The criterion for evaluating them is moral or poetic [sic]."[1]

According to White, this conclusion is suggested by narrative theory, the ways in which scholarly intentions are betrayed by the structure of language, but it is also suggested in a more concrete way precisely by the heterogeneity of populations, the variety that turns up on all sides of a historically significant struggle and that cannot be accounted for in terms of accident or coincidence, whether it is the English Civil War, the American or French revolutions, the Nazi or Bolshevik movements, or any other such complex event. It is this heterogeneity of populations that makes it so difficult for social scientists, historians, psychoanalysts, philosophers, and other interpreters of human experience to find a way of assessing interpretively people's motives, intentions, or reasons. If especially the forms of social and psychological theory on which interpretation rests could allow for the reasonably precise assessment of people's intentions in either a social or a dynamic sense (on the assumption, e.g., that mental outlook can be inferred from class or from any similar conception of social location or accounted for in such terms as internalized morality or national character), there would not be this interpretive problem. As it is, interpretive standpoints proliferate from all sources in the attempt to encompass the stubbornly heterogeneous data, with no basis yet for asserting the primacy of any one of them, except on the grounds suggested by White.

The empirical consequences of people's actions, as they have taken sides in unexpected ways in a succession of struggles over time, are sufficient to lend credence to White's claim that choosing one interpretation of why people behaved as they did over another is a matter of ideological preference or, as the writer and critic Cynthia Ozick also recently put it, of "whatever selection most favors your cultural thesis." [2] These consequences, which may be identified initially with the attempt to achieve religious tolerance on the basis of a tradition that emphasized salvation as a matter of private conscience rather than public authority and then, subsequently, with the obligation placed on people to participate in an ever-increasing variety of markets, have in fact proved too difficult for historians and theorists to account for. The reason is that the form of social change ("modernization") enhanced the everyday importance of a variety of social locations, institutional arrangements, and ideological perspectives, and not just in terms of class or family. People got involved in or were affected by struggles on successive institutional levels from a number of vantage points, with contradictory and heterogeneous results. These struggles, over expanding or contracting the social space within which people could act and over the extent of autonomous and inclusive practice in which people could engage, made life difficult for them at the time and for historians and social theorists afterward.

Writers and observers have been alert to the significance of these problems for a long time. Indeed, we could hardly do better on the crucial subject of heterogeneity than Robert Musil has already done in his celebrated novel *The Man Without Qualities*. Musil was not the first writer to turn his attention to this subject, but he was among the first to challenge the conventions of the traditional novel form because of it. In any event, his sense of what it implied for Western culture and history is so acute on two sides, dynamic and social, that we would do well simply to quote from his work: "It is always wrong to explain the phenomena of a country simply by the character of its inhabitants. For the inhabitant of a country has at least nine characters: a professional one, a class one, a geographical one, a sex one, a conscious, an unconscious and perhaps even too a private one; he combines them all in himself, but they dissolve him. . . . Hence every dweller on earth also has a tenth character, which is nothing more or less than the passive illusion of spaces unfulfilled."[3] The unhappy result of so many dynamic and social elements occurring in so many people is multiple and competing perspectives and multiple and discontinuous bases for action, certainly by the eighteenth century a matter of repeatedly expressed concern as writers deplored the sense of fragmentation and discord and anxiously pondered how social order could be held together. As Musil wrote for his own time,

> Nobody knew exactly what was on the way: nobody was able to say whether it was to be a new art, a New Man, a new morality or perhaps a reshuffling of society. So everyone made of it what he liked. . . . The Superman was adored, and the Subman was adored; health and the sun were worshipped; the delicacy of consumptive girls was worshipped; people were enthusiastic hero-worshippers and enthusiastic adherents of the social creed of the Man in the Street; one had faith and was skeptical, one was naturalistic and precious, robust and morbid. . . . Admittedly these were contradictions and very different battle-cries, but they all breathed the same breath of life.[4]

The problem of assessing subjectivity was also long ago perceived to be a significant one, particularly for historical interpretation. Indeed, Musil's contemporary, the noted American historian Carl Becker, had also by then presciently concluded that historians' interpretations and explanations were epistemologically suspect, putting the matter this way in his well-known presidential address to the American Historical Association in December 1931. Insofar as historians organize data without any larger interpretive purpose, their work might be factually accurate and interesting as narrative, but it could not be culturally relevant, could not, that is, serve interests or provide emotional consolations by establishing the significance of the past for people. Insofar as historians express a larger interpretive purpose, which they do by clarifying the subjective intentions, reasons, and motives of people, their work becomes culturally relevant but also suspect, as all interpretations of subjectivity seem to involve inferential leaps not warranted by evidence.

Thus, Becker explained to his colleagues that the history that "Mr. Everyman" imaginatively recreates for the sake of orienting himself "in his little world of endeavor" is inevitably "an engaging blend of fact and fancy, a mythical adaptation of that which actually happened. In part it will be true, in part false; as a whole perhaps neither true nor false, but only the most convenient form of error." Becker then went on to say that the history imaginatively recreated by historians is similar in character, itself "a convenient blend of truth and fancy." What is truthful is the archival work accurately reported; what is fanciful is the interpretive significance of that work; what is convenient is the interpretive language of historians, which fills a need for people whether that language accurately describes reality or not.[5]

It is important to recall here that from time to time Becker acted on one of the possible implications of his insight: he would write fictional accounts of historical events. In his preface to *The Eve of the Revolution,* to cite an instance, Becker wrote that he had frequently resorted to the literary device of telling the story by means of

> a rather free paraphrase of what some imagined spectator or participant might have thought or said about the matter in hand. If the critic says that the product of such methods is not history, I am willing to call it by any name that is better; the point of greatest relevance being the truth and effectiveness of the illusion aimed at—the extent to which it reproduces the quality of thought and feeling of those days, the extent to which it enables the reader to enter into such states of mind and feeling. The truth of such history (or whatever the critic wishes to call it) cannot of course be determined by a mere verification of references.[6]

Or again, when Becker was asked in 1926 to give a talk on "The Spirit of '76," by way of commemorating the 150th anniversary of the American Revolution, he said that he did not have any clear notion—and he did not think that the people who had asked him had any clear notion—of what was meant by the phrase. The paper that Becker delivered, entitled "The Spirit of '76," was a fictionalized account of how people thought and felt about the American Revolution.[7]

Of course, Becker also wrote proper histories despite his skepticism, *The Heavenly City of the Eighteenth Century Philosophers* being a notable example. In that familiar work, Becker had argued that French Enlightenment philosophers and revolutionaries were sustained by an emotional impulse, that their visions of progress and perfectibility were a compensation for the limitations and frustrations of their everyday lives, that their quest was religious in nature, based on a mystical faith in humanity and not at all, as the philosophers, revolutionaries, and successive generations of historians have supposed, on reason. But Becker must obviously have realized that, had he been challenged to defend his interpretation by reference to evidence, he would have been hard pressed to do so.[8]

In short, Becker assumed the insufficiency of historical accounts that were not interpretive, concluding as well that interpretation presented problems to which intuition and common sense provided no solution, especially not with respect to the kinds of events he was interested in, principally the American and French revolutions. Finally, Becker saw no solutions in the social theories then available either, notably Marxism. Becker did not foreclose on the issue because it was too complicated to permit any final judgments, and the times did not permit it in any case. From his point of view, history had an important role to play in the unfolding political and ideological struggles of the 1930s.[9]

It should perhaps be said that Becker is interesting in this context more for professional than for philosophical reasons, having been all at once so perceptive, ideologically engaged, ambivalent about his enterprise, and restrained in his criticism. The reasons for Becker's ambivalence and restraint, however, no longer appear so compelling. On the contrary, social and language theorists, historians, philosophers, critics, and novelists have been busily promoting a variety of critical positions, including the one noted at the outset. These positions have affected what historians do, the main reason being that the experiences with conventional forms of social theory, especially as they were employed in interdisciplinary programs after the Second World War, have been both more extensive than anything Becker could have foreseen and quite discouraging. So-called objective accounts of events have time and again proved inadequate, as neither the most precise descriptions nor the most systematic accumulation and analysis of data can allow for the interpretation of events apart from the subjective perceptions and feelings of the people who lived through them on any but the simplest levels, while the problem of assessing and explaining such subjective perceptions and feelings is not yet close to being solved because of the heterogeneous responses.[10] Many social psychologies have been developed to address the problem, but the ability to make plausible statements from a half dozen and more of these standpoints without being able to discriminate better from worse among them in terms of data only underscores the seriousness of White's claim, as I have stated.

The history that people have lived, then, challenges the imaginative capacity of historians and theorists to account for it, and this is why we are more likely to find discussions of heterogeneity and discontinuity in the writings of critics and novelists than in the writings of historians or the theorists from whom they have borrowed. These critical and novelistic discussions are intended to bring the audience closer to the "real world" of people, to the turmoil, divisions, and conflicts that they experience in their everyday lives. By contrast, historians and social theorists, as a means of establishing a sense of order in the world, have constantly searched for underlying unities, sometimes in one or another structuralist form (linguistic, developmental, biological, social), but much more often in the conventional, less grandiose forms of the professional social sciences. However, the poor results produced by social scientific endeavor have mostly served to bolster the argument that any approach to reality as consistently unable to encompass historical data as this one ought to be abandoned, that neither the further accumulation of data nor the further refinement of the kind of theory social scientists and their historian colleagues interpretively employ could remedy the deficiencies.

Indeed, Charles Lindblom and David Cohen, themselves workers in the field, addressing people responsible for the formation of public policy (in 1979, capping an interesting period of self-scrutiny and criticism), argued correctly, I think, that social scientific knowledge cannot be used for the formation of public policy, that what social scientists actually know is quite meager, and that the results of all social scientific investigations have yielded but an insignificant quantity of findings of questionable value.[11] Lawrence Stone, too, in what is less of an overstatement than might at first appear, addressed then both the seemingly imminent "intellectual disintegration and collapse" of the professional social sciences (sociology, economics, psychology, political science) and the "revival of narrative," by which he meant a move away from "thick" academic, theoretically grounded depictions of causes and conditions to a "thinner," more storylike depiction (including especially the abandonment of the scholarly apparatus of the social historians whose work had been so influential in the preceding years, the charts, graphs, tables, in general, the mathematized form of expression that social historians had so routinely deployed in their work).[12] Of course, one can also find the counterargument that the social sciences have "significant achievements" to their credit and are making good progress. But the points of view or the fields of endeavor that sociologists, for example, might put forward or identify in support of such assertions are not at all encouraging. The only exception that I can see is the study of emotion in sociological terms, a very particular interest that some sociologists currently share with some historians, psychologists, and, in a larger way, psychoanalysts.[13]

There are powerful features of Hayden White's critical standpoint, just as there are of the more conventional critical standpoint that I have also briefly introduced.[14] At the same time, however, the problems of history and theory, or of interpretive histories grounded in the work of one or another of the major theorists, are too complicated to be fairly encompassed by any of these standpoints. Interpretive histories, after all, are complex things, characterized by a defined problem, that is, an arbitrary construct, a rationalized belief that one series of events or one systematic development is more important than another, justifying a particular research strategy or providing a basis for organizing data; a vantage point, which dictates the method, the way that the problem will be dealt with, which may be numerate or literate or emphasize social or institutional interactions, cultural or ideological contents, or unconscious motivation; a language, whether of class, gender, ideology, internalization, perception, or something else, which serves to unify the project; and a conclusion, which affords closure, partly in terms of the data presented but partly also in terms of the moral commitments that are at least implicit in the project. However, interpretive histories characterized by this network of problem, vantage point, language, and conclusion are not vulnerable to criticism or do not fail in the same way, and it is important to observe the differences.

The most famous network, the one provided by Marx, does not require any significant elaboration here, although it is worth emphasizing that Marx's network has failed particularly in terms of the conclusion. Marx's belief that capitalism is compelled to make life excessively harsh considering the enormous productive capacity that the system generates, apart from what anyone wishes or intends, with the strong implication—which to the best of my knowledge no one has ever missed, though it is nowhere elaborated and is based on no evidence—that the reorganization of the means of production will permit harmonious, nonconflictual social development, has been persistently and radically contradicted by events. Other aspects of the network nevertheless remain more or less useful for various kinds of research strategies: one can always learn something, for example, from the numerate analysis of class relations. But it has been evident for a long time that inferences about people's intentions and motives based on such an analysis are not warranted in terms of the expected conclusion: there is evidently more that goes on in the social world than can be revealed by class interests and class antagonisms, regardless of how these concepts are conceived or employed.[15]

There are a number of such networks that either are suggested by or can be plausibly derived from the work of the other major theorists, including Alexis de Tocqueville, Max Weber, Emile Durkheim, Sigmund Freud, and Talcott Parsons. These too can be demonstrated to have failed in significant ways. However, the only one among them that I want to address at this point is the one suggested by Talcott Parsons, because Gerald Platt and I had employed it in two earlier books, *The Wish to Be Free* and *Psychoanalytic Sociology,* and it is necessary to point out why it could not be sustained.[16]

The problem suggested by this network is the struggle over the expansion or contraction of spheres of autonomous, inclusive activity, the capacity for which is adumbrated developmentally and then subsequently actively elaborated insofar as any culture obligates people or imbues them with the desire to establish an independent household or source of livelihood or, after the Reformation, a personal relationship to God based on autonomous conscience in the absence of the mediating role of clergy. The vantage point is the inferred response to forms of social change that were not under the control of authoritative leadership, such as the establishment of national markets or the bureaucratic organization of society, that is, the normative perception of people affected by such change that authoritative leaders bear the responsibility for the violation of internalized moral commitments, releasing them for action, either to restore what they perceived as lost or to strike out in novel directions. The language is derived eclectically in part from Weber, Durkheim, Tocqueville, and Freud (e.g., internalized morality, perceived transgression of morality, the lapse of socialized restraint on aggressive strivings as a result of such perceived transgression), and in part from the post-Freudian ego psychology, which was focused particularly on ego and superego control over aggressive as well as libidinal drives and on such notions as "primary" and "secondary" (culturally informed) autonomy. The conclusion is that, although tension exists between passive-dependent and autonomous strivings, and although there were great struggles and notable failures at different times along the way, involving class, age, gender, race, religion, and ethnicity, there is a discernible process of demands for and expansion of autonomous, inclusive activity on successive institutional levels.

There have been a number of interesting general commentaries on the shortcomings of this Parsonian network,[17] but these commentaries aside, Platt and I had our own doubts and misgivings—about vantage point and language, however, not about the way the problem was posed or the conclusion. In part, the reasons for doubt and misgivings were theoretical, including our inability to anticipate or account for the different ways that perceptions of loss and recovery could be experienced because of the emphasis on instinct and the implied unity of motivation that lay underneath the variety at the surface. In part, too, the reasons were empirical: the populations involved in social situations of all kinds were so heterogeneous, unanticipated situations were so affecting and occurred so rapidly, and responses were so discontinuous that the explanatory value of such a factor as internalized morality was radically compromised.[18] Put another way, the effects of the heterogeneity problem on the ability to sustain autonomous activity, that is, of the multiplicity of interests, perspectives, and social locations, were too palpable to ignore any longer, although it was also clear that no conventional sociological or sociopsychological standpoint, whether based in interest or in morality, could adequately address the issue.

Thus, the reference to "the Fall" in the title of this book refers not to any conclusive philosophical-linguistic critique of unity and coherence based on perceptions of heterogeneity and discontinuity and of the systematic repression of division and unpredictability. Rather, the reference is to the failure of a particular kind of social theory to address these issues, which are real and are possible in principle to address. The difference in emphasis is significant because the situation in history and theory should be viewed as paradoxical rather than closed. For, if we follow René Descartes in his radical reductionism, doubting and discarding everything not clearly self-evident to see whether anything certain remains, we are left with the fact that historically, for most people most of the time, societies organized around particular versions of order and change were perceived to be working and that, when they were perceived not to be working, organized groups arose to challenge these versions. It seems reasonable to suppose still that we ought to be able to describe how this occurred in a systematic way, taking into account the significance of the surface, that is, the ability of people to generate meaning in terms of their own interests and perspectives, from all the social locations they inhabit, and the problems of heterogeneity and discontinuity that follow as a result.

Accordingly, I have addressed the problems of heterogeneity, discontinuity, and interpretation, relating them to each other in terms of four essential themes. The first theme is the capacity of people to construct versions of the world in terms of their own needs and interests that are more solid in imagination than they ever are in reality. I have discussed this initially in the context of interpretive claims that appear in fiction, psychoanalysis, the social sciences, and history, to show how problematic interpretation is, regardless of the standpoint that is adopted, but also to show that, in order to make sense of events in a world in which "change follows upon change with unparalleled speed," the assessment of the intentions of others is nevertheless so important that people are compelled to look for and to use the interpretive schemes that come to them from all these sources, even when they are not particularly compatible with each other.[19]

The second theme is the inevitability of multiple perspectives, based on activity in multiple social locations, the technical source of the heterogeneity problem, particularly in the sense that no one lives or acts—even in the course of a day—in a single structural reality. There are specific tendencies, to be sure, but nothing that recurs consistently enough from one instance to the next to be deemed determinative either predictively or in retrospect. This multiplicity served finally to undermine the regulative constructs of the founding theorists and the professional social sciences that followed in their wake,[20] all of which failed to realize their initial promise because they cannot account for the ways in which people construct versions of the world situationally in terms of their own needs and interests as defined by a sense of adequacy and continuity. It is ironic, in fact, that those societies that made some attempt to acknowledge and assimilate the heterogeneity problem in practice did better with it than any of the theorists who have thus far tried to account for how they managed to do so.

The third theme, then, is adapted from Clifford Geertz's view of ideology as a cultural system, a network of authoritative concepts that render politics coherent by providing a means of orienting heterogeneous groups to a common goal.[21] In these terms, people use ideology to construct multiple and even conflicting views of the world and also to absorb the contradictions that result and that always appear so insignificant to the people who live with them and so compellingly incompatible to outsiders. It is important to add, however, that ideology is a necessary but not a sufficient solution to the problems of heterogeneity, discontinuity, and interpretation. Hence the fourth theme, which is derived from D. W. Winnicott's concepts of transitional objects, transitional phenomena, and transitional space.[22] This transitional language is heuristically useful for focusing attention on the ways that societies both facilitate and constrain behavior, given the heterogeneous construction of reality; but it is especially and additionally useful for focusing attention in a crucial way on the persistent (and perhaps unexpected) need that people have for authoritative leadership, even in the most democratized societies, and for access to or possession of objects like money and property.[23] That is, insofar as people have been able to take a step away from authoritative leadership historically, to pursue a more independent course of action in a heterogeneous world, often perceived as fragmented and chaotic, they have been able to do so only by substituting other objects of support such as property and money. In sum, then, it is the way that the potentially or actually threatening effects of heterogeneity and discontinuity are contained (illustratively, but most importantly) by ideology, authority, property, and money that I will explore here in the expectation that it is possible to discriminate better from worse interpretations by reference to evidence or, at least as a useful first step, to narrow down the possible choices.[24]

1

The Problem of Interpretation

History and Fiction

Among the liveliest and most persistent critics of historical writing recently have been contemporary novelists, any number of whom have expressed, in pursuit of their own literary projects, a wish or need to expand historical consciousness, or to affect moral consciousness in terms of historical events, or to change our way of looking at life, character, or language in terms of historical events. Unlike earlier generations of novelists who did not like history or historians, for whom history was a nightmare from which they were trying to awake and who would have escaped from history into a world of art, not only are there novelists currently who have come to appreciate the uses of history (if not historians), but a number of them want to claim history for their own.[1] In part, as one critic observed, this posture has emerged among writers who had no choice but to reject any idea of the novel freed of the obligation to tell a story, to interpret motive or portray reality, in an attempt to make sense of current conflicts by discussing how things could have gotten to such a point—in South Africa, Latin America, the Middle East, or Eastern and Central Europe, places where they know that "history is the nightmare from which . . . they cannot awake."[2] Such writers are anxious to repudiate the legacy of modernism because, as V. S. Naipaul has written, modernist fiction does nothing to enhance the novelist's "interpretive function," having degenerated into narrow, formalist experimentation.[3] But in part it has also emerged from a more general search for content and audience, and where better than history to find "a resource for writing," to look for content, "to load up on adventures" for the sake of recapturing an audience.[4] Indeed, there have been so many novels rooted in historical themes recently, such a rush to occupy this space, which in a spirit of competitive urgency is being advertised by some novelists as empty, that one historian and critic was moved to reflect on this exceptional preoccupation with history that has occurred "not, alas, in the academic world but in the imagination, speculation and writing of novelists, all kinds of novelists."[5]

The highly publicized experimentation with faction, true-life novels or nonfictional novels, has resulted in the attempt, from different perspectives and for different purposes, to break down the distinction between the real and the imagined, "between formal fiction and the actual, palpable sense of life as it is lived," and especially between literature and history as art forms.[6] Novelists reconstruct events, often as accurately and carefully as any historian, putting real people in imaginary situations, imaginary people in real situations, and imaginary situations in documentary narratives, augmenting the significance of historical events by plausible, internally consistent, but obviously unverifiable depictions of the subjective intentions of people.[7] E. L. Doctorow has declared, in a statement that has achieved some notoriety, that "there is no longer any such thing as fiction or non-fiction; there's only narrative": "What's real and what isn't—I used to know, but I've forgotten. The book [*Ragtime*] gives the reader all sorts of facts—made-up facts, distorted facts—but I happen to think that my representation of historical characters is true to the soul of them."[8] As a reviewer of one of Doctorow's subsequent novels has pointed out, by flaunting the "artificial line dividing the true from the imagined," not only does Doctorow suggest that the process of remembering is by definition one of invention, but "he rejects altogether the notion that imagination and memory are ever pure of each other."[9]

Moreover, this confounding of the real and the imagined, this "breaking down of genres, the elevation of puzzle, paradox, mystification and Borgesian sleights of hand," is woven into discussions or reviews of different works and made available to a wide audience in journals of opinion without too much reflection or discrimination of points of view, even as the audience is assured that the collapse of the distinction between the real and the imagined does not matter all that much because any depiction of reality is a fictional construct regardless of the source or, by contrast, because so close to life are imaginative works, so accurately are lives depicted in fiction, that the real and the imagined are "virtually indistinguishable" in any case:

> Norman Mailer's "Executioner's Song," subtitled "A True-Life Novel," and E. L. Doctorow's "Ragtime" (which locates Emma Goldman, J. P. Morgan, Henry Ford, Evelyn Nesbit and Harry Houdini in imagined circumstances) treat verifiable events as if

they were "texts" to be "deconstructed." "A visitor from another planet," Doctorow has argued, "could not by study of the techniques of discourse distinguish composed fiction from composed history."[10]

Thus we read of Mario Vargas Llosa's *The Real Life of Alejandro Mayta* that, "like one of Magritte's paintings of a landscape within another painting, the book opens out to disclose layer after layer of realities that become so intertwined with imaginative constructions that by the end the reader can no longer distinguish between what is 'real' and what is invented—indeed, has been compelled to re-examine the very definitions of literature and history."[11] Or again, "Where does autobiography end and fiction begin? Bestseller lists and publisher's catalogues assume we know the answer to this question, as they assume there is a clear-cut difference between fiction and non-fiction."[12]

The claim that it is hard "to distinguish the point . . . at which history leaves off and fiction or fantasy begins" is becoming routine, just as the idea that a work of fiction can also be a historiographic achievement is not as contradictory as it might once have appeared to be.[13]

Then, too, the recent republication of Nicola Chiaromonte's *The Paradox of History* should be viewed in this context. For in that work Chiaromonte argued,

> It is only through fiction and the dimension of the imaginary that we can learn something real about individual experience. Any other approach is bound to be general and abstract. My aim in this book has been to present the question of the relation of men to historical events as it appears in different contexts. And I felt that this could only be done on the basis of that particular kind of historical truth which is fiction and, more especially, great nineteenth century fiction, whose avowed purpose was to provide the true, rather than the official, history of the individual and society.[14]

Or, as Hayden White put it, by way of amplifying Chiaromonte's point, "These literary artists give us truer, because they are more honest, representations of the human experience of historical events than do historians themselves."[15]

There are obviously several important messages being broadcast. One is that historians have failed to provide people with the appropriate language that they need to make sense of the world, specifically, a "postmodernist" language that emphasizes "fear and flux, unsureness, inward chaos, self-surprise," a standpoint that has challenged in fiction the stability of self-conception and "the myths of coherence and conti-nuity," which have now also been challenged in history as well.[16] On this view, the absurdities of contemporary history "transcend the con-fines of naturalism and traditional narrative technique," reveal the elu-siveness and "utter subjectivity" of truth, and justify "an independence from the old fashioned American concern for factual fidelity." Writers of this "mythopoeic historical fiction" share "a sincere feeling that truth is a good deal more than merely factual and often may contradict the facts." Because there is no conventionally conceived historical reality "out there," and because our ordering of history, or what we make of history from our own perspective, is a matter of arbitrary construc-tions, the novelist, who is better able to see through the problem and more innovative in the manipulations of language, may use "familiar mythic or historical forms to combat the content of those forms and to conduct the reader . . . to the real, away from mystification to clarifica-tion, away from magic to maturity, away from mystery to revelation."[17]

The second important message is not only that there is a historical reality capable of being described but that novelists should have the primary responsibility for describing it because of their superior intui-tive access to the intentions and motives of people. It is not just that the kind of perception that gets "concretized" in history "is just as valid in a [novel]," or even that "realistic fiction can effectively augment his-tory," presenting facts "not to be found in any archive, but no less valid or important." It is that fiction could perhaps provide a way for us to master history rather than continuing to be its "gulled audience."[18]

We might recall in this connection that, when Hannah Arendt wanted to explain the virtuous intransigence displayed by revolution-aries, their unswerving devotion to principle, their ability to kill while protesting their innocence, perhaps even claiming at the same time a higher sense of compassion, she did not turn to historians or to social scientists for confirmation; she turned to Dostoyevsky and Melville:

> The classical story of the other, non-theoretical side of the French
> Revolution, the story of the motivation behind the words and
> deeds of its main actors, is "The Grand Inquisitor." . . . The sin of
> The Grand Inquisitor was that he, like Robespierre, was "attracted
> towards les hommes faibles," not only because such attraction was
> indistinguishable from the lust for power, but also because he had
> depersonalized the sufferers, lumped them together into an aggre-
> gate.

Melville in turn had demonstrated in *Billy Budd* that "virtue finally in-terferes not to prevent the crime of evil but to punish the violence of absolute innocence."[19]

However, it is one thing to make use of the insight of imaginative writers as Arendt did, citing some famous instances in order to heighten the impact of her own work. It is quite another to claim that this ought generally to be done, that historians, lacking the intuitive capacity, should have no primary, independent responsibility for their subject, a claim currently being made for a variety of reasons but primarily because historians (and the social theorists whose work informs their own) have failed to bring their audience close enough to the subjective intentions of people, their perceptions of themselves and their world, their reasons for doing things, and especially how they feel about things. Put succinctly, it is at the level of "the turbulence, the corrupting claims, the seductions of ideological and class conflicts," or the "imagining of motives and a depiction of personal tensions" that fiction not only meets but supersedes history.[20] Saul Bellow has stated, for example, that the novelist is "an imaginative historian who is able to get closer to the contemporary facts than social scientists possibly can," by which he clearly meant closer to their emotional significance.[21] The critique at any rate is consistently directed at the evident inferiority of the intuitive or interpretive capacity of academic writers and the contrasting superior capacity of imaginative writers: "Non-fiction gives you the facts. Fiction gives you the truth"; "history tells us what happened; fiction tells how it felt"; "Fiction is the best place to express the emotional truth."[22] A newspaper account (and by extension a historical account) can tell you what happened, Nadine Gordimer has said, "but it's the playwright, the novelist, the poet, the short-story writer who gives you some idea why."[23] Even when interested novelists are being generous in this respect, they are still claiming a special, more elevated role for themselves. Thomas Fleming has written that, in the historical novel, "the gifted, imaginative writer is able to enhance his fiction by uniting it with a version of the past that embodies a vision of America, an interpretation of our experience that has relevance for our own time. This, and not its utilitarian function of informing the reader about America's past, is what makes the historical novel so important."[24]

Of course, it is easy to show that novelists, with their high regard for the power of literature to enhance perceptions of the world, have been using historical events and real characters in historical fictions and romances for a long time.[25] But this current claim that historians have no primary role (in some versions not even necessarily an archival one) is something else again. For what is implied in all these statements about history is that there are no solutions to the problem of assessing subjectivity that vexed Carl Becker or to the other real problems raised by postmodernist critics, especially discontinuity and heterogeneity. Historians have seen arguments about history as the impossible profession before, from Henry Adams and Henry James to Carl Becker and beyond.[26] But there is an order and a logic to history writing that is rendered problematic in a different way by these several notions of subjectivity, discontinuity, and heterogeneity, and the kind of knowledge that academics and their audience thought possible in history and the social sciences, particularly in the heyday of interdisciplinary studies after the Second World War, may not in fact be forthcoming. A number of novelists have therefore suggested that, given the problems that historians have now been shown to be up against, perhaps it is time for people to look for knowledge in the one place still uniquely able to provide it, fiction. As Norman Mailer characteristically boasted, "Only great fiction can save the world. . . . For fiction still believes that one mind can see it whole."[27]

It is in this context that we should understand Gore Vidal's claim that he is chronicling American history or that "like Doctorow he is persuaded that he excels historians . . . in accurate portrayals of real figures." Harold Bloom has stated that Vidal's imagining of American politics "is so powerful as to compel awe": "No biographer, and until now no novelist, has had the precision of imagination to show us a plausible and human Lincoln. . . . Vidal . . . does just that, and more: he gives us the tragedy of American political history, with its most authentic tragic hero at the center."[28] Moreover, we should understand similarly Kenneth Lynn's observation that John Dos Passos's trilogy *U.S.A.* is "a dazzling mixture of biography and fiction, of prose-poetry and journalistic documentary," a work that has told us more about the "twentieth century American experience than any historical synthesis ever has."[29] We may add to these statements of high praise the following depictions: of Robert Coover's *The Public Burning* as an attempt "to cram the whole sprawl of American history into its mythic narrative"; of Graham Greene's *The Quiet American* as "the most comprehensible and predictive account of the origins of the Vietnam war"; of Robert Critchfield's *These Days,* which "mixes fact and fiction," as encompassing "an amazing chunk of American history"; of Thomas Flanagan's *The Year of the French* as recreating, from "barroom to manor hall, the entire intellectual and emotional climate of the time" (of Flanagan's more recent *The Tenants of Time,* the same reviewer wrote that, "even as we wholeheartedly agree with his characters that the true history of the times cannot be written, we are aware that he has just done it, in a work of fiction"); of Mario Vargas Llosa as beginning "a complete inventory of the political, social, economic and cultural reality of Peru"; of Carlos Fuentes as "the palimpsest of Mexican history and culture," an artist "who contains and illuminates all the layers of all the times and cultures of a nation"; of Augusto Roa Bastos's *I the Supreme* as "an impressive portrait . . . of a whole colonial society," one that offers much for students of African and Asian decolonization to reflect on.[30] The reason that these writers are capable of such exceptional insight?

> Fiction gives us the names and symbols in a grammar of experience, synchronizing feeling with event into an understandable order. The truth about people can best be known as people know it. It is a package deal, and the package best adapted to convey a sense of the human condition is the novel. . . . No analysis that separates human emotions from event can tell us as full a story as the one that joins them.[31]

Novelists and critics are unarguably free to make any claims they like, including claims for some presumed, specially enhanced "penetrative power" of imagination and intuition. But why should anyone accept at face value what may be little more than self-serving belletristic wishfulness? Perhaps one can learn more about twentieth-century American history from Dos Passos than from historians, a questionable proposition in any event. But why should anyone believe that novelists as a group are any better able to cope with the complexity of events than historians or social scientists; or, by the same token, why should anyone believe that a talent for narrative, language, and the depiction of character translates into a singular ability to understand history or society or that such a talent is the source of an "imaginative truth which transcends what the historian can give you?"[32] Ernest Hemingway insisted that the novelist's "standard of fidelity to truth should be so high that his invention, out of his experience, should produce a truer account than anything factual can be."[33] But what is such a statement as this last one supposed to mean—that novelists are possessed of immaculate perception, that as distinct from other kinds of writers they have an immediate, unmediated access to reality, an unobstructed perception of historical subjects' thoughts and feelings or of the inner significance of historical events?[34]

Hayden White explained that historians should not too hastily separate themselves from writers of fiction because "the process of fusing events, whether imaginary or real, into a comprehensive totality capable of serving as the *object* of a representation is a poetic process. Here the historian must utilize precisely the same tropological strategies, the same modalities of representing relationships in words, that the poet or the novelist uses."[35] But this situation must be viewed from the other side as well, at least in one important sense, because no writer, whether historian, social scientist, psychoanalyst, or novelist, can make complex statements about the subjective intentions of people without some organizing preconception of how mind and society work. Every writer willing to make such statements therefore functions as a theorist, or at least we might say that his preconceptions share the characteristics of theory, even if they are not derived from any particular viewpoint or are said to derive from intuition (which often enough turns out to be the residue of some theorist's design—who these days is innocent of theory anyway?). This simply underscores the problem presented by historical subjects who responded continuously to events but who did not themselves have an adequate conception of the significance of events or the reasons for their particular response.

The result is that any writer armed with social or cultural theory of any kind, or with intuition or common sense, must interpret other people's interpretations of events by supplying from outside their recorded experience the links that permitted and fostered collective action. Any writer, regardless of standpoint, must approach historical problems as theorists do, abstracting from the welter of events in terms of some preconceived scheme, which is why claims for the virtues of intuition or common sense are evasions of the problem rather than any kind of solution to it. The novelist's preconceptions, like the theorist's or the historian's in this case, serve to transform the character of the empirical world; they facilitate abstraction, allowing events to be presented in an ordered and unified way, either in terms unavailable to the people who lived through them or in terms of language, feelings, and thoughts that were invented for them. The novelist's interpretive preconceptions, in short, are as problematic as any other writer's, and the fact that they can render an ordered depiction of reality or that their work can be consoling for an audience does not make them right in the sense that they are conveying. On the contrary, novelists trying to fathom historical and social conflicts are faced with the same logical and empirical problems as any writer is faced with and are as likely for that reason to be getting things wrong. Occasionally, we may read that the novelist "no longer pretends to be any less baffled or blind than the rest of us."[36] But for the most part this is not true, as we have just seen: novelists have recently been making just such claims more vigorously than ever before, as if such problems did not exist for them.

It is important to emphasize, however, that the claims are not only or primarily about fiction, history, and theory or about better or worse interpretations of the past; they are about politics and power in the present, about access to the public and the right to address the present needs of the public that history and theory are perceived as having failed to do. Of course there is a better argument for the uses of fiction in history than the one presented here and a better place to find it than in popular journals of opinion. But I have taken this approach in order to make clear that one familiar, almost routine mode of interpreting historical events has failed and another is not yet in place and that both the form of argument and the forum are evidence of a struggle over what and whose interpretive mode will replace it and what the relative shares of the turf will be. I have deliberately chosen a crude version of the argument just because it has appeared in this popular form, because it is so evidently a matter of ideology (or discourse) and not merely an abstract academic debate over ways of interpretively assessing the subjective intentions of historical actors.[37] The claims that novelists have a greater capacity to crystallize and convey meaning, to make life coherent for people, which historians, social theorists, and especially (given the emphasis on interpretive assessment) psychoanalysts have consistently failed to do, are not politically neutral or innocent; they favor one side of an important conception of how the world works over another. This political and ideological issue is a crucial one, and it is crucially related as well to the issue of heterogeneity. But in order to see how these two issues are related it is necessary to consider first the ways in which psychoanalytic and historical interpretations in particular are perceived to have failed.

The Problem of Psychoanalysis

It is not surprising that, if history as a discipline has been taken to task for its failures in terms of interpretive assessment, psychoanalysis should have been too. For, if especially the problem of interpreting the subjective intentions of interacting groups could be solved in abstract terms, then psychoanalysts should have been better able to indicate how than they turned out to be. Their failure to have done better results from the inability to make systematic sense of the subjective responses that they are able to elicit in the special therapeutic environment that they have developed. This environment makes personal strivings, desires, impulses, and evasions more accessible, revealing a dynamically heterogeneous world. But the fundamental psychoanalytic insistence that this dynamic world is nevertheless "at bottom" a homogeneous one makes very remote the possibility of a unified theory, one that is intended to carry beyond the therapeutic environment to explanations of larger cultural attainments and conflicts.

For our purposes, the most interesting work of fiction that explores connections among historical events, different responses to events, and psychoanalysis is D. M. Thomas's *The White Hotel*, in which Freud, psychoanalysis, and European culture in the period between the two world wars are treated as centrally as they have been in any number of histories. Thomas undoubtedly had his own literary purposes in dealing with history and psychoanalysis, but it is not hard to see how his uses of fantasy, his depiction of a particular therapeutic encounter and of the Holocaust, provide significant elements of a critique of psychoanalysis, apart from whatever else might have been intended.[38] Thomas's construction of a fictional case study, his ability to recreate Freud's language and imagination and mingle it with his own, allows him to examine ways in which Freud's personality and language could have served a healing and integrative purpose in therapy, and even in the larger culture, without ever becoming scientific or objective or acquiring the explanatory power that Freud had envisioned.[39]

Starting with Thomas's premise that whatever "cure" occurred in Freud's "analysis" of "Anna G." resulted from the relationship between patient and analyst and not from the analyst's interpretations (which the patient more often than not rejected), we may make the following observations as well. The reconstruction of events in a patient's past by a psychoanalyst, a patient's guess or a psychoanalyst's suggestion about something that "must have happened," might well be confirmed by independent observers who happen to recall the events in question. But confirmation is not the only standard for correct interpretation. Quite often, as Freud wrote, "[we] do not succeed in bringing the patient to recollect what has been repressed. Instead of that, if the analysis is carried out correctly, we produce in him an assured conviction of the truth of the construction which achieves the same therapeutic result as a recaptured memory." That is, Freud assumed that "our construction is only effective because it recovers a fragment of lost experience," so that, if an interpretation or construction of his evoked a visible sense of conviction in a patient, then likely it was true whether it was confirmable or not. But Freud had no grounds for making such an assumption, which shares the logic and vulnerability of the kind of historical inferences that Carl Becker was so skeptical of. For integrative, healing, therapeutically effective thoughts are not necessarily true ones, and the sense of conviction could just as easily have arisen from the transference relationship as from the correctness of the interpretation. The kind of response that Freud identified is readily elicited by authoritative figures; it is a relief for people to think that someone authoritative knows the inner significance of things.[40]

In addition, we might easily infer from Thomas's description of

Freud's relationship with Anna G. that any or every analysis is incomplete, that patients evade the fundamental rule, that they always know more than they say about the things that are important to them, and that what is important changes over time anyway as they face different tasks in life. It is not hard to imagine, as Donald Spence has suggested, that links between ideas in clinical practice are often imposed, that psychoanalysts impose more structure on material than they like to admit, that consensus among psychoanalysts is not a criterion of validation, that a patient's agreement with one or another interpretation is more often a mark of passivity than a mark of confirmation, and that psychoanalytic reconstructions are usually but a poor approximation of what might actually have happened.[41]

Thomas's fictional portrayal of a case history, of psychoanalysis, and of certain themes and events in European history is framed by his sense not only of the preordained failure of the therapeutic encounter but of the insufficiency of psychoanalytic concepts with respect to the kind of world that people have created for themselves. Psychoanalysts have available to them the language of patients, including body language; they are able to observe constantly the formation of associative links, the expression of different kinds of idiosyncratic symptoms, and the fleeting but indicative mood swings that people experience. They have also established a unique environment that, involving the suspension of the sense of time and of the social world, facilitates the play of the mind, and they have the advantage of the transference relationship as it is buttressed by the setting and by the cultural authority of the psychoanalyst. But, even so, they still find it difficult to acquire knowledge and especially to use what they have acquired in a social or cultural sense for the reasons that Thomas referred to (all of which, incidentally, have been explored in the psychoanalytic literature itself) and for the one additional, crucial reason already referred to that has not been explored: they cannot effectively account in a general theoretical way for the primary result of clinical experience, dynamic heterogeneity.

More interesting in this critical context than Thomas's fictional commentary, therefore, particularly because it also appeared in a popular form intended to be much more widely disseminated than is the case with purely academic efforts, is Bruno Bettelheim's essay *Freud and Man's Soul*. Anxious to redeem Freud and psychoanalysis from a failed positivist orientation by locating the "authentic" psychoanalysis in a hermeneutic-spiritual tradition, Bettelheim emphasized that what Freud intended, which is revealed by the language he chose to use, was obscured and distorted by the English translators of Freud's work, especially by James Strachey, chiefly responsible for compiling the *Stan-*

dard Edition, a result of his inclination, as well as that of his colleagues, to promote the natural science side of things, the side closest to their own tradition.[42] Given a choice between positivist and hermeneutic traditions, the translators nearly always chose the positivist, and these distorting, defective translations have led to erroneous conclusions about Freud's work.

This is by no means Bettelheim's opinion alone; on the contrary, it is by now a matter of some concern that what is commonly accepted as the structural theory is more Strachey's invention than Freud's, and the possible need for a newly revised edition of the complete works of Freud, as great a task as that would be, has already been publicized.[43] But Bettelheim felt a special responsibility in the matter and he took on the corrective task for a wider lay audience, to the degree at least of making people aware of what was entailed. Bettelheim felt himself peculiarly suited to do this, having shared Freud's cultural background and being "closely acquainted with the language as Freud himself used it."[44]

However, the positivist view of Freud's work that Bettelheim deplored, the view that appears in English "as abstract, depersonalized, highly theoretical, erudite and mechanized,"[45] was most heavily promoted by Anna Freud, Heinz Hartmann, and some notable others who also shared that cultural background, particularly in the leading publication devoted to the development of psychoanalytic theory and practice after the Second World War, the *Psychoanalytic Study of the Child* (which began to appear well before the *Standard Edition*). The managing editors of that distinguished series included Anna Freud and Heinz Hartmann as well as Ruth Eissler and Ernst Kris. Their task in this publication was the elaboration of the ego psychology, the development of a concept of aggression equivalent in sophistication and explanatory power to the developed libido theory, the resolution of certain contradictory tendencies (choosing to emphasize the organizing functions of ego as opposed to the determining and disruptive power of the drives), and the integration of these and other aspects of theory (e.g., narcissism) in a more coherent whole, a task, they suggested, that Freud would have attempted had he had the time.

The language used by Anna Freud, Hartmann, and many others was resolutely abstract and mechanistic, full of such notions as neutralized or "deaggressivized" psychic energy, quantitative fluctuations (or variations) in energy levels, and the like. One example of the use of such language says as much about this as needs to be said here: "It may be that structural analogies are less useful in describing the early psyche than estimations of function in terms of energy, i.e., the quantities of unmodified instinct passing through the psychic system."[46] Now it is possible to imagine a lot of things, but among them is not that Anna Freud or Heinz Hartmann had trouble with Freud's language or failed to appreciate his cultural milieu. On the contrary, the almost universal acceptance of the Strachey edition of Freud's work was reinforced by the authority of Anna Freud.[47] Freud's coworkers may have chosen to resolve a particular ambiguity in his work, a tension between humanistic and scientific concerns, but they clearly perceived themselves to be fulfilling Freud's ambitions for the future of psychoanalysis. There are even grounds for claiming that Freud himself preferred this emphasis, given the role that he played in earlier translations of his work.[48] Hence Roy Schafer's conclusion that "the terms of Freudian metapsychology are those of natural science. Freud, Hartmann and others deliberately used the rhetoric of forces, energies, functions, structures, apparatus, and principles to establish and develop psychoanalysis along the lines of physicalist psychology."[49] This is to say not that there are no bad or misleading translations of Freud's work but rather that even good ones, or even a special emphasis on the humanistic side of Freud such as Bettelheim offers, cannot reverse this conclusion.[50]

Thus Bettelheim's approach to psychoanalysis is in some respects forceful and correct, and it is certainly current; but in other respects it is evasive, and I have no idea why he proceeded the way that he did.[51] Still, in the context of his discussion, Bettelheim made two points vital for the issues raised here, the relationship of psychoanalysis to history and theory and to the specific problems of subjectivity, discontinuity, heterogeneity, and self-conception mentioned earlier. First, Bettelheim claimed that Freud's psychoanalysis is "plainly" an idiographic science, by which he meant that the contents vary and change diachronically while the underlying processes remain constant.[52] According to Bettelheim, psychoanalysis utilizes

> unique historical occurrences to provide a view of man's development and behavior. Whether Freud analyzes his dreams, which are unique to him, or establishes the past history of patients, or discusses what constitutes the essence of a work of art and how it relates to the life and personality of the artist, or analyzes the origin of religion or rituals, the psychology of the masses, or the basis of society or of monotheism, he is working within the framework of the *Geisteswissenschaften,* applying the methods appropriate to an idiographic science.[53]

This is a strange claim because Freud undoubtedly attempted to establish the universal basis of law, religion, morality, and social order in *Totem and Taboo;* he persisted in promoting the universal validity of his standpoint, basing it finally on phylogenetic (Lamarckian) grounds. Freud was interested not in the surface variety for the purposes of theory but only in the underlying unities, and there was nothing idiographic about his intentions or his treatment of contents.[54] The fact that psychoanalysis could be recast in a variety of terms, stressing historical development or the primacy of society or language, does not contradict the fact that Freud refused to budge from this position.[55] Earlier, in *The Psychopathology of Everyday Life,* Freud explained how a psychology of the unconscious could be used to investigate "the myths of paradise and the fall of man, of God, of good and evil, of immortality, and so on, and to transform *metaphysics* into metapsychology."[56] Later, in 1917, Freud wrote to Karl Abraham,

> Have I really not told you anything about the Lamarck idea? It arose between Ferenczi and me, but neither of us had the time or the spirit to tackle it at present. The idea is to put Lamarck entirely on our own ground and to show that the "necessity" that, according to him, creates and transforms organs, is nothing but the power of unconscious ideas over one's own body, of which we see the remnants in hysteria, in short, the "omnipotence of thoughts." This would actually supply a psychoanalytic explanation of adaptation; it would put the coping stone on psychoanalysis.[57]

Moreover, the theme of *Totem and Taboo* was repeated again in phylogenetic terms in *Civilization and its Discontents,* while Ernest Jones reported that he pleaded with Freud to omit from *Moses and Monotheism* a passage confirming the Lamarckian view, arguing that no responsible biologist any longer regarded the Lamarckian theory as tenable.[58] Freud's response was that they were all wrong.[59] In his very last work, Freud was still claiming that "the phylogenetic foundation has so much the upper hand over personal accidental experience that it makes no difference whether a child has really sucked at the breast or has been brought up on the bottle and never enjoyed the tenderness of a mother's care."[60] Nothing could be clearer than Freud's desire to "reduce symbolism to universal, fixed sexual contents and to prefer an explanation of recurrent meanings in terms of phylogenetic, inherited contents."[61]

Bettelheim's claim that Freud meant psychoanalysis to be an idiographic science is strange, then, because it is so easily contradicted: there is nothing obscure, remote, or ambiguous about the pertinent materials. The point is, however, that Bettelheim is nevertheless right:

from the standpoint of clinical experience, the observational basis of psychoanalysis, it is an idiographic discipline. Of course, the hermeneutic position that Bettelheim promotes, concerned with meaning rather than with causes and mechanisms, does tend to make the individual the ultimate guarantor of the meaning of his own reality so that all psychoanalysis may then come to be seen in terms of the idiosyncratic features of individual patients. But this is only an abstract statement about what in fact happens. The course and resolution of any dynamic problem is unique, or, as Oliver Sacks put it, "We may be biologically similar, but we are each of us biographically unique."[62] This, moreover, is a very common sort of observation made by psychoanalysts:

> Although the Oedipus complex has shared characteristics that can be communicated, it is essential that this not eliminate the fact that each person experiences the Oedipus complex uniquely.[63]

> The direction of our search and our words is always towards singularity.[64]

> There is no more reason to expect that all patients who are sad constitute a homogeneous group than to expect that all patients with a fever do so.[65]

> Theoretical knowledge as well as the seeming repetition of psychoanalytic constellations dull our senses to the unique qualities of each psychoanalytic experience.[66]

> It is neither general explanations nor obvious positive instances of psychoanalytic hypotheses that appear to be especially important to either psychoanalyst or analysand. Rather, what is given special weight by both is the emergence of circumstantial detail, having an astonishing degree of specificity and idiosyncratic nuance. . . . Such details have not been previously remembered by the analysand . . . and almost certainly have not previously been imagined or guessed in advance by the psychoanalyst. A psychoanalysis without surprises cannot properly be termed a psychoanalysis at all.[67]

There are of course more such statements, but adding reasonably to the number provided would not constitute proof; it would only prove tedious.

The second claim made by Bettelheim on Freud's behalf, following from the first one, is that psychoanalytic knowledge can be established only on the basis of the actual reporting of individuals.[68] Freud,

wrote Bettelheim, "had decided that to different persons the same symbol could have entirely different implications—that only a study of the
individual's unique associations with a symbol permitted understanding of what it signified. He had become convinced that each psychological event had its own unique history, existed within a unique context, and could be understood only in that context."[69] Two important
conclusions follow from this claim. First, psychoanalysis (and, for these
purposes, psychohistory too) is a communicative discipline. If the subject does not say, the analyst or historian cannot know, and the communication cannot be just symbolic, an observation of behavior in particular circumstances, because we can never make assumptions about
what people meant or intended by any thought or action unless their
associations are available and interpretable by clinical standards. Second, symbols are not universal; they cannot even have consistent meaning through a culture by definition. Symbols are powerful because they
can absorb and reconcile a variety of meanings imputed by a dynamically heterogeneous population, not because they mean the same thing
to everyone.[70] Indeed, what emerges in practice from clinical psychoanalytic investigations of patients' subjectivity is a strong sense of just
how dynamically heterogeneous people in fact are.

This dynamic heterogeneity, moreover, reinforces a tendency toward the dissolution of psychoanalysis as a unified discipline, diminishing its relevance in current forms, except as different concepts may be
used in a heuristic sense, to cultural history or to social theory, a tendency that is not reversed by the "science" half of Bettelheim's phrase
"idiographic science." To begin with, psychoanalysis at the present
time, far from being a monolithic entity that can compel loyalty to a
single standpoint, as critics still sometimes laughably picture it, is too
fragmented to be constituted as a unified discipline. There was a time
in the United States, even rather recently, when proponents of "mainstream psychoanalysis" could insist on the primacy of Freud's drive
theory and the version of the world associated with it, man as pleasure
seeking. There were other possible versions of the world, especially one
that emerged from the British psychoanalytic tradition established by
Melanie Klein, W. R. D. Fairbairn, Ian Suttie, John Bowlby, D. W.
Winnicott, Joseph Sandler, and others, man as object seeking.[71] This
version, given space in the principal psychoanalytic publications, the
International Journal of Psychoanalysis and the *Psychoanalytic Study of the
Child,* nevertheless remained a secondary one, not happily but practi-
cally so. Then the hermeneutic critique of psychoanalysis promoted by
Paul Ricoeur in addition to the efforts of certain anthropologists, no-
tably Clifford Geertz, fostered still a third psychoanalytic version of the

world, man as meaning seeking.[72] Now all three stories have their proponents, and there are variations within each (e.g., Klein, Fairbairn,
Suttie, Bowlby, and Winnicott are all object relations theorists in
the British tradition, but they are still different from each other).[73]
Through all the frequently bitter experiences with C. G. Jung, Alfred
Adler, Wilhelm Reich, Melanie Klein, Otto Rank, Karen Horney,
Harry Stack Sullivan, and Erich Fromm (not to mention the special
contribution of Erik Erikson), there was something that could still be
called "mainstream psychoanalysis." But that situation no longer exists:
psychoanalysis lacks the kind of unifying, authoritative core that the
proponents of the drive theory had so persistently provided. In Thomas
Kuhn's terms, psychoanalysis lacks a disciplinary matrix that can provide the basic concepts constituting a context for its activities as a science. The absence of any agreed on way to evaluate all the different
psychoanalytic versions of the world is one important criterion of this
lack.[74]

There is little any more that is central or common to psychoanalytic imagination. The different theories "are not translatable," as one
psychoanalyst expressed it; the different points of view share little more
than concepts of unconscious mental processes, repression, and transference. It is well known that Freud once set down rigid standards for
what qualifies as psychoanalysis, involving particularly the centrality of
the Oedipus complex; but at different times Freud set down a variety
of standards both flexible and rigid (the concepts just referred to are
quite close in fact to the standards that Freud set down for psychoanalysis in 1914). Besides, only a foolhardy person these days would try to
insist on rigid standards, and it is not hard to see why: Freud's drive
theory is no longer nearly as decisive for psychoanalysis as Freud
thought it must forever be, and it gets less so with time.[75]

Joseph Sandler, prominent British psychoanalyst and former editor of the *International Journal of Psychoanalysis,* has long since substituted affect for drive as the motive force in human behavior; Arnold H.
Modell has also argued that "affects are at the heart of the problem of
psychoanalytic knowledge"; while Robert R. Holt has exclaimed that
"drive is dead."[76] The Oedipus complex as Freud valued it has also
become much less important than it used to be, especially because of
the variety of object relations theories that stress preoedipal factors in
different ways (Harry Guntrip, another well-known British psychoanalyst, has claimed that he never came across a patient in which oedipal
phenomena were of major significance);[77] because of the stress on social factors in a variety of terms, including Heinz Kohut's self psychology (a psychology of deficits rather than of conflicts as Kohut, too,

disputed the centrality of the Oedipus complex); because of the stress on other factors such as loss and restitution (as "all behavior can be construed as an attempt to prevent losses of objects and to regulate some fundamental susceptibility to depression"); and because of the need for synthesis that follows from the proliferation of standpoints, including, for example, Modell's attempt to synthesize the work of Kohut and Sandler, focused on conflicts between people and their social world conceived of in Sandler's terms as a "background of safety."[78]

Finally, it is necessary to add a word on D. W. Winnicott's contribution to psychoanalytic developmental psychology. Winnicott, who rarely referred back to Freud in his own work and whose reputation has been steadily rising since his death in 1971, had an entirely different clinically derived conception of development (where Freud claimed that childhood experiences are determinative, to cite an instance, Winnicott might—and did—respond by emphasizing that "early is not deep"); this led in turn to a conception of art, illusion, creativity, and reality very different from Freud's. Nor is this all. Systematic interest in id processes has radically declined (the last major discussion of the subject appeared in 1966), and other aspects of psychoanalysis that were then also considered very important (e.g., economic and regulatory factors) have suffered a similar fate.[79]

But, even if psychoanalysis could be reconstituted as a unified science of development or a developmental psychology, there is no way back from the kinds of idiosyncratic experience reported by therapists to an exclusively psychoanalytic theory (i.e., a drive theory in terms of man either as pleasure seeking or as object seeking) relevant to social and cultural events.[80] Freud's claim in *Group Psychology and the Analysis of the Ego* that individual psychology "is at the same time social psychology as well" cannot be defended, whether this refers to assumptions about familial socialization or internalization, or phylogenetic assumptions, or to other possible assumptions, for example, that drive is structured by organized social relationships and is not the source or cause of such relationships.[81] The problems of religion, law, morality, and social order that Freud had hoped to have solved become insoluble not only in Freud's preferred drive terms but in all other psychosocial terms as well, including age-graded theories, theories of cohorts, theories of shared traumatic experiences, and so on. Current research, moreover, suggests strongly that this is the case.[82]

The significance of Bettelheim's treatment of psychoanalysis is that, no matter how heuristically valuable psychoanalytic observations of attraction, affect, memory, fantasy, loss, morality, impulse, ideals, self-regard, and the like may continue to be in drawing attention to

certain kinds of problems, social phenomena or the phenomena of collective behavior cannot be explained in systematic psychoanalytic
terms: neither the logic of (inherited, genetic, programmed) structures
nor the logic of categories derived from a different conception of theory
and practice (culturally derived orientations to age or gender) is sufficient to deal with the heterogeneous dynamic reality as depicted by
Bettelheim and confirmed by clinical experience (or with the heterogeneous social reality either, a problem I will return to below). Both
psychoanalytic standpoints have always contradicted the data of clinical
experience and other kinds of empirical data by collapsing heterogeneous tendencies into "underlying," "deep" unities, an imperious gesture meant to colonize refractory data as a means of finding a basis of
order or stability or explaining how social relationships work, either in
structural terms or by attempting to apply numerate standards to psy-
choanalytically informed categories, which then turned out to have less
explanatory power than the sociological categories that they were
meant to replace.

At the same time, however, by stressing man's dependence on
"extragenetic outside-the-skin control mechanisms" for ordering behavior, Clifford Geertz's version of cultural anthropology does provide
a solution of sorts to this problem. Geertz views human thought as
basically social and public; thinking consists not of "happenings in the
head"—although, as he writes, something occurs there—but of a traffic
in significant symbols that are used to impose meaning on experience
and in the absence of which people would be more helpless "than the
beavers." The task for ethnographers, or historians, is twofold: "to un-
cover the conceptual structures that inform our subjects' acts" and to
construct a system of analysis and a vocabulary in terms of which what
is implied for subjects by symbolic action can be expressed.*

---

*It is of course a convention of psychoanalysis and psychohistory to refer to "in-
ternal" and "external" worlds. This phrasing of the matter as a spatial metaphor raises
problems that, from a psychoanalytic standpoint, Roy Schafer has addressed in particular.
Schafer prefers to use the language of "private" and "public" worlds rather than the language of "internal" and "external," and I have tried to follow this practice. I emphasize,
however, that whatever the language, private, internal, dynamic, or something else, the
reference is to idiosyncratic versions of the world, to unique mental constructs that provide individuals with a sense of adequacy, continuity, and connection. The prospect that
people uniformly share versions of the world in the sense of sharing feelings and wishes
about people and things (or mental representations of people and things), or that they
experience or express with constancy over time the same degree of fidelity to standards
and expectations, or that they uniformly share perceptions of or a sense of loyalty to
variously located and empowered authorities, is too remote to consider. Hence, the emphasis on ideology as a public means of orienting people to each other, to social tasks,

This is an important suggestion because it bypasses the dynamic problem, orienting people to ideological contents external to themselves. But it is also a problematic one, for it must still be decided how socially heterogeneous individuals and groups remain oriented to each other and to a symbol system because perceptions of such a system are always multiple and more or less constantly changing. That is, people are not just the passive receptors of a symbol system that directs their behavior; rather, they actively construe the significance of the system for themselves, in developmental terms, however idiosyncratic, and in terms of the various social locations they occupy (with respect to class, age, gender, occupation, religion, region, ethnicity or nationality, language, and so on). Then, too, because neither the numbers on any side of a conflict involving inevitably competing, contested versions of a symbol system nor the system itself is constant over time, it becomes necessary to address another problem mentioned earlier, discontinuity. Geertz did also suggest that it is necessary to look "for systematic relationships among diverse phenomena, not for substantive identities among similar ones." But it is not clear yet how all this might work itself out in the study of history. This kind of project, as Geertz later wrote, "now that easy assumptions about the convergence of interests among peoples (sexes, races, classes, cults, . . .) of unequal power have been historically exploded and the very possibility of unconditioned description has come into question, does not look nearly so straightforward an enterprise as it did when hierarchy was in place and language weightless."[83]

The Problem of Interpretation in History and Social Theory

Among the taken-for-granted pieties of the historical discipline are the notions that historians must respect the evidence and not go beyond it and that they are obligated to prove the things they write.[84] Lawrence Stone, declaiming against the identity of history and fiction, has stated that both history and fiction are constructs of the mind, "but the historian is tied and bound by respect for his archival data. The novelist is free to create events. Imagination does play a very important part in the writing of history but there is a reality principle out there." However, faithful adherence to these ideal standards would put an end to

---

and to cultural norms, one that is capable of absorbing the inevitable variety and that permits both socially and dynamically heterogeneous people to pursue goals in common. (Clifford Geertz, *The Interpretation of Cultures* [New York, 1973], 27, 44–45, 99. Roy Schafer, *The Analytic Attitude* [New York, 1983], 88.)

history as a professional discipline, except perhaps in a narrow moral or narrative sense. What keep history from being mere morality tale or antiquarian narrative, in other words (and what government-endowed institutions are paying for, if not privately endowed institutions also), are the interpretations of peoples' intentions or of the significance of events to an audience, and historical interpretations, except in simple instances, do not involve data. Although these interpretations are intended to appear explanatory and are presented to students in the typical lecture course and to the reading audience as addressing "why" questions (why things worked out as they did in terms of cause and effect), they actually involve an imaginative leap from social relationships and events to mind or mentality, a leap that is rarely confirmed or, under current conditions, confirmable by evidence.[85]

The kind of imaginative leap I am referring to can be quickly identified because the form is so familiar, requiring no more than a few examples chosen (for their interesting content rather than for any special vulnerability to criticism) from popular journals of opinion as well as from current and classic historical texts to see not only what professionals think they are doing but also what their audience is encouraged to believe they are doing. Accordingly, some few pertinent examples follow:

> Why does the phenomenon of health anxiety emerge in 1830? At that time . . . the grounds of both pessimism and optimism were shifting in the American mentality. On the one hand, the Calvinist fatalism about redemption was giving way to a more optimistic and entrepreneurial belief that stressed man's free will and the importance of individual action. On the other hand, Americans were facing a crisis of confidence in a democratic social structure that was widely thought to be unworkable. The last of the founding giants had died, and it was left to people of much smaller stature to secure the Union. Fearing the social fabric might disintegrate, some individuals turned for reassurance to mending their own bodies.[86]

Or again,

> Economic depression threatened victorian sex roles, since white men found they were less able to provide materially for their families. They compensated for their growing economic powerlessness by emphasizing their role as protectors of white womanhood.[87]

One more familiar kind of example from a different historical tradition:

The peasant uprising represented a terrible warning and an inducement to abandon their enlightened liberal ideas; but at the same time they could not contemplate a return to the previous matter-of-course acceptance of the exploitation of the peasantry by the upper classes. What remained was flight into the realm of individualistic self-perfection, the "inner life of the soul," or . . . the Masonic Lodge.[88]

These interpretive statements are obviously characterized by plausibility and closure, but they all raise a question about causal connection. How do these transitions from objective situation to subjective response occur, what is the process by which these different substitutions are achieved, and what language would one use to describe the process?

There are important reasons for raising these questions, but, before commenting on them, we should explore this form of argument a bit further. We may recall, for example, that Karl Marx argued, in *The Eighteenth Brumaire of Louis Bonaparte,* that the French revolutionaries of the eighteenth century found in the "classically austere traditions of the Roman Republic . . . the ideals and the art forms, the self-deceptions that they needed in order to conceal from themselves the bourgeois limitations of the content of their struggles and to keep their enthusiasm on the high plane of the great historical tragedy."[89] This remarkable interpretation of the subjective intentions of French revolutionaries, involving concepts of cognitive lack, lapse, or failure, the moral rationalization of interest, the power of moral strivings to determine appropriate latitudes of behavior and insight, involving even a concept of censorship of some sort, is deficient in only one respect: Marx provided no evidence for his interpretation, no basis, that is, for the independent assessment of his argument. Of course it could be claimed that this text of Marx's was polemical and not scholarly, but Marx's arguments take this form regardless of context.

In the same vein, Jean Paul Sartre argued in his work on Flaubert, *The Family Idiot,* that the French bourgeoisie, who had invented the idea of a universal human nature as a weapon against the particularizing tendencies of the aristocracy, were faced in turn, in 1848, with a proletarian underclass that they could not recognize unless they conceded to that class a share of power. The bourgeoisie solved their problem by becoming Victorian, repressing the animal and physical nature that they seemed to share with the proletariat, and by transforming their earlier humanism into a misanthropic positivism. This is also a very interesting assertion, obviously, but not only is no evidence provided here either, it would be hard to say what exactly would constitute evidence. On the other hand, Sartre did refer to his work as a "true novel," implying that it was meant to serve moral rather than analytic purposes anyway.[90]

It is important to emphasize that this kind of inference occurs in "objective" studies as well, as it must if such studies are to avoid a sort of numerate antiquarianism. Michael Haines, for example, in a study of fertility and occupation, has stated that mineworkers tended to marry younger and to have higher marital fertility rates than workers in other occupations, that they were well paid, but that their income tended to stabilize at a relatively early age. On the basis of these data, Haines concluded that mineworkers married at a younger age and had more children because the earnings of teenage children could supplement family income when the head of the family grew older. Haines acknowledged that people have children for many reasons and that there is a great deal of personal, individual variation in such decision making. Still, Haines could not come to any conclusions about the group on the basis of idiosyncratic strivings, even if an appropriate kind of documentation existed; he therefore solved his problem by suggesting a commonsense reason for his subjects' behavior. This occurs because there would be no point to collecting such data if this kind of inferential statement could not be made.[91]

There are in fact an endless number of examples to choose from, but there is only one more that I want to introduce here because of its particular content. Edmund Morgan, explaining the disappointment felt by Puritans as a result of their experience in the New World, had this interesting thing to say:

> But this disappointment in America required sublimation into disappointment in oneself. And American Puritans became expert at disappointing themselves. Without the surrounding wickedness of the Old World to combat, they contended with their own continuing sins and corrupt nature. Lifelong anxiety and self-deprecation became the hallmarks of the American Puritan. He made a virtue of uncertainty until he came to identify feelings of assurance about salvation as signs of its absence. The only way to be sure was to be unsure. The only distinction it was safe to claim was that of being the chief of sinners, and one of the primary sins to be bewailed and repented was disappointment in America. Nor was it necessary to have made the trip from England to be guilty of it: those who were born in New England could also be taught to mourn their failure to appreciate it. Thus there developed a curious love-hate attitude toward the land, combined with self-abasement for failing to live up to the opportunities it offered.[92]

The reason that it is important to raise questions about causal connections, about the process by which the transition from observed event to mental response occurs, or about the language that might be used to describe the process, is the absence of any substantial difference between any of the statements that we have just reviewed and fictional ones or, better yet, psychohistorical ones, about which so much critical fuss is made. For all these interpretive statements are characterized by some conception of mental activity that was unavailable to historical subjects for conscious examination but that can nevertheless be retrospectively identified. All these statements, including Marx's and Sartre's, are based on a social psychology as phantom as the hand that Adam Smith thought must regulate the play of the market for the sake of the common good. It is in this sense that we should consider Michel Foucault's observations, first, that

> the problem of the unconscious—its possibility, status, mode of existence, the means of knowing it and bringing it to light—is not simply a problem within the human sciences which they can be thought of as encountering by chance in their steps; it is a problem that is ultimately coextensive with their very existence. . . . [An] unveiling of the non-conscious is constitutive of all the sciences of man;

and, second, that

> whereas all human sciences advance towards the unconscious only with their back to it, waiting for it to unveil itself as fast as consciousness is analyzed, backwards, as it were, psychoanalysis . . . points directly towards it, with a deliberate purpose . . . towards what is there and yet hidden.[93]

These remarks of Foucault's underscore the irony of historians' complaints either about the identity of fiction and history or about psychohistory and, with respect to the latter, particularly the complaints of the most outspoken critics of psychohistory, Jacques Barzun and David Stannard. Both authors have argued that psychohistorians do the kind of work they do in theory and history because they do not have the nerve to tolerate a complex reality, preferring to simplify reality for the sake of closure or a sense of certainty. However, this is not what psychohistorians say about the matter either in personal or in theoretical terms. If that is the case, then there is no evidence for Barzun's and Stannard's assertions, which can be understood only in terms of their insight into unconscious mental processes (i.e., psychohistorians should be able to see the point of such persistent criticism of their efforts and change their thinking, but for the reason they suggest, which is quite different from a conscious desire to be stubborn, they cannot).[94]

Moreover, these remarks also underscore the difficulty of making statements about people's motives and intentions from any point of view, and it is especially in this context that historians should reconsider the concepts of ideology and relativism. By *ideology* I mean any network of high- or low-level ideas—including scientific, religious, mythic, or commonsensical ideas—that serve the moral rationalization of interest or that are characterized by a moral as distinct from a cognitive emphasis or are more readily brought to bear on moral issues than on cognitive ones and that are further characterized by contradictions, logical gaps and lapses, incongruities, and a remoteness from the real social relations these ideas are intended to account for. By *relativism* I mean the notion that interpretations of historical events change as generational needs and expectations change—the novelty of every future demanding a novel past, as George Herbert Mead put it. For, if all we have is, as Gore Vidal has recently stated, "a mass of more or less agreed-upon facts about the illustrious dead and each generation tends to rearrange those facts according to what the times require," then the authors who express these requirements must be making judgments about people's intentions different from the ones people themselves made at the time.[95] These authors must be claiming that people did things for reasons that they were not aware of, very often, as we have just seen, in terms that suggest they could have known more but for "symptomatic" reasons they did not. The reason for reconsidering these terms is, then, to have clearly in mind what historians and theorists are doing when they claim a discrepancy between the intentions of people as they expressed them and their own interpretations of these intentions as they are rendered subsequently and successively. After all, there is no better way to account for this discrepancy than by assuming, as authors routinely do, whether they say so explicitly or not, the existence of unconscious mental processes in some form.*

* An alternative approach is to conceive of people as objects of some kind of structural process in which questions of agency or subjectivity are secondary and derivative. But this approach is even more definitely the one-sided construction of an observer than is the routine kind of interpretation of unobserved intentions. It should be noted that one of the things that Carl Becker explained in "Everyman His Own Historian" is that "in the history of history a myth is a once valid but now discarded version of the human story, as our now valid versions will in due course be relegated to the category of discarded myths. With our predecessors, the bards and storytellers and priests, we have therefore this in common: that it is our function, as it was theirs, not to create, but to preserve and perpetuate the social tradition; to harmonize, as well as ignorance and prej-

These observations should be taken less as an endorsement of psychoanalysis than as a comment about routine modes of interpreting the subjective intentions of people. At the same time, however, it could be noted that, when psychoanalysis was based on an instinctual view of people as pleasure or object seeking, it was possible to distinguish these several different interpretive statements from psychoanalytic statements. But once there developed in psychoanalysis a social as distinct from an instinctual concept of relatedness, and especially once psychoanalytic authors began to view people as meaning seeking too, then such statements as I have reviewed are readily accommodated to one or another psychoanalytic standpoint.

To be sure, there is one outstanding difference between psychohistorical and other sorts of texts, if there is not that much difference in interpretive logic. Psychohistorians typically attempt to describe or to understand in theoretical terms the process by which such contents as I have reviewed achieved their effect.[96] But this approach to the question of process, however clumsy, stilted, artificial, and failed any version of it may be, is on principle the correct one because, if a theory that allows us to specify the process by which such contents became effective cannot be developed, specifically, a theory about intentions that can encompass problems of subjectivity, heterogeneity, and discontinuity, then any interpretive claim about content becomes moot. The question of evidence raised earlier is in the first place a question of theory, in other words, and as long as it remains unanswered there is no practical basis for verifying or assessing the merits of any one of these statements against a number of other possible, equally plausible ones. This may be an unwelcome conclusion to historians who want to keep their discipline theory free. But, if history is only a matter of intuitive or commonsense judgments, and if there is no way to discriminate among a

---

udice permit, the actual and the remembered series of events; to enlarge and enrich the specious present . . . [so] that 'society' . . . may judge of what it is doing in the light of what it has done and what it hopes to do" (in *Everyman His Own Historian* [Chicago, 1966], 247–48). Critics have fastened on the relativism of Becker's statement, but relativism was by no means the most serious implication. Rather, we should understand Becker to have implied by his reference to myth that there is something unreal and made-up about history that is nevertheless socially purposive, serving to link past, present, and future, preserving thereby a culture's sense of continuity and adequacy. (For structuralist conceptions of the kind noted, see, e.g., Louis Althusser and Etienne Balibar, *Reading Capital,* trans. B. Brewster [London, 1970], esp. 180. Becker once posed the question, "What is the good of history?" But he was capable of answering his own question in terms of coherence and closure. See Michael Kammen, ed., *"What Is the Good of History?" Selected Letters of Carl L. Becker, 1900–1945* [Ithaca, N.Y., 1973], xxiii.)

number of plausible conclusions, then why not leave the enterprise to novelists on the grounds that it is all imaginatively constructed anyway and for the greatest part they really do write better?

It must be emphasized that I am not referring to verifiability or assessability in the lofty sense that might occupy the attention of a philosopher of science. These observations are not a lament over the inevitability of approximate descriptions of reality rather than absolute ones or over the unattainability of true descriptions of reality. I am referring to verifiability or assessability strictly in terms of the question of evidence. The argument that no scientific theory, not even Newton's universal mechanics, has ever been established or verified is so well known that it might cause some confusion, and there should be no confusion on this point. A scientist may claim that there is no such thing as absolute knowledge, that all empirical hypotheses are "conjectural" in the radical sense that we shall never be able to "know" them for certain, and that there can be only probabilities. A physicist might therefore say that atoms as real objects in the form we imagine them cannot be proved absolutely; the most anyone can say is that the universe acts as if it is made of atoms as conventionally imagined. By the same token, an astronomer can say that we know stars as grains of light exposed on a photographic plate but that absolute proof of what they are is lacking. Still, the high quality of modern technology stems from the ability to make practical use of theoretical observations. In science, at any rate, there is an experimental basis for deciding whether particular assertions are worth agreeing with. History and the social sciences are not by any stretch of the imagination in or near to the same position. On the contrary, by inferring reasons, intentions, and motives inappropriately from "objective" data, or by supplying reasons, intentions, and motives from outside the conscious, reported experiences of people, or by simply guessing at reasons, intentions, and motives on no basis other than what appears currently plausible to colleagues, authors of interpretive statements such as the ones reviewed above preclude the possibility of a strategy of verification or assessment.

Historians (and social scientists) are, by their own criteria for evidence, far from any but a trivial explanatory capacity; there is little empirical basis for any of the middle terms that they have so far employed, linking social relationships and events to mind or mentality, a statement that is confirmed by the inability to account for the heterogeneity of groups, the variety that turns up on all sides of a social conflict.[97] We should therefore think of such familiar middle terms as class or generational conflict, internalized morality, national character, a paranoid style, patriarchalism, and the like as important because they imply to academics and to their audience that there is a unity to people's reasons, intentions, and motives that is revealed in an objective way by these terms. The terms, however, are ideological in the sense explained above, legitimating in this context the notion that people's subjectivity is accessible in a particular way, that subjective responses are more or less unified through the culture, and that assessments of them are based on some knowledge of the process by which social relationships are linked to mental activity. Psychoanalysis in its different forms is still a very important source of language and strategies for focusing attention on and explaining the deeper significance of people's behavior, but there are other languages and strategies, especially in the social sciences and in history as well.[98] The moral or ideological point of these languages is that the dynamic and social heterogeneity apparent at the surface should not be perceived as threatening because mind and society are unified at a deeper level. The various languages and strategies may differ, but the underlying premise does not.

The Social Function of Interpretation: The Homogenization of Motive

All the different points of view, fictional, psychoanalytic, historical, and social, are concerned with assessing and explaining people's motives and intentions, and they are all equally problematic. At the same time, however, the ability to assess or explain the intentions of others in everyday life is so important that any or all of these different points of view are used by the variety of audiences to achieve such explanation. The novelists' preference for their intuitive interpretations of human endeavor is vigorously promoted, but their standpoint is still in an everyday sense a secondary one. The standpoints of psychoanalysis and the social sciences, from the professional literature down through academic popularizations to the mass media (television, newspapers, magazines), are still the primary ones. The slight, uncertain grounds on which these interpretations are based are made clear to the public only rarely.[99] Otherwise, statements similar in form to the ones I have referred to in the historical literature are offered every day from every source and allowed to stand with little or no reflection, examination, or commentary, as if their truthfulness or accuracy were self-evident.

Thus it is that people are constantly being instructed in the "inner" significance of behavior, trained to expect, accept, and themselves employ a particular kind of language and interpretive strategy. Moreover, if some action is especially challenging, puzzling, threatening, or disruptive (e.g., the mass murder and suicide at Jonestown, serial murders in different places, the abuse of children and women, a terrorist attack or hijacking), or if there is a real or imagined trend of longer-range significance (the effects of large numbers of women in the work force or in positions of authority or the significance of successful career women making decisions to stay home and raise children), a psychiatrist, a psychoanalyst, a clinical psychologist, or some other "expert" will appear on the television screen or in the newspaper with a language legitimated by authoritative sources and made recognizable by repetition ("Stockholm syndrome," "stress management," "role model," "identity crisis," "significant other," "the me generation") to explain its significance, that is, to reassure the audience that these things are really comprehensible and that they fit into a known scheme of one sort or another. Note, for example, the following statements. First,

> The coldly calculating bombplanter or assassin is impervious to the restraint of ordinary emotions like empathy or compassion. . . . His ideology deadens his emotions.

Then, by contrast,

> Those who train terrorists . . . seek recruits who are more emotionally stable than others in the group and who are willing to follow rules and are able to develop strong bonds with their comrades. Under the stress of a terrorist act, such as a hijacking, those bonds within a small unit of terrorists are more crucial than the initial commitment to the movement's ideals.[100]

All the different branches of the media have their experts or have access to experts whose task it is to explain the subjective significance of whatever compels the public's attention, hula hoops and Rubik's cube, the fan wave at the ball park or fan violence at soccer matches, the attractiveness of Cabbage Patch dolls, the purchase and display of art by banks and corporations, the significance of glass towers, illegitimate adolescent pregnancy, suicide among adolescents or the elderly, and family disputes over the remote control television device. One of the television networks has even supplied a sports psychologist to "deepen" the commentary on professional football games. Questions are raised or statements made in a similar vein ("Why Are Women Psychotherapy's Best Customers?" "Why Do People Want to Be Scared Silly?" "Why Sherlock Holmes Fascinates Americans," "Why Athletes Turn to Drugs," "Why Youth Revolt").[101] Explanations of a conventional sort are provided—as if there could be a single explanation for any of these complicated questions—as with this explanation of why American youths turn up at college football games wearing body paint: "In late adolescence, teen-agers have moved away from their parents as role models and have switched their identification and allegiance to subjects that are culturally in vogue, such as rock groups or athletes. . . . When the sports fans paint themselves, they are engaging in a fantasy in which they identify with the players. But it is a safe and time limited fantasy." [102]

Every day, in subtle or blatant ways, the reading and viewing public get explanations of this sort, sometimes more technically refined, using a distinctive academic language, and sometimes less refined, using a commonsense language, as in these statements:

> An Oreo is part of America. . . . As kids people peeled it in half or dunked it. It's that nostalgia. Especially if you live in Yuppiedom, where everything is brand new, the Oreo is adding the stability that people are wanting so much.

> When the economy tightened up, people looked for jobs that would earn a lot of money. . . . Now, because the economy has loosened up and everyone's a little more relaxed, the pendulum is swinging back.

"It's a fad," said a psychologist, commenting on the popularity of a commercial computerized cowboys and Indians or hunter and hunted game played with toy guns that shoot beams of light. "It's a game for the Yuppie generation who hated to give up their toys." [103]

The form and context of these explanations allow the audience to infer that there is or could be a single, shared, unified reason or motive that emerges from social relationships within the discrete groups of people referred to and, most often, all things considered, from familial relationships, what the family did or failed to do or was compelled or allowed to do or could no longer do given the larger imperatives of the economy, the market, late capitalism, instinctual development, and so on. Of course, the situation described earlier still obtains: that a single dynamic reason could emerge sufficient to account for the shared behavior of groups defies all experience; the subjects have not themselves reported; and there is no middle term, no reference to the process by which these things have occurred, because there is no knowledge of the process. Authors explain that these are complicated issues, and they often provide disclaimers. But these disclaimers are not nearly as effective in appealing to the imagination as the summary, codifying languages that people look for and use. These languages are evidently appealing, not least if they are technical, because they then have the authority of "science," inviting people to invent a coherent world for themselves and others, whatever that might subjectively entail.

However, the many journalists and commentators who have instructed the public in this way reflect only palely the much more serious political and ideological issues that pervade history and the social sciences, the persistent struggle over the language and concepts that should define and guide orientations to the social world. We may recall in this connection the successive interpretations of American character, family life, and culture that these journalists and commentators must themselves have read as part of their education, provided by Erich Fromm, T. W. Adorno, Erik Erikson, David Riesman, Herbert Marcuse, Kenneth Keniston, Philip Rieff, Charles A. Reich, Christopher Lasch, and many others in the period following the Second World War.[104] The interpretations of these authors do not follow one from the other, they often contradict each other in crucial ways, and, taken together, they suggest a more discontinuous and heterogeneous world than any individual author meant to convey. Still, they were all taken up and used when they appeared, particularly in college classrooms, because they provided a sense of where people stood and where they might be standing next and they also provided a way of thinking about how to assess events and prospects.

The brilliance of this literature is not in question, but it is important to consider how we can reasonably get from one depiction of reasons, intentions, and motives to the next, even, for example, how we can get from Kenneth Keniston's *The Uncommitted* in 1960 (a discussion of deeply disaffected young men whose alienation extended to virtually every encounter with the world) to his *The Young Radicals* in 1968 (who may have been alienated from the American mainstream in their aggressive repudiation of the Viet Nam war and racism but who were certainly integrated and committed from their own point of view) or from Charles Reich's *The Greening of America* in 1970 (a discussion of an elevated level of consciousness that had arisen spontaneously, according to the author, in the period 1965–69 and was characterized by "energy of enthusiasm, of happiness, of hope") to Christopher Lasch's *The Culture of Narcissism* in 1979 (a discussion of a degraded level of consciousness, characterized by an indifference to past and future, a compelling desire to be admired, contempt for those manipulated into fulfilling the desire, fears of intimate relationships, fears of old age and death, and by an unappeasable hunger "for emotional experiences with which to fill an inner void".[105]

It also pays to recall, on this subject, that the contemporary discussions of narcissism began with Herbert Marcuse's *Eros and Civilization,* in which Freud's notion of primary narcissism was held by Marcuse, "beyond all immature autoeroticism," to denote a "fundamental relatedness to reality, which may generate a comprehensive existential order." Primary narcissism, Marcuse explained, could contain the germ of a different reality principle, the source for a new cathexis of the objective world, "transforming the world into a new mode of being."[106] Fifteen years later, in 1971, Marcuse was described by Henry Malcolm as having "provided a rational context" in which youthful Americans could understand that their desires for a different reality are not just "immature struggles against adult reality" nor yet a "childish rebellion against adult reality." Rather, the affluent background of many of the youths provided them with radically different opportunities that, along with technological developments, made the world more accessible to them and made their narcissistic strivings an affirmative force. Malcolm nevertheless simultaneously admonished society's managers to provide an environment in which people can live up to their ideals and establish the relationships that permit this affirmative force to assert itself. Otherwise, they will be faced with a narcissistic revolt, initiated by people who would possess, as a result of their failure, "a true mixture of emotional health and deeply pathological conflict." By 1979, with the appearance of Lasch's *Culture of Narcissism,* Marcuse's elaboration of primary narcissism was no longer part of the discourse, not even in terms of the tension perceived by Malcolm. Lasch's attention, by contrast, was directed toward the effects of secondary narcissism in the manner I have already described.[107]

It would no doubt be easy to disparage this work or to dismiss it as merely speculative or as ephemeral pop sociology, not to be taken seriously. But this would be a grievous error because to disparage this work would be, in effect, to disparage the process by which people have thus far managed to hold themselves together in a complicated and scary world, a little like disparaging the weather, which, good and bad, we live in and need. These authors had taken on themselves the serious task of attempting to develop moral or ideological positions not only in terms of changing interests and perspectives but also in terms of defining the meaning of such change and the direction that society must pursue to correct and improve the results. They are important political and intellectual actors who were intent on shaping approaches to the social world, and what they accomplished had serious political consequences, as revealed in the degree to which their concepts penetrated and permeated the discourse of different groups, especially by way of the classroom as well as the popular press and television.

However, the authors could not have succeeded in imposing a particular direction, regardless of their arguments, because the society was far too fragmented in terms of class, gender, religion, region, and ethnicity to permit it. Any one of them could have criticized current practises and suggested prospective ones, promoting, for example, a notion of community, as Robert Bellah and his coauthors recently did in *Habits of the Heart*. But even so apparently unobjectionable a wish for a more harmonious and integrated community, recalling to mind the expectations of older biblical and republican traditions (absent their exclusionary principles and practices, of course), provoked a sense of anxiety and scorn among feminist and other groups. The changing content of this literature and its reception are echoed in the shifting coalitions and alliances among disparate and even conflicting groups in the political arena, which has often been commented on, underscoring the heterogeneity of interests, perspectives, and wishes that precludes the achievement of less conflicted, more unified social relationships, let alone communal relationships.[108]

This argument about the moral or ideological intent of a familiar form of literature in the light of the heterogeneous composition of contemporary society is easily expanded in terms of historical data and a body of historical literature that also emphasizes the heterogeneity problem. Consider, for example, Gordon Wood's characterization of the American Revolution:

> Men were only half aware of where their thought was going, for these new ideas about politics were not the products of extended reasoned analysis but were rather numerous responses of different Americans to a swiftly changing reality, of men involved in endless polemics compelled to contort and draw out from the prevailing assumptions the latent logic few had foreseen.[109]

Or Eugen Weber's characterization of the French Revolution:

> Roused in their revolution to obtain a representative assembly, then a constitutional monarchy, the French drifted by 1793 into dictatorship based on police terror and the guillotine. The French revolution—meant to establish freedom of enterprise, trade, speech, and careers "open to talent" rather than birth—soon turned to social war.[110]

There are many other such characterizations that could be addressed, not least among them Stalin's "second revolution," which certainly had as one of its principal targets the heterogeneity of interests and perspectives. But just to cite one more interesting example, consider the remarks of C. Vann Woodward on the American South during the Civil War. According to Woodward, slavery, originally declared to be the "cornerstone" of the new nation, was replaced by independence as the true aim of the war. However, because the attempt was made to recruit slaves in the South as frontline soldiers with the promise of emancipation afterward, this was not the end of the story either:

> For to confess emancipation to be right, slavery wrong, and the war unjustified would to some be to dishonor the graves of thousands. . . . Unable to endure such an indictment of the past others continued the fight, they said, for the defense of the South's honor.[111]

These events and these views of events are additionally in part the source for and in part the result of the recent discussions or elaborations of discontinuity in literature, in the work of such a writer as Robert Coover, and in theory, criticism, and history, in the work of such writers as Michel Foucault and Edward Said who have emphasized

> the historical abruptness of transformations in ways of knowing and thinking, and the sheer discontinuity involved in "beginning" anything. What all these movements—literary, philosophical and critical—have in common is a determination to make us see that the reality . . . so effectively imposed on Western thought [by Darwin's evolutionary conception] is in fact only a set of conventions, it is a myth serving its own political and ideological functions, as all myths do.[112]

This standpoint, too, must have a political and ideological function, considering especially the writers who promoted it. But, whatever their purpose may have been, this standpoint does bring us closer to reality, and the challenge is to see what use can be made of it.

Defining the Problem for History and Theory

The problem of interpretively assessing people's intentions is now even more complicated than perhaps it initially appeared to be, requiring first of all a discussion of the specific problem that undermined the strategies of the social sciences, psychoanalysis, and history to deal with it, dynamic and social heterogeneity. The enduring tendency of people to turn up in unpredictable and changing numbers on different sides of issues, to behave in unexpected ways, contradicts the main premise of all the disciplines, that there is an underlying cause or reason for behavior that, once correctly identified, will serve to unify the variety at the surface. The most interesting thing about the historical and critical literature that we have reviewed, along with the examples from journalism, is that it all exists as so many attempts to provide a moral and ideological basis for different interpretations that, just because of their variety and even contradictoriness, can serve a heterogeneous audience looking for conceptions of process that can explain to them the baffling and often threatening forms of social change that they experience. The Western concepts of history and society, especially after the legitimation of competitive autonomy and the emphases on reasoned analysis, on the sanctity of the individual, and on widening the spheres of independent activity, invite competing interests and multiple interpretations (the source of Hegel's notion of "subjective freedom"—which is anything but free—or Jacob Burckhardt's emphasis on the subjective side of things once people recognized themselves as "spiritual individuals").[113] In a social context that is constantly changing and that survives disintegration or dictatorship only on the ability of people to reconcile multiple and antagonistic versions of context, this means creating an arena for multiple interpretations and for the constant development of concepts and images appropriate to the experience of change and of heterogeneous response.

That is to say that, once faith in the capacity of people to pursue independent forms of activity was morally justified and encouraged, multiple and competing interpretations of the reasons for participation and exclusion were bound to follow, along with a focus on one's own and others' intentions and motives as a means of maintaining a stable orientation to the world. The competing concepts and images that appear in fiction, various forms of theory, and history (or journalism) become, paradoxically, one of the ways by which a perception of reality as chaotic among a heterogeneous population is forestalled. All descriptions and analyses of mind and society, whether cast as fiction, theory, or history, are therefore intended and used to make sense of the present in the service of particular interests and perspectives. It is certainly the case that the conventional, homogenizing concepts of psychoanalysis and the social sciences, whether they appear in scholarly or popular form, have a much greater impact on people's imagination and their ability to interpret events continuously than the empirical data on which they are based could possibly warrant.

Indeed, the body of literature taken together, the fiction, the psychoanalysis, the history, the social science, and the journalism, is integrated by this ideological function. All this literature, interpretively focused on the intentions and motives of people, is readily accessible to a variety of audiences, and all of it is used by these audiences as a means of orienting themselves, constituting one form of evidence of the impact of heterogeneity and discontinuity on people and of the importance of the interpretive process to them. And there are still other forms of evidence, as people have reported and continue to report on their perceptions of fragmentation and breakdown, on the difficulty they have absorbing the variety of people and acknowledging the legitimacy of their claims, and as different social agencies labor to instruct the variety of people in the virtues of pluralism. However, the most obvious kind of evidence, it seems to me, is the widespread use of all forms of psychotherapy. Philip Rieff noted in the *Triumph of the Therapeutic* that therapies devoted to individual improvement were bound to proliferate in this kind of society, displaying their wares, passing in turn by "the psychological reviewing stand," as people search for some sense of inner unity and a capacity for integration. But the number and variety of therapies is surprising and constantly increasing (including human potential and New Age therapies that stress variously the release of untapped energies, holistic health, meditation, practical spirituality, grass-roots activism, and the like and that are based in older therapeutic forms as well as newer ones.)[114] One observer has claimed that by now one American in three has been in some form of psychotherapy and that, in 1987, some 15 million Americans will have made "roughly 120 million visits to mental health professionals." All this occurs, moreover, apart from the great and enormously appealing variety of fundamental and evangelical religious groups that are themselves overtly hostile to the pluralism of the society and therapeutic and integrative in intent.[115]

Thus, although the ideological process of integration and repair is constant over time and the problem—how to orient a heterogeneous population to a common goal—is also constant, the contents directed to this purpose are varied and changing. The most interesting of these contents at this point are those provided by certain European and American writers and activists whose work was intended to address the problem, approvingly, angrily, despairingly, derisively, because their lives were so deeply affected by it. It pays to take another look at some of these contents, however familiar they may be, not so much for their own sake, as for what they reveal about both the problem and the process.

2

The Heterogeneity Problem in Practice and Theory

Perceptions of Discord and Fragmentation

One crucial facet of Jean-Jacques Rousseau's many-faceted career as social theorist, artist, and critic involved his perception of subjective strivings as a social force and of the dangers for social order of multiple interests and perspectives. Rousseau was not the first to condemn and he was not alone in condemning the effects of self-seeking and the antagonistic activities of competing groups, the degeneration of social life, as he saw it, that followed from the formation of private property and the division of labor.[1] Alexis de Tocqueville, who was himself interested in the problem, pointed out that A. R. J. Turgot had complained, too, that "the nation is an aggregate of different and incompatible social groups whose members have so few links between themselves that everyone thinks solely of his own interests; no trace of any feelings for the public weal is anywhere to be found."[2] But, by dwelling on the affective vices of envy, pride, greed, resentment, and vanity, on alienation, narcissistic self-absorption, false desires, distinguishing between "true self" and "false self," by condemning the desire to stand out, to climb, to achieve notoriety, and especially to shine in the corrupting environment of Paris, or to promote one's interest by organizing factions, combinations, or special associations, the source of contentious bickering, of plots and cabals, division and discord, Rousseau did a great deal to establish the perceptual and semantic space within which Western observers and critics undertook to construct their versions of the modern world, focused particularly on the absence of a unifying principle.[3] Rousseau was looking for a way out of pluralism and diversity, a way to counter the effects of social change, inequality, and complexity, and his solution was the promotion of a condition of agrarian simplicity defined by a freely chosen, morally binding suppression of the narcissism of all differences, great and small, for the good of the community. For, if the community could not find a single unifying moral standard for conduct and ensure compliance with it, then it would fail in its primary responsibility, to provide an arena for the development of character as the necessary basis for the establishment of freedom and equality, and everyone would become a victim.

The principal convention in the Western world over the last two centuries has been to ascribe the source of this discord to capitalist relations of production and exchange and the division of labor, perceived either as the bourgeois promotion of individual self-seeking, exploitation, exclusion, and class conflict or the rationalization and bureaucratization of life involving further, from various points of view, noble or ill-conceived and damaging attempts to integrate diverse religious, racial, ethnic, or linguistic groups in formerly homogeneous societies. The different attempts to justify these activities—whether John Locke's notion of majority rule based on individual consent, or Adam Smith's notion of a useful degree of economic inclusion as compensation for personal and social division, his vision of a host of seemingly random individual transactions guided to a socially integrative result by the workings of an "invisible hand," or James Madison's notion of the inevitability of competing interests and perspectives nevertheless absorbed and mediated safely by well-conceived representative forms of government—did not inspire confidence in concerned observers and critics. Much less, needless to say, did the combative claims of heterogeneous populations pursuing their own interests and perspectives regardless of how others were affected in the course of the French Revolution: the legal-institutional politics of the bourgeoisie, compromising in some forms, intransigent in others, the eruptive street politics of the sans-culottes, the violence of the peasant jacquerie, and the bitter opposition of the monarchy, aristocracy and church to the lot, only confirmed the worst fears of a writer like Rousseau and led important revolutionary activists to urge and attempt to implement the suppression of factions.[4]

It has often been argued that the French Revolution occurred and kept changing its shape because of the absence of a morality (or ideology) that could legitimately reconcile the material interests of these contending groups or integrate them in the processes that affected their lives. It is important to keep in mind, however, that what was for some a situation of increasing access to resources in potentially favorable circumstances was obviously for others a situation of threatened or actually decreasing access to resources in unfavorable circumstances, a situation that was further aggravated because no group was unified within itself. Hence Tocqueville's subsequent accounting for the breakdown in French society: "Once the bourgeoisie had been completely severed from the noble, and the peasant from both alike, and when a similar differentiation had taken place within each of these three classes, with the result that each was split up into a number of small groups almost completely shut off from each other, the inevitable consequence was that though the nation came to seem a homogeneous whole, its parts no longer held together."[5] This meant, according to Tocqueville, that nothing could stop the centralizing French monarchy, but nothing could support it either, and that is why, in the crisis of the late 1780s, the whole structure collapsed. But it also meant that the solution to the problem caused by the collapse could have been neither communal, in Rousseau's terms, nor institutional, in Madison's, at least not without the constant resort to force. The short-term solution that the French finally arrived at was based on personality, the chance appearance of a charismatic leader, Napoléon, who unified the society temporarily around his military genius and political vision, which gave some substance to his claim that he could satisfy the competing interests of the different groups. To be sure, when Napoléon was defeated, the conflicts and divisions reappeared, and the succession of monarchies, empires, and republics that followed underscored the tenuous grip that governments in France have had ever since over the variety of contending groups.

This perception of division and discord in all domains (including eventually historical relativism, "the contemporary historical dissolution of all that is substantial, absolute and eternal in the flux of things, in historical mutability") was discussed by any number of critics in terms of the effects on character, outlook, and social relationships.[6] On Tocqueville's view, the main problem was the abolition of privilege and the intermingling of ranks, which detaches people from each other and forces them to live constantly with change—of place, feelings, and fortunes—as they rise and fall on the social ladder.[7] Friedrich Schiller, on one side of Tocqueville, was just one of many observers who complained that people were isolated from each other, fragmented, and able to experience only "partial and paltry" relationships, while Nietzsche, on the other side, explained that, as a result of this kind of social change, there were no longer any viable communal formulas (the significance of Freud's work as well, according to Philip Rieff, for, if there are no longer any viable communal formulas, then there is nothing left for people to do but achieve a personal sense of integration).[8]

Nietzsche also observed in this context that, just as we know of no fact independent of interpretation, so too there is no vision of reality uncontaminated by prejudice and perspective: "As long as the word 'knowledge' has any meaning at all, the world is knowable. But it can be *interpreted* differently; it does not have a meaning behind it, but innumerable meanings. . . . It is our needs that interpret the world."[9] Max Weber further elaborated this standpoint in his discussion of value-bound and value-free points of view. Weber argued that it was impossible for any observer to capture the world in all its concreteness and detail from any single point of view and that therefore "All knowledge of cultural reality . . . is always from *particular points of view.*" Weber perceived the absence of structure in the social world, which he referred to as a "heterogeneous continuum," "an amorphous detritus of appearances," or a "chaotic stream" that becomes ordered in our own terms, as our own composition. That is, social reality is chaotic as such, but not for us because we bring order to it, although we then struggle over the different conceptions of order. Weber believed that any argument to the contrary, specifically Marx's expectation of the development of a monistic proletarian culture, a shared perspective emerging from a single interest, was a morally suspect evasion of reality.[10] In any event, this kind of observation had long since become part of the critical common sense of the Western world, as we may infer from the following conversation in George Eliot's *Middlemarch:*

> "When I was young, Mr. Lydgate, there never was any question about right and wrong. We knew our catechism, and that was enough; we learned our creed and our duty. Every respectable Church person had the same opinions. But now, if you speak out of the Prayer-book itself, you are liable to be contradicted."
>
> "That makes a rather pleasant time of it for those who like to maintain their own point," said Lydgate.[11]

Clearly, it was the heterogeneity of populations, movements, and perspectives and the sense of disintegration and fragmentation that this heterogeneity impelled that was the principal specter haunting Europe and America. Consider Herman Melville's depiction of an American scene on a Mississippi river boat, aboard which, as he wrote, "there was no lack of variety": "Natives of all sorts, and foreigners; men of business and men of pleasure; parlor men and backwoodsmen; farm-hunters and fame-hunters; heiress-hunters, gold-hunters, buffalo-hunters, bee-hunters, happiness-hunters, truth-hunters, and still keener hunters after all these hunters." There were, besides, English, Irish,

German, Scotch, Danes, Quakers, soldiers, slaves, Spanish creoles, old-fashioned French Jews, Mormons, Papists, Sioux chiefs, hard-shell Baptists, clay eaters, teetotalers, convivialists, and more—"in short, a piebald parliament, an Anacharsis Cloots congress of all kinds of that multiform pilgrim species, man." Nathaniel Hawthorne, wanting to take a closer look at the Civil War, visiting at Willard's Hotel in Washington, D.C., in 1862, also observed the exceptional "miscellany of people" there, including governors, generals, statesmen, orators, and other illustrious men, mixed up with "office-seekers, wire-pullers, inventors, artists, poets, prosers (including editors, army-correspondents, *attachés* of foreign journals, and long-winded talkers), clerks, diplomatists, mail-contractors, railway-directors, until," as Hawthorne put it, "your own identity is lost among them." [12]

The variety was obviously impressive—and there were more such lists.* But consider also Tocqueville's first impression on arriving in America: "No sooner do you set foot on American soil than you are stunned by a kind of tumult; a confused clamor is heard on every side; and a thousand simultaneous voices demand the immediate satisfaction of their social wants. Everything is in motion around you." Nothing, Tocqueville wrote, was more striking to him than the "tumultuous agitation," the "constant agitation," of social and political life. In America, men, things, and opinions are forever changing, the "heterogeneous and agitated mass," given to "extreme fluctuations," are intent on pursuing only their own petty interests, their feelings turned in on themselves. [13]

American society was distressing to observers because it appeared so vulnerable to "personalist fragmentation," which is why Weber emphasized to his contemporaries that America was not just a formless sandheap of individuals "but rather a buzzing complex of strictly exclusive, yet voluntary associations." [14] But, in any event, America represented only a novel and startling instance of a general condition in which, as Emile Durkheim described it, "there is no firm ground under the feet of society. Nothing any longer is steadfast. And since the critical

---

*On the subject of lists, fragmentation, the loss of identity, and the potential for chaos, Saul Bellow's Artur Sammler also observed the variety of people, this time on Broadway: "All human types reproduced, the barbarian, redskin, or Fiji, the dandy, the buffalo hunter, the desperado, the queer, the sexual fantasist, the squaw; bluestocking, princess, poet, painter, prospecter, troubador, guerilla, Che Guevara, the new Thomas à Beckett. Not imitated are the businessman, the soldier, the priest, and the square. . . . They sought originality. They were obviously derivative. And of what—of Paiutes, of Fidel Castro? No, of Hollywood extras. Acting mythic. Casting themselves into chaos, hoping to adhere to higher consciousness, to be washed up on the shores of truth" (*Mr. Sammler's Planet* [New York, 1970], 147–49).

spirit is well developed and everyone has his own way of thinking, the state of disorder is made even greater by all these individual diversities. Hence the chaos seen in certain democracies, their constant flux and instability." Henry Adams, too, wrote that people had managed to keep control of their minds by assimilating bits of the seemingly chaotic situation and blocking out the rest of it. But in 1900, Adams arbitrarily continued, "a new avalanche of unknown forces had fallen on [the mind] which required new mental powers to control. If this view was correct, the mind could gain nothing by flight or fight; it must merge in its supersensual multiverse, or succumb to it."[15]

All this movement appeared especially threatening to people in the modern cities, completely unprepared for the kind of development that they were undergoing. London, Paris, Vienna, and New York seemed to have nothing to offer people but separation, isolation, and a constant, despairing, insupportable assault on the senses. There are books and chapters within books devoted to the experiences of people in cities and the different languages scientists and artists used to describe what they thought they were witnessing. Authors employed the language of degeneracy (the morbid deviation of an organism from its original type), of urbanization as a form of racial poison affecting the health and mental stability of people, of the second law of thermodynamics translated into cultural terms, or of entropy, the universal tendency of things to get more and more disordered. But there was also the language of shipwreck and castaway, of volcanic explosion, earthquake, and whirlpool, of the city as a place of shoals and terrors where threatening mobs spill over and workers sink and drown, a "noisy, thunderous" place and a dark one, limned in gray and brown colors.[16]

Rousseau, whose feelings presaged this more general condemnation of urban life, spurned Paris, "the illustrious city, the city of noise, smoke and mire where the crowd is a waste-land." Samuel Johnson had boasted that whoever was tired of London was tired of life, but London nevertheless made many people tired. Alexander Herzen, living in this "city of cities," could not believe that such a place had a future. Henry James explained why London could appear so insupportable: "The fogs, the smoke, the dirt, the darkness, the wet, the distances, the ugliness, the brutal size of the place, the horrible numerosity of society, the manner in which this senseless bigness is fatal to amenity. . . . You may call it dreary, heavy, stupid, dull, inhuman, vulgar at heart and tiresome in form." James, who thought that "a 'subject' may very well reside in some picture of this overwhelming, self-defeating chaos or cataclysm toward which the whole thing is drifting . . . the deluge of people, the insane movement for movement, the ruin of thought, of life, the negation of work, of literature, the swelling, roaring crowds," also thought that London was still magnificent, "on the whole the most possible form of life," an opinion that he did not hold of New York, which appeared fatally and senselessly big to him without any of the redeeming qualities of London.[17]

Beatrice Webb wrote that people in London had "no roots in neighborhood, in vocation, in creed, or for that matter in race." Others bemoaned the loneliness (Matthew Arnold's often-quoted line "We mortal millions live *alone,*" is just one famous expression of it), the "transcendental homelessness" of modern man (a theme of Georg Lukacs's as well as of Jean-Paul Sartre, Albert Camus, and Franz Fanon and of the American authors David Riesman, Peter Berger, and Richard Sennett), bereft and abandoned, camped in cities (in Joseph Conrad's image) "like bewildered travellers in a garish, unrestful hotel." Rousseau's vision of the city as the abyss, Lukacs's vision of city life, "the anarchistic tendencies to tear everything asunder, to dissolve everything into spiritual atoms," and Georg Simmel's equally unhappy vision of the alienating consequences of this life as people are deprived of any unifying relationships and are rendered unfit to cope with the complex mental states required by it underscore the widely shared sense of "urban degeneration." Henry Adams wrote of New York in 1905 that "the city had the air and movement of hysteria, and the citizens were crying, in every accent of anger and alarm, that the new forces must at any cost be brought under control." But recall as well Adolf Hitler's impressions of Vienna as he related them in *Mein Kampf* or Sigmund Freud's brief reference to the contemporary literature in *"Civilized" Sexual Morality and Modern Nervous Illness.*[18]

This situation was viewed by some as irreversible but remediable. Tocqueville, despite expressed fears of the tyranny of the majority in democratic societies or the power of the state to crush civil society or, under other circumstances, to sap civic will, rendering people passive before authority, envisioned a solution in civic participation, social activism, and voluntary association. Tocqueville believed that the right of association is as inalienable in its nature as the right of personal liberty, and, in any case, people, especially in democratized societies, had no choice but to exercise this right "to prevent the despotism of faction or the arbitrary power of a prince."[19]

By contrast, Max Weber viewed the process as irreversible and irremediable, except perhaps by the intervention of a charismatic figure, arguing that nothing could forestall the rationalization of culture or the bureaucratization of society. Bureaucracy is the most efficient means of organizing large-scale tasks, and, in industry, whether organized by capitalists or socialists, or in the work world generally, that meant the separation of workers from their tools and the vulnerability of workers to bureaucratic officials. Weber believed in the virtues of individual autonomy, and he favored the capitalist organization of production over the socialist on the grounds that sustaining autonomy under these conditions was more promising. But it is hard to see, given Weber's terms, how ordinary people in either case could fail to become victims of bureaucratic domination.[20]

Ferdinand Tönnies argued similarly with regard to the rationalization process that, in the earlier "organic" *Gemeinschaft*, people were bound to each other by a special sympathy, a social force essentially of the kind that binds families, nurturant, solicitous, and communal. In the "mechanical" *Gesellschaft* that supplanted it, everyone is isolated and alone, each opposed to the other, bound together only by abstract laws and the decisions of a numerical majority. Life in towns had formerly been characterized by the "fellowship of work, the guild or corporation, and the fellowship of cult, the fraternity, the religious community," which, taken all together, represented "the last and highest expression of which the idea of *Gemeinschaft* is capable." Now, Tönnies explained in obviously intentional Hobbesian terms, "the relation of all to all may be conceived of as potential hostility or latent war." In the *Gemeinschaft*, people were essentially united in spite of all the factors that worked to separate them; in the *Gesellschaft*, people are essentially divided in spite of all the factors that might work to unite them.[21]

But there was yet a third view, the possibility of recovering or establishing anew a unified community based on the discovery of a moral mechanism capable of guaranteeing the necessary development, whether determined objectively, by history or blood or laws of energy or attraction, or subjectively, by some kind of animating, integrating myth, which proved more compelling. The most potent expression of course was that of Karl Marx, whose work inspired people to imagine that the conflicts inherent in bourgeois modes of production must provide a real basis for a future communal life. The terms are too familiar to require great elaboration here: it is enough to say that the establishment of a unified social world was assured by the historical and emancipatory role of the working class, whose interests and perspectives would prevail as a matter of structural necessity, eliminating the social basis of conflict, allowing thereby the development of a monistic culture. Critics have pointed out many times that Marx understood the historical situation to be more complicated than this scheme allows, that human perceptions and motives are contingent and cannot be mechanistically conceived, that tendencies do not automatically work themselves out independent of the subjective assessment by people of their circumstances, and that there is nothing inevitable about historical development, all of which is readily enough documented.[22] Still, Marx wrote for an audience whom he hoped to convince, who were distressed in the many ways and places already noted, and who were only too eager to read Marx's observation of "tendencies working with iron necessity toward inevitable results" in a one-sided, deterministic way.[23] Indeed, Marx is as much a man of his own time as he thought only as he is misread in these terms. This other, two-sided reading of Marx, the emphasis on meaning as well as structure, makes of him what he in fact was, a highly idiosyncratic thinker whose conception of community could not possibly have been understood correctly by the audience for whom he was writing.

The sense of discord and fragmentation, the powerlessness of the individual in a bourgeois society supposedly devoted to the enhancement of the individual, accompanied by expressions of anger, alarm, anxiety, disgust, disappointment, and fear, was also accompanied by imagined solutions, the supersession of the bourgeoisie, the overcoming or suppression of the rationalization process and the reintegration of feeling into everyday life, a return to the countryside, or, certainly not least, the elimination or exclusion of Jews or other racial, ethnic, religious, or linguistic minorities.[24] We may recall in this last connection T. S. Eliot's comments to students and faculty at the University of Virginia in 1933 that a population should be homogeneous, especially in a religious sense, "and reasons of race and religion combine to make any large number of free thinking Jews undesirable." But Eliot was one of those who believed that people are not able to tolerate much reality, by which he meant the disordered and chaotic world into which they are born. (Eliot, of course, was not the only writer to express such feelings—Ezra Pound and George Santayana did as well).[25]

In addition, the sense of discord and fragmentation was accompanied by the appearance of substantial social movements based on claims and expectations of the sort that Marx promoted, of harmony and unity, of release from a degenerate and immoral past and the final achievement of justice and equality. The exalted claims and expectations of these movements or of the social revolutions that sometimes followed from them, notably in France, Germany, and Russia, particularly the world-embracing claim for the realization of a communal spirit and practice aimed at purifying a contaminated body, are not the whole story, but they are one of the principal parts of the story as it unfolded. These claims and expectations obviously constituted for large numbers of people the real purpose of the movements and revolutions, which was not the solution to particular conflicts or the support of particular interests but rather, as expressed especially by authoritative leaders at the time, the ultimate solution to discord and the establishment of life on a new moral plane. Hence Robespierre, whose goal was to protect the mass of French citizens, pure, simple, and virtuous, from the mob of ambitious, impure intriguers and scoundrels, said that the Jacobins intended to "fulfill the will of nature, accomplish the destiny of mankind, realize the promises of philosophers, and absolve providence of the long reign of crime and tyranny," effecting thereby "an entire regeneration," the creation of "a new people."[26] Lenin also declared that the Communists would "transform the conditions of life of the whole of humanity," that they were going to "rebuild the world" and would achieve "the complete end of the very division of society into classes."[27] At the other end of the political spectrum, Hitler, for his part, said that, if the Aryans were triumphant, the world would witness a period of unprecedented achievement based on the promise of Aryan blood but if they were not, the planet itself would grow cold.[28]

These are all rather characteristic expressions of particular expectations and fears, but it is necessary to discriminate among the different elements involved. One element that was especially affecting in the nineteenth century, the subject of conservative as well as radical criticism, was the chaotic economic conditions, the fact of urban mass poverty imposed by the novel practices of the bourgeoisie, in which people were related to each other only in terms of money and were otherwise isolated. Another element, however, was the fact of heterogeneity or diversity as such, whether conceived in Robespierre's terms of virtue and vice, public morality and corruption, unity and division; or in terms of bourgeois relations of production, which compel class conflicts and antagonistic perspectives; or in terms of Protestantism, which was also perceived as separating people from each other by fostering adherence to the dictates of individual conscience and reason; or in terms of the readiness of liberal-bourgeois societies to be deceived into integrating hitherto excluded alien races, principally the Jews. The common strategy of theory and practice was to infer the existence of heterogeneity and its contentious consequences from one of these sources and to suggest that the elimination of the source (the bourgeoisie, Protestantism, the Jews) would guarantee the disappearance of the consequences. But, of the two elements, heterogeneity was at least as compelling as poverty, the prospect of unity as compelling as that of distributive justice, especially to those capable of articulating the problem. Critics unaffected by poverty or capable of justifying its existence still felt vulnerable to the threat of diversity, which they experienced or perceived as disorder.[29] What all the different conservative and radical perspectives shared was the promise or expectation of community and not necessarily a concern with poverty. As Joseph de Maistre put it in his own terms, people need beliefs, not problems, and there should be an absolute and general national dogma, a "national mind" capable of forestalling the consequences of individual reason, which is the enemy of moral association.[30]

The Heterogeneity Problem in Practice: Comments on Two Revolutions

One of the fundamental requirements of republican ideology is a homogeneous population, and republican moralists undertook the American Revolution with expectations of "organic social homogeneity."[31] Such homogeneity was considered not only essential to good order (there was a shared republican belief that this kind of unity was indispensable, that competing interests and factional rivalries would engender the kind of turmoil destructive of liberty).* It was a practical prospect as well because of America's unique historical situation. As one often-quoted observer put it in 1776, "America is the only country in the world wholly free from all political impediments at the very time that it is laid under the necessity of framing a civil constitution. Having no rank above freeman she has but one interest to consult."[32]

But this wished-for unity based on the prospect of a single interest, however conceived, could not have lasted, and it did not last. In fact, as the compromises that went into the drafting of the Declaration of Independence revealed, American society was already too complex and conflicted to permit the kind of unity republican moralists assumed to be necessary in order for a republic to be sustained. It did not take long for Americans to become alert to the many reasons for—even the

---

*Of course one cannot infer from the use of republican language, evident also in the statement of Robespierre above, how people felt about it or about the prospects for republican morality in different places. The expressed sense of outrage of Robespierre (and Saint-Just), their contempt for hypocrisy and moral weakness, their willingness to punish people who failed to live up to their high standards, their sense that unity was achievable, a function of implacable will and resolve, especially in a revolutionary period when the immediate world seemed capable of fundamental change, their peculiar combination of defiance and despondency, certainty and vulnerability, their passionate urge to risk everything and their indifference to life itself when people refused to follow, all this was quite different from anything that happened in the United States, where prominent leaders were also disappointed, frustrated, anxious, alarmed, and fearful because of the moral laxity implied by their inability to implement republican standards in the postrevolutionary society.

necessity and inevitability of—division: alliances unraveled, moderates and radicals split, leaders and factions split among and within themselves. The most common and durable source of this division, as James Madison explained in his *Federalist* paper no. 10, is the various and unequal division of property. But property is not the only source: religious differences, differences relating to the organization of government, and attachments to different leaders, all these things and more have always divided mankind: "Those who hold and those who are without property have ever formed distinct interests in society. Those who are creditors, and those who are debtors fall under a like discrimination. A landed interest, a manufacturing interest, a mercantile interest, a moneyed interest, with many lesser interests, grow up of necessity in civilized nations, and divide them into different classes, actuated by different sentiments and views." Madison suggested further, ungenerously but not untruthfully, that, even where no substantial differences present themselves to people, "the most frivolous and fanciful distinctions have been sufficient to kindle their unfriendly passions and excite their most violent conflicts."[33]

It follows, Madison argued, that, because it is impossible to remove the causes of this division, the only choice that people have, apart from submitting to tyranny, is to control the effects. The main problem to solve if the revolution was to survive and America to flourish—the same problem that was shortly to undermine the best intentions of the French—was how to mobilize the diversity and orient the different factions to a common goal, preserving the republic by reconciling reality to principle, given the unlikelihood that the ensuing conflicts could be resolved by the activities of virtuous leaders or, more to the point, given the need to accept the manipulations of self-interested individuals and groups and the need to control the activities of government itself. The constitutional solution that the Americans arrived at from a variety of motives—miraculously, according to Madison—permitted a contentious politics based on competing political parties, themselves a mixture of factions and interests, organized to confront each other on local and national levels.

The result was unexpected, but it solved a problem, considering the kind of society that Americans had already developed. There were differences everywhere, and, while leaders and followers may have united for a while against a common enemy, employing a common language, they never saw things the same way. As Daniel Webster later remarked, "All the great men of our Revolutionary epoch necessarily had a circle of which they were, severally, the centre. Each, therefore, has something to tell not common to all. Mr. [John] Adams and Mr.

Jefferson, for example, tho' acting together, on a common theatre, at Philadelphia, were nevertheless far apart, when in Massachusetts & Virginia, & each was at home, in the midst of men, & of events, more or less different from those which surrounded the other." [34]

Madison's discussion of the problem of heterogeneity and of the kind of government necessary to control its effects, regardless of the source (David Hume or Bernard Mandeville) or the ulterior purpose (segregating people from the operations of government), is still as good a one as there is: no one yet has perceived the problem more acutely or phrased it more succinctly than he did. Madison did typically locate the "cause" of faction in "nature," but he may be forgiven this locution. [35] Besides, dwelling on it deflects attention from the more crucial point that he made, one that we should be able to appreciate all the more with hindsight: heterogeneity is an intractable problem that occurs for more reasons than the unequal division of property, or, to put it another way, even if private property in the means of production were eliminated, there would still be competing perspectives and a need for some institutional means to mediate the differences.

It is important to consider that, once the Americans had settled on the form of government, their main concern was to preclude the expression of any residual passive strivings among the public or any seeking after nurturant and dependent consolations. Their main fear was the ignorance and weakness of those people "susceptible of influence, and of the irregular passions." They worried about the failure of character (typically expressed as servile dependence or slavish submission) and the tyranny of government. Americans protected themselves from this possibility in different ways, primarily by enhancing the power of those deemed capable of autonomous activity, "the wise, the uninfluenced and steady," and by forbidding the right to participate in decision-making processes to all people deemed incapable of exercising self-control, personal mastery, and will (i.e., women, workers, children, blacks, etc.). [36] Americans had no tolerance for the kind of political or social ideology that justified dependence and hierarchy and that appeared among conservative writers and authoritative public figures in Europe, where people were urged to choose the right to belong to an exclusive if hierarchical community over the right to pursue independent activity and personal gain in a more open and inclusive one. The West European bourgeoisie hoped to achieve primacy over their conservative opponents (and Americans were pleased never to have to deal with such opponents) by guaranteeing the rewards of personal effort, by integrating and elevating those who did succeed by dint of such effort, by organizing a political environment in which vital concessions could be made to the interests of this particular class, and by repudiating for as long as they could, and especially in America, all aspirations for communal endeavor or communal solutions. As Tocqueville had already observed, and as we may still observe in the widespread appeal of lotteries in a period of economic uncertainty, there are no communal solutions in America; there are only private and personal ones.[37]

In these terms, the Bolsheviks, on coming to power in Russia, had a double task. First, they had to overcome what they conceived of as the cultural inertia of the masses, their servile and submissive habits, their passive acceptance of conditions, a problem that they addressed typically by contemptuous references to "oblomovism." It was most characteristic of Lenin, who approached the problem with all the fervor and anxiety of the best republican moralists, to complain about the laziness, carelessness, and indiscipline of the people, to condemn what he called their "asiatic" or "semi-asiatic" slovenliness, their inability to submit to the requirements of plans and systems; and it was characteristic also to insist on focusing energy on prosaic tasks in everyday life, the mastery of practical detail. But, second, not only did even Party people need to struggle constantly against such expressions of personal weakness (to learn that the Party was not a "family circle," that sentimental strivings were no substitute for disciplined behavior and objective analysis), but they also had to struggle against what were called bourgeois or petty-bourgeois tendencies compelled by past history and class background; that is, members of the Bolshevik party, let alone the public at large, had themselves to suppress the desire to promote their own interests, to indulge the selfish pursuit of personal gain or narrow group interests.[38]

In the more spontaneous and free-spirited decade of the 1960s, Lenin was criticized from the left for being too bourgeois because of his concern with discipline and control, strict accounting and businesslike attitudes.[39] The fact remains, however, that he and his colleagues refused to accept the bourgeois "either/or," either the right to be a dependent, passive participant in a hierarchical but exclusive community or the right to pursue personal gain in a more open, inclusive one. The Bolsheviks insisted that there had to be a third way, based on the universally inclusive, integrating, communal vision that Marx had made so compellingly real for them and that for the most part they all shared. But they also had to figure out how they were going to achieve this ultimate goal.

The Bolsheviks realized of course that there were objective problems that they would have to deal with, particularly in the economy, unintegrated in terms of the division of labor, industrially backward by any modern standard, characterized by the antagonistic activity of hostile classes, all rendered more serious by their isolation in the world. They also realized that there were subjective problems that they would have to deal with, not only among the so-called backward masses, a reference that included those among the working class who had survived the civil war and had not joined or been drafted into Party or government work, but also among Party members as well. The Bolshevik leadership was obviously concerned with both inadequate task performance and inadequate moral performance (careerism, opportunism), coming to view the leadership of the Party as a limiting agent needed to control such illegitimate tendencies.

However, there was another still more serious problem that the Bolsheviks did not expect to have to deal with, and that was the constant expression of competing and conflicting perspectives among Party members at every level and the organization of factions to promote them. The Bolsheviks simply could not speak with one voice, no matter how much they narrowed the basis of decision making, because they could not agree on the significance or implications in practice of what Lenin called the "essential unities." Lenin acknowledged the existence of splits and divisions within the Party, claiming at an earlier point that they were a sign of health and vitality. Expecting such things to occur in a heterogeneous and predominantly peasant society, Lenin said that these splits would nevertheless prove to be self-correcting because they occurred on the basis of an agreed on rock-hard foundation.[40] But, by the time of the Tenth Party Congress in 1921—at which, typically, there were so many platforms presented on the current trade union controversy that Lenin said that he could not read them all even though it was his responsibility to do so—he was not so sure and no longer so tolerant either of interminable debates, fights over shades of opinion, and "shades of shades."[41]

In short, the Bolsheviks stumbled on the heterogeneity problem, more unexpectedly even than the American and French revolutionaries before them. For example, one of Lenin's primary organizational rules was to allow the smallest possible number of the most homogeneous possible groups of professional revolutionaries to organize among the greatest possible number of diverse groups.[42] Belief in the efficacy of such an approach is affecting; it molds expectations and affords a sense of control. It was hard to imagine as a result that fraternal Bolsheviks could not combine as a unified group, no matter how small the number, not even among the most prominent leaders or in the face of danger. The anticipated ability of Bolsheviks to organize an overall plan based on an objective assessment of specific situations and on a unified con-

ception of working-class interests was never even remotely realized. On
the contrary, the problems of the economy, political organization, and
foreign relations led constantly to the expression of conflicting view-
points. The Bolsheviks had expected to achieve a high degree of agreement on the significance of events in the sense that events in this last
revolutionary period must all but reveal their own significance to experienced Marxist revolutionaries; they never expected to differ radically on every single issue. Lenin was forced to abandon his initial belief
that splits and divisions would prove to be self-correcting, concluding
as well that it was becoming dangerous for the Bolsheviks to continue
the struggle among themselves, reminding his colleagues in 1922 that
the policies of the Party were being determined not by the character of
its membership, except in a negative sense, but only by a small group
of leading members, "the Old Guard of the Party." He warned that even
a slight rift within this group might be enough, "if not to destroy
[their] prestige, at all events to weaken the group to such a degree as
to rob it of its power to determine policy."[43]

Nothing the Bolsheviks did, however, was sufficient to achieve a
unified approach, a definite plan that could project people, even the
small group of leaders, into a shared vision of the future, reconciling
and absorbing the antagonistic elements in the Party and in the society
at large. They adopted a self-denying stance on the issue of factional
politics and debate, they kept narrowing the basis of decision making,
searching for that rock-hard core of "irreproachable communists" who
could organize matters among themselves, and they reified the concept
of the Party, which came to stand as a source of discipline and authoritative control outside and above the people who belonged to it.[44] This
last was important not only for what the subsequent acts of revolutionary self-effacement seemed to reveal but because it was a last-ditch effort
to locate Bolshevik activity and decision making in an "objective" structure and to avoid the conclusion that, for whatever reason, Bolshevik
efforts had become linked again to subjective standpoints, to personality, and that their position was no better and perhaps worse than that
of the socialists of the Paris Commune.[45] But none of this availed to
stop the constant infighting, which Stalin described at one point as a
"factional orgy," threatening constantly to dissolve the Party into "a
conglomerate of heterogeneous elements," compounding in a dangerous way the grievous problems of agriculture and industry.[46]

These problems of internecine struggle and of the economy sig-
naled the failure of Lenin's version of Marxism to serve as a mobilizing
public force, a unifying ideological position, insofar as that entailed
even certain minimum standards for the control of people and events,

the capacity for objective, predictive economic and class analysis, and the capacity for organizing urban and rural workers in an integrated process of production. Leninism was insufficient to encompass the heterogeneous interests and moral perspectives on any level of the society or otherwise to encourage people to participate in the economic struggles in a communal spirit. The criterion of that failure, by the standards of the Bolsheviks themselves, was the retreat that was about to occur from structure to personality. Split among themselves, unwilling to give in to the principal implication of multiple and antagonistic standpoints, the establishment of a party system, much less to resort to military dictatorship, the Bolsheviks proved unable to control the process that led them backward to the "cult of personality," the last thing that the Bolsheviks in 1917, in pursuit of their revolutionary goal, had expected ever to have to deal with again.

Moreover, these two problems, heterogeneous groups and a faltering economy, retain their significance for Soviet society to the present day, accounting for the persistent reliance on leadership to establish economic and social policy. To be sure, the current version of Soviet leadership has felt compelled to emphasize openness and public awareness and discussion of problems as a way of coping with the contradictions of late Marxism—including the bureaucratic organization of society, the stultifying effects of which have often been observed; the inability to arouse a sufficiently high degree of worker morale and hence of worker productivity; the need to educate successive generations of young people in greater numbers and the inability to absorb the ideological and characterological consequences of the educational process; the reluctance to give up the paramount role of leadership as a technique of mobilization, not the least reason being the need to forestall the legal organization of conflicting parties addressing issues of production and the distribution of resources, especially among these same educated people; and the inability to control, or even to locate, the link between productive processes and ideological processes. This current leadership then represents yet another strand in the varied and discontinuous Bolshevik tradition, one that hardly resembles its Leninist or Stalinist forebears of some decades ago: no one could claim for it the intellectual ferocity, the passion, the vanity, the omnipotent and grandiose idealism, the exalted expectations, or the destructiveness that characterized these earlier versions of Soviet leadership.

At the same time, once the policy of openness was taken seriously, then all kinds of groups emerged to take advantage of new opportunities—not only did the existence of a variety of political positions from right to left become publicly manifest, but ethnic, racial, religious, and cultural groups with all kinds of concerns (social, national, artistic, environmental, historical) also appeared. The intensity and variety of this public activity indicates in the first place that the socialization of the means of production is in no way sufficient to account for the source or variety of ideological expression. Marx's expectations for the emancipatory role of the working class have long since been abandoned. Any discussion of the issue after Lenin is much more likely than not to privilege the cultural dimension over the social, ideology over class, superstructure over base—or, finally, to conceive of ideology as part of the base—as a way of explaining why these expectations were never realized. Still, this other expectation, that social location and modes of production are the source of ideological expression and conviction, which turns out in practice to be as incorrect as the notion of the emancipatory role of the working class, still retains its hold, and it is not hard to see why: without a moral mechanism like socialization in a cooperative context, there is no way to imagine how the kind of morale on which voluntary productive labor is based will ever appear, no way to conceive of how a deeply held, unreflected commitment to the communal ideal could occur, no evident basis in practice for the end of the dictatorship, no reason to continue to believe that socialism will develop in the unified, harmonious way that Marx had suggested.

In the second place, and more significant, the appearance of all these groups mentioned above coincided with the preliminary development of a strategy announced by Central and East European activists that acknowledged and encouraged heterogeneous participation. The point of this strategy, which followed from the earlier failures of the Hungarians, the Czechs, and the Poles to implement a variety of reforms, most notably in this context a multiparty system, was to avoid any direct challenge to the Communist party, the bureaucracy, the police, and the military, but to bypass the dictatorship by filling up the civic arena with all kinds of groups, while emphasizing that no one intended to organize any competing political parties and that all this civic organization was meant to be accomplished in a strictly legal manner. The expectation was for people to take over public life, to carve out a sphere of autonomous activity and inclusion, legitimating the right of participation, accustoming people to a sense of their own efficacy. No single group would have been significant enough to threaten any government, but the activity of all the groups taken together over a period of time could have changed cultural practice. That is, in the words of a London-based Czech émigré observer, "Certain glasnost principles, if taken up by independent democratic groups outside each country's Communist Party, especially in Eastern Europe where democratic traditions are much stronger than in the Soviet Union, could be used to erode the power base of the establishment. . . . International cooperation among the opposition groups will inevitably lead to the growth of de facto pluralism from below, which could in turn pave the way for a gradual democratization of the Soviet bloc."[47] Obviously, matters have progressed beyond this point in many places, while the whole initiative may yet be challenged. But all these current and prospective issues aside, this suggestion was the first major innovative attempt to imaginatively absorb and work politically with the problem of heterogeneous participation since the American Constitutional Convention of 1787 and the party system that emerged from it. Typically, moreover, it is closer to the expectations of so-called bourgeois social theory, to Tocqueville and Durkheim, than it is to Marxism. Or, as Durkheim wrote,

> The inference to be drawn from this is simply that if the collective force, the state, is to be the liberator of the individual, it has itself need of some counter-balance; it must be restrained by other collective forces, that is, by those secondary groups. . . . It is not a good thing for the groups to stand alone, nevertheless they have to exist. *And it is out of this conflict of social forces that individual liberties are born.* Here again we see the significance of these groups; their usefulness is not merely to regulate and govern the interests they are meant to serve . . . , they form one of the conditions essential to the emancipation of the individual.[48]

Still, the radical activists' dream of reconciliation and harmony, whether of the left or the right, whether based on a notion of a single interest, of unity of moral or religious perspective, or of racial strivings, has not been much affected by this or by any of the revolutionary experiences: no matter how often attempts fail, fall short, or are contradicted by events, there remains the wish, and there remain those who are committed to the vision of an undivided self living in communal concord in a social order that can allow people, beyond division and discord, to take up in common the struggle for mastery over nature and fate. It seems not to matter that, regardless of the severity of force or the stringency of rule, leaders and parties have been unable to solve the problem of heterogeneity and diversity that persistently recurs.

The recurrence of the heterogeneity problem seems not to matter either for routine perceptions of the American Revolution, which, especially from various radical standpoints, is still considered a minor and not-too-revolutionary episode, compared to the revolutionary upheavals that followed in Europe and elsewhere. However, if Madison was right, and the conflicts that arise from multiple interests and perspectives are inevitable, and there is no evidence anywhere to demonstrate otherwise, then the American attempt to solve the problem, the organization of a form of representative government, and the ideological and moral emphasis on distancing people from impulse on one side and authority on the other, whatever the hypocrisies and failings, were revolutionary and in no sense minor.

The Heterogeneity Problem in Theory

The heterogeneity problem that gave revolutionary governments so much trouble, and that any number of governments since have failed to solve short of dictatorship, is the same problem that social theorists have had so much trouble with and have also for the overwhelming part failed to solve. Social theorists and governments alike have wanted to know how compliant social order occurs, and the answer that both have sought for, indeed, the answer that governments have come to expect from social theorists, is that the diversity at the surface is only apparent and that locating the unities at a deeper level is largely a matter of the further refinement of particular kinds of theory—sometimes structuralist but more often what is conceived of as professional social science—and the further accumulation of data in these terms.

Consider in this context the authoritarian personality syndrome, which is still one of the most recognizable concepts to have emerged from the social scientific literature. Heavily influenced by Erich Fromm's synthesis of Marx and Freud and by his delineation of a "sado-masochistic resolution of the Oedipus complex," the "authoritarian personality," characterized by rigid thinking, splitting the world into polar images of good and evil, submissive fear as a reaction to coercive rage, yearnings for passivity and submission masked by contempt for tender feelings and by a rough, tough, "manly" exterior, a lack of education or intellectual sophistication, and intolerance of ambiguous situations, was derived from a particular conception of familial socialization marked in the European context by the vulnerability of the lower middle classes to the vicissitudes of the marketplace and to the threat represented by big business on one side and big labor on the other.[49]

In his well-known *Escape from Freedom,* Fromm had argued that Hitler was able to recruit a following from among such people because he shared their character structure. According to Fromm, Hitler's ideology stemmed from his personality, which, "with its inferiority feelings, hatred against life, asceticism, and envy of those who enjoy life, is the soil of sado-masochistic strivings; it was addressed to people who, on account of their similar character structure, felt attracted and excited by these teachings and became ardent followers of the man who expressed what they felt."[50] However, not only is it impossible to infer the character of the followers from the character of the leaders (or to infer shared wishes from shared behavior), but the different features of authoritarian behavior are in fact related to a variety of adaptive and defensive postures. Indeed, the authors of *The Authoritarian Personality* themselves noted that there were many character types in Germany who exhibited this behavior, and they identified, in addition to Fromm's sadomasochistic type, "rebel," "crank," "psychopathic," and "manipulative" types. Ernst Roehm, for example, was considered a "rebel" type, and Heinrich Himmler was considered perhaps an example of the "manipulative" type.[51]

The question then arises, if there were five different character types (not only was this number arbitrary—there could have been more, for all the authors knew—but the anti-Semitism that they shared was not a single thing either), why focus on only one, why dwell on or imply a fundamental unity and ignore the problem created by the variety?[52]

The answer to this question is twofold. First, the authors, especially Adorno, were promoting a particular ideological position, as Edward Shils pointed out in his critique of their work. Shils took exception to their emphasis on the failures fostered by the capitalist mode of production and the insufficient emphasis on similar authoritarian aspects of left-wing behavior.[53] Second, the authors had to locate their work within the context of a professional social science; they had to "operationalize" the concept, stress the saliency of a particular causal variable, and turn it into a quantitative generalization that they hoped would exhibit an acceptable range of variation in subsequent studies. If they had tried to cope with five (or more) different types, given their assumptions about familial socialization, they would have failed in any event. Thus, the authors ignored the dynamically heterogeneous composition of the Nazi movement (as well as its socially heterogeneous composition), focusing on an apparently unifying factor because, within their frame of reference, there was no other way to explain how people were linked to each other, and to a leader, to form a movement.

That the authoritarian personality concept did not survive as rigorous social science is not surprising, for historical data have rarely broken conveniently for the sake of this kind of conventional social science. The primary reason for the failure to survive is the standard mode of analysis based on the logic of social location or of categories such as class or occupation. This logic, whether intended as objective analysis independent of questions of character or whether it encompasses characterological questions, as the authoritarian personality studies do, actually depends on a series of unwarranted inferences about the subjective sources of action. As Gerald M. Platt has pointed out, social scientists who interpret events in this manner must assume that individuals in their subjective experience act in a manner consistent with the category employed to describe their action, that people use such a category as class as the basis for perception and interpretation of the people and events that affect them, and that a particular social location shapes their experiences and feelings without reference to specific situations because there are invariant rules of interpretation embedded in it that "predispose" people to act in expected ways. This logic, except in very simple matters, is constantly belied by the heterogeneous composition of social movements and social relationships and by the changing numbers, often very substantial numbers, of people involved on different sides of an issue over time.[54]

The expectations of social scientists to be able to identify underlying unifying principles in this manner have been no better realized than the expectations of radical activists. Their attempts to locate or specify such principles have always yielded a confound: although some portion of a population may act consistently in terms of class or some other category, some portion, which cannot be accounted for by accident or coincidence, also does not. The use of categories and the inferences that they permit is linked to the actual composition of social movements only by partial and statistical relationships, and the only way to make a larger argument of these relationships is to take a part for the whole or to violate scientific logic in another way, by multiplying entities.* All this results from the fact that people are rooted in

*It is important to emphasize again in this context that there are simple problems that this frame of reference can address, e.g., the stance of a particular interest group on an issue like tariff regulation or the voting preference of an ethnic group in a particular neighborhood. Beyond that, the problems get too complicated in ways most conspicuously revealed by interpretations of the rise and influence of Nazism in the Weimar period and after. Nazism, indeed, is still being defined as primarily a movement of the lower middle classes while workers are typically described as "underrepresented" in it and elites as "overrepresented." The questions that follow are, given what is typically said interpretively about the attractiveness of Nazism to lower-middle-class people, why significant numbers of people from these other classes were attracted by Nazism at all, how the participation of people from these other classes can interpretively be accounted for except by multiplying entities, and how the different groups can then be understood to be related to each other and mobilized to pursue a common goal, considering additionally and unavoidably factors of age, gender, religion, region, and educational attainment. It is necessary to ask, too, how this issue of class is related to what is distinctive about Nazism as a movement, i.e., not so much the ferocity of the assault on people per se as the deliberate and systematic quality of it. Was this assault also effected primarily by lower-

multiple social locations and are characterized by multiple identities (as workers, parents, friends, neighbors, and members of ethnic, religious, regional, linguistic, and other groups), and it is not possible to know prospectively, and it is difficult to know retrospectively, the basis on which people will respond or have responded, as workers or as parents, or as workers one time and as parents the next, and so on.

To set out to calculate, for example, future relationships from the knowledge of current or past relationships raises questions of how well the latter are actually known, and this is problematic because, while people may share a language to interpret anticipated and unanticipated events, they do not necessarily share feelings about events or a sense of adequacy in coping with them.[55] Such things are variable, and so too are people's responses. To put it another way, similar starting points in history or in the social world do not lead to similar end points because people are capable of evaluating their situations from a variety of social and dynamic standpoints. This accounts for the discontinuities referred to earlier, and it also accounts for the inability of social scientists to accommodate larger theories to the details of particular instances.

In a much larger sense, the great social theorists of the nineteenth century and the early twentieth primarily responsible for the language and concepts that guided the development of the social sciences, Marx, Tocqueville, Weber, and Durkheim, approached their task in a spirit similar to that of the authors of *The Authoritarian Personality.* These theorists appreciated the real complexity of social organization and re- lationships: as events unfolded, especially the major events that com- pelled universal attention, the great social movements and revolutions, industrialization and urbanization, along with the widely shared sense of discord, fragmentation, and insecurity, it was not hard for them to see that people were affected at the same time in different ways, that in any given instance it was for some people primarily a matter of dimin- ishing chances or declining access to material resources, for others a matter of improved chances or increasing access to material resources, for others a matter of the failure of a moral perspective to continue to serve as a guide to action, and for still others a matter of the absence of

---

middle-class people, or did participation in it cut across class lines in significant ways? (On Nazism defined still as a movement primarily of the lower middle classes, see Michael H. Kater, *The Nazi Party: A Social Profile of Members and Leaders, 1919–1945* [Cambridge, Mass., 1983], 117, 127, 236–37. Kater also discusses here the representation of workers and elites. On the interpretive significance of lower-middle-class participation in the Nazi movement, see Seymour Martin Lipset, *Political Man: The Social Base of Politics* [New York, 1963], 114–16, 137.)

such a perspective.[56] Not only that, but the revolutions in politics and production could not have had the enormous impact that they did if people in one situation had not been able to recruit or to evoke a sense of loyalty among people in the other situation.

We may recall in these terms Tocqueville's description in *Democracy in America* of the tensions that arise between masters and servants in "those sad and troubled times at which equality is established in the midst of the tumult of revolution," when new beliefs have not yet become a matter of settled conviction and it is not clear why one has the right to command or what compels the other to obey. The moral order is knocked askew: masters still think that they are superior, but they dare not say so. Domestic service has become a temporary thing, a matter of convenience and contract, so that obedience loses its moral significance for the servants. The masters are weak, considering their former class position; the servants are resistant to claims, considering their new status as citizens. Servants continue to serve because it is in their interest to do so, but they dislike the moral stigma attached to service. They do not necessarily dislike the work, but they dislike the master, "or rather, they are not sure that they ought not themselves to be masters, and they are inclined to consider him who orders them as an unjust usurper of their own rights."[57] The situation is dangerous, according to Tocqueville, because the masters' access to resources is threatened at the same time that the servants see increased opportunities for themselves. The masters have abandoned their paternalistic obligations, thus enlarging the field in which the servants can act. The servants are insubordinate and disobedient, but that is a result of the failure of the masters' traditional morality. The servants imagine their disobedience justified; their problem is the still-unsettled belief in a moral standpoint that can legitimate and dignify the novel practices that they are about to engage in.

Tocqueville's version of the complexity of social relationships, the stress on both the failure and the absence of moral perspectives and class relationships, is made even more explicit in his subsequent work, *The Old Regime and the French Revolution*. In that work, Tocqueville depicted the French bourgeoisie as experiencing unprecedented and increasing prosperity even as they are becoming more restless and discontented. The government promotes their prosperity and frustrates their expectations at the same time because of its exclusive practices. The more their situation improves, the more hostile the bourgeoisie become: rentiers, merchants, manufacturers, businessmen, and financiers, typically cautious and conservative people, finally prove "to be the most strenuous and determined advocates of reform."[58]

At the same time, however, the bourgeoisie were ignorant of affairs, remote from any real experience of governing, as they were also lacking a moral standpoint of their own. They were thus vulnerable to the appeals of Enlightenment writers, seduced by the abstract speculations of men of letters who had the cultural field to themselves, though they were also bereft of any experience in the art of governing. As a result, the bourgeoisie filled the experiential and moral void with the most radical conceptions of how things ought to be.[59]

The peasant masses, for their part, were going through a period of increasing hardships of both a moral and a material sort. Abandoned in spiritual and practical ways by church, nobility, and monarchy, isolated and abject, their agriculture backward, they were living in a state of ignorance and destitution worse than that of their serf ancestors. But peasant rancor was also focused by the Enlightenment attack on government and society, which they came bitterly to experience as arbitrary and punitive, and by the Enlightenment ideals of equality, all of which had the effect of stirring their most primitive emotions, envy, malice, and cupidity.[60]

As for the nobles, they were "spiritually estranged," alienated from everyone by virtue of having remained a privileged class after having lost their power as a ruling class. Social change—the centralization and bureaucratic organization of the state, the increasing prosperity of the bourgeoisie, and the declining condition of the peasantry—affected them perhaps most adversely of all:

> The French nobility had stubbornly held aloof from the other classes and had succeeded in getting themselves exempted from most of their duties to the community, fondly imagining that they could keep their lofty status while evading its obligations. At first it seemed that they had succeeded, but soon a curious internal malady attacked them. . . . The more their immunities increased, the poorer they became. On the other hand, the middle class . . . grew steadily richer and more enlightened . . . at their expense. Thus the nobles, who had refused to regard the bourgeoisie as allies or even fellow citizens, were forced to envisage them as their rivals, before long as their enemies, and finally as their masters.[61]

Tocqueville's view of class relationships is richly textured, encompassing material interests and moral perspectives, "the mentality of the rulers and the ruled." But it is also contradictory: Tocqueville writes that class is the most important aspect of social organization, but, in practice, as the French Revolution itself occurs, participation cuts across class lines—those who have much are joined by those who have little, in pursuit of a common goal. In the period of the Reformation, Tocqueville writes, the ruling class adopted the new form of religion out of ambition or self-interest whereas the common people adopted it out of conviction. By contrast, the elite sponsored the revolutionary cause in France out of conviction whereas the masses joined out of interest—their impoverished condition, in fact, compelling them to act. But, in either case, Reformation or revolution, how were these disparate groups able to combine and remain connected to each other long enough to accomplish such significant change? Tocqueville's answer is ideology—French revolutionaries, at any rate, were guided by the abstractions of the philosophers. In Tocqueville's depiction of the revolution, elites and masses soon fell out, as competing interests overrode all other considerations. Nevertheless, if social order ever works at all in a heterogeneous world, then the general answer to the larger question must be the same: ideology must take precedence over class, and, failing that, authoritative leadership must intervene.[62]

Things work this way because, as Max Weber later pointed out, "the 'masses' as such, at least in their subjective conception and in the extreme case, have nothing concrete to lose but their lives. The valuation and effect of this danger strongly fluctuates in their own minds. On the whole, it can easily be reduced to zero through emotional influence."[63] This is just to say that, under certain conditions, poor peasants or workers may attempt to seize property, or they may perceive a need to support monarchy, church, landlord, or employer, as nationality, ethnicity, religion, family, or some other factor takes precedence in their imagination over any objective notion of interest or class, or even over life itself. The problem for social theory is that there is no way to say with any degree of precision how people will respond to events. Moreover, what is true for the subjective conceptions of the masses is true also for elites. If this were not the case, "servants" would never find articulate leaders from the masters' class to take their part, just as the masters could never find followers among the servants in sufficient numbers ready to do the same.

Marx's work can be similarly viewed. The bourgeoisie revolt, according to Marx, because of a damaging discrepancy between their increasing productive capacity, their ability to generate wealth, and their access to political power. In order to realize the greatest advantage from their productivity, the bourgeoisie revolutionize not only social and political processes but the moral order as well, the "immense superstructure," the legal, political, religious, aesthetic, and ideological forms that orient people in the everyday world. By contrast, the impoverished workers, called into being by this victorious class and then reduced to the status of a commodity, are so bereft of everything that makes life worth living that there is nothing that they can do finally but reverse the main tendencies of bourgeois social relationships, employing the greatly expanded industrial base for the benefit of the entire community. The two revolutions, one accomplished, one prospective, occur in entirely different circumstances, but there is no contradiction implied, for the bourgeoisie, intent on pursuing their narrow class interests, are forced to cut short their revolutionary enterprise; they cannot possibly pursue all the ramifications of their familiar slogans of liberty and equality, not even in imagination, let alone in everyday life. By contrast again, the workers have no need to curb their revolutionary enterprise or cut it short, and, just as the bourgeoisie supplanted a failed morality with one of their own, so too would the workers supplant a failed bourgeois morality with one of their own.

Thus, in Marx's work, social change occurs, or is expected to occur, in situations of increasing or decreasing access to material resources and in situations of failed or absent moral perspectives.[64] All the dimensions of social theory (social-interactive, cultural-symbolic) are represented in or strongly implied by Marx, a point that is confirmed by Engels, who scornfully dismissed the "amazing rubbish" that adherents were putting forward in Marx's name (history, social process, and class consciousness as fully determined results of a particular organization of the means of production). Hence Engels asserted that all he and Marx ever really meant to propose was the idea that production and reproduction of real life is ultimately the determining element in the development of social relationships. In the meantime, all kinds of moral, religious, legal, and philosophical ideas can "exercise their influence upon the course of historical struggles and in many cases preponderate in determining their form."[65] Of course, Engels's emphasis on an "ultimate determinant" of social relationships has in practice the same logical status as religious expectations of the last days.

It would not be difficult to show, mutatis mutandis, that all the major theorists were aware of this kind of complexity.[66] Yet, in order to make sense of the social world, for ideological or operational reasons they followed one of two courses. Either, like Marx, they ignored for practical purposes the subjective capacity of people to generate meaning and to change meaning, in favor of causally a priori choices based on one of the categories, usually class, in terms of interest, privileging the social over the cultural, an approach that is continued by the greater number of professional social scientists who followed their lead. Or, like Weber, they acknowledged the significance of meaning but failed to address adequately the complications that arise when they do.[67] Behavior is still fixed in these terms by such notions as "base-superstructure," or by other familiar notions such as socialization or internalization, which accounts for "class consciousness," "value integration," "national character," and the like, or by a variety of structuralist notions. The implication is that there is some regulatory, controlling, directing, or unifying center that monitors, orders, and integrates social behavior. To be sure, professional social scientists try to choose empirically manageable problems as compared to the encompassing ambitions of the founders. But they must imagine in the end that the social world is unified around some principle and that the process, particularly in social-interactive terms, is continuous. They do this by inventing concepts that have a logical but not an empirical status ("latent function") or by ascribing motives successively to particular segments of the population without drawing attention to the inevitable result, the multiplication of entities with no clear idea of how they are linked to each other.[68]

Such a unified theory cannot be achieved in these terms, however, because the social arrangements that shape imagination and constrain behavior are themselves too varied. People respond to events in cognitively or morally disciplined or wishful terms on one side and in terms of class, gender, age, occupation, religion, ethnicity, nationality, and the like on the other. People are capable of evaluating their circumstances and chances in any of these terms and of changing the terms. The ability to be cognitively and morally disciplined, or for certain purposes and on certain occasions to be wishfully engaged, or the need to make choices, pursue alternatives, juggle primacies, to figure out when and whether disciplined or wishful responses are most appropriate, the need to discriminate instances or to discern prospects while coping with impulsive, peremptory, "alien" thoughts and feelings, or with different crises through the life cycle as Erik Erikson has described them, or with random, accidental, and unexpected events, or with legitimate forms of social change that are nevertheless often difficult to justify or accept, or even with threatened or actual conditions of rapid and violent change, makes heterogeneous responses a certainty and the development of a unified social theory in any conventional sense unlikely.

This complicated business, the inability to achieve a critical degree of control over data, especially in terms of a "sensitivity to initial conditions," that is, in terms of assessing how the subjective basis of decision making actually affects outcomes even from one instance to the next, is clarified by a brief review of a recent instance of turbulence, "Black Monday," the shocking and massively disrupting stock market collapse of 19 October 1987, and the rationalized, reparative responses to it (often cast in the language of "chaos theory," which had just then become publicly and popularly visible). Not only did concepts of numerate rationality yield to psychodynamic concepts, suggesting a degree of mental turbulence equivalent to the turbulence of the market;* and not only did politics and history appear to be involved in very subjective ways;† but the following equally pertinent ideas were also expressed: a stock price is an abstraction driven by the minds of market participants, and minds can change instantaneously; specialists who control the setting of prices for individual stocks are obliged to maintain the appearance of continuity, even when it is little more than appearance; not only do economists repeatedly find themselves unable to distinguish good news from bad, but the same data often result in "decidedly different forecasts"; because nonlinear relationships produce surprising behavior, both their direction and their timing can run counter to ordinary intuition; and, finally, economics is about people and their "often unpredictable reactions to events."[69] All these statements about mind, perception, continuity, complexity, the insufficiency of ordinary intuition, and the unpredictability of responses are as necessary for historians and social theorists to consider as they are for economists, in terms of aggregate responses to unanticipated events and in terms of how people get along in the everyday world considering all the social locations that they inhabit and the subjective basis of decision making with respect to them.

The revolutionary actors in the political world of the eighteenth century and after achieved two solutions to the practical problems of governance, one based on the expectation of unity, the other acknowledging the variety, each promoting a different form of social organization. Social theorists faced with the same evident disorder in their own domain have not paralleled the political experience; rather, they have constantly tried for a solution based exclusively on the expectation of

---

* "But statistics cannot come close to measuring Wall Street's anxiety. Despite the fact that Wall Street lives by the numbers it is ruled by emotions" (Lawrence J. De Maria, "Analysts Try to Put Plunge in Context," *New York Times,* 16 October 1987, sec. D, 1). "Market turns are often characterized by extreme levels of fear or greed" (Anise C. Wallace, "Money Managers Still in Shock," *New York Times,* 20 February 1988, sec. B, 3). Characteristically looking for the underlying unity, Wallace continues, "When everyone is most frightened, for example, the market often moves sharply higher, and extreme levels of greed often characterize market tops."

† "But unlike any physical system, economics exists in a world with politics and history. It has the doubly entangled complexity that comes with human behavior: the same people who are trying to understand the stock market are quite capable of influencing the variables they seek to predict" (James Gleick, "When Chaos Rules the Market," *New York Times,* 22 November 1987, "Business" section, 1, 8).

unity. There are the "terrible simplifiers" who provoked Tocqueville, Jakob Burkhardt, and others (although Tocqueville himself had trouble with questions of centralization and socialism).[70] But then there are the more modest simplifiers, trying patiently by the application of a particular kind of logic to locate the order they imagine to exist under the surface disorder.

The problem they are up against is not only the "two nations" of Benjamin Disraeli or the "two cultures" of C. P. Snow: two would be relatively easy. Rather, they are up against the world whose existence we may infer from John Locke's argument for religious tolerance within a tradition that emphasizes salvation as a matter of private conscience rather than public authority, a world characterized by the division of labor with its novel tasks and hierarchies and rapid pace of change, by life in the cities, which depends also on the ability to live with constant change, novelty, and anxiety, and by the expansion of knowledge that paralleled the unprecedented social change, especially of the kind associated with Marx, Darwin, Freud, and Einstein, which itself promoted multiple worldviews by way of an explanation of the situation. Justice Oliver Wendell Holmes offered one solution to the multiplicity, to put the truth value of any standpoint to the test "in the competition of the market." But even those movements that denied the necessity for such competition, that were intended to provide a haven in the guise of authoritative leadership and unitary ideology, whether religious or political, could not avoid splitting into feuding factions.

The only valid approach to the social sciences and social theory, if the goal is to account for the variance in a reasonably precise way, at least retrospectively, is to reverse the conventional logic, to ask how heterogeneous populations are oriented to a common goal or how they can continue to perceive the world as orderly or maintain a sense of adequacy and continuity. The most immediate result of posing the question this way, however, is to reject the primacy of "base" over "superstructure," the social level of activity over the cultural, or to reject even their equivalence, privileging the cultural over the social, the world of meaning over the world of structures, ideology, and authoritative leadership as mobilizing forms of public activity over such a social factor as class. The point is not to disparage class as an analytic tool or to deflect attention from conflicting interests or from the fact that some people have much more in the way of resources and access to power and most people have much less. The point is that those people who have more can nevertheless recruit and command loyalty among those who have less, while those who have less have still consistently been able to find champions among those who have more, a fact that cannot be deemed insignificant.

The point is additionally, therefore, to examine why the results of social conflict, when it has occurred, have fallen so far short of the high expectations that had already been so significantly elaborated by the first half of the nineteenth century. It pays to recall here that Robert Owen, in an address published in 1827, had declared that "during the French revolutionary war you passed a boundary never before reached in the history of man, you passed the regions of poverty arising from necessity and entered that of *permanent abundance* . . . you have attained the means to ensure the 'Wealth of Nations,' the object so long sought for by legislators and political economists."[71] And Moses Hess, in his essay "On the Essence of Money," had expected that ideological ("theological and philosophical") speculation would cease with the cessation of commercial speculation, once the economy was taken out of the realm of competition; then religion would give way to genuine politics. Marx integrated these and a number of other observations in his work, concluding subsequently that the period of man's prehistory was just about over and that the bourgeois mode of production would be the last antagonistic mode.[72]

The answer to the question, What happened? is not primarily in a social category like class, which by itself is insufficient to an explanation of how social order occurs or fails to occur. It is true that there is as yet only the beginning of a more adequate explanation, but, whatever the form such an explanation may finally take, providing that it is not just a slogan or a label like "false consciousness," it will be sufficient to reveal why the social level is not primary or why a Marxist like Herbert Marcuse wrote a book like *Eros and Civilization* and did not discuss class, although he did refer to the persistent fact that

> each revolution has been the conscious effort to replace one ruling group by another; but each revolution has also released forces that have "overshot the goal," that have striven for the abolition of domination and exploitation. The ease with which they have been defeated demands explanations. Neither the prevailing constellation of power, nor the immaturity of the productive forces, nor the absence of class consciousness provides an adequate answer. In every revolution, there seems to have been a historical moment when the struggle against domination might have been victorious—but the moment passed. An element of *self-defeat* seems to be involved in this dynamic (regardless of the validity of such reasons as the prematurity and inequality of forces). In this sense, every revolution has also been a betrayed revolution.[73]

Whether Marcuse is correct here in the details, whether it was self-defeat or something else, does not matter. Marcuse was right in principle, there is something going on that a category like class cannot encompass, and nothing has happened since this appeared in 1955 to encourage one to believe that this particular corner has been turned.

The argument is important not only to emphasize the obvious, that any ruling class constitutes only a fraction of the population and that rulers must be able to count on the loyalty of people whose interests they do not share or represent, but also because it compels attention to the process by which this occurs, to the problems of perception and feelings, to the ways in which people become and remain attached to ideology and authoritative leaders. What this process entails must still be decided, and I can discuss only aspects of it here, in particular those aspects of the common culture such as ideology and leadership that serve to organize meaning, memory, intelligibility, and structure, that sustain for people a link between past and future, that provide the materials out of which they can construct a sense of order and closure, a task that is rendered all the more difficult by commitments to and struggles over principles of autonomy and inclusion. For, while ideology and leadership help create a situation in which narrative order becomes possible, people are obliged to put the narrative together themselves, which they do in terms of their own interests and perspectives. Thus, events and decisions taken in respect of them, especially those that are unexpected from the standpoint of cultural standards, are bound to have an effect on conceptions of past accomplishments and future prospects, confirming or violating the sense that individuals and groups have of what is necessary, appropriate, and just, affecting them in different ways as workers or parents or as religious or ethnic loyalists, and so on, eliciting from them different responses, depending on how they evaluate their prospects or how they perceive and feel about their ability to cope.

These different responses are then the source of the problems of heterogeneity and discontinuity as they exist for history and theory. It is not exactly correct to say that the past is prologue or that the past is never really past: the past lives on only in particularized versions that are affected by current exigencies, meaning that commitments to these versions are subject to change, even to rapid change. This is why the only historical knowledge that we can have is "local knowledge." That is, we can perhaps know in a systematic way about the process, the microstructures, the cultural practices, and social arrangements, and the directive and defensive systems that lend order to everyday life; and we can more definitely know about the fundamental problem that people have been struggling with for a long time that makes order so problematic (degrees of autonomy and inclusion, what "true" independence is and how it is achieved, who is in and who is out, who is worthy and who is not, and why). But the specific instances of struggle over the different aspects of the problem on different institutional levels always vary, which is why Donald Barthelme was moved to offer as a hopefully enlightening slogan, "The fragment is the only form I trust."[74]

In addition, it becomes more understandable in this context why the grand theories of the founders ultimately proved inadequate as a basis for the social sciences, why it is, in other words, that, the more observers stressed interest in terms of social location, the easier it became to explain social change, but the more remote were such explanations from the actual responses of people, their sense of alarm, outrage, anger, anxiety, intolerance, suspiciousness, grandiosity, their devotion and loyalty to or their fear of leaders, their ability to attack formerly sacred institutions and practices and to become attached to new ones, their sense then of renewed prospects or of disappointment and disgust with failed expectations, and so on. It was also, conversely, why it was that, the more socialization and internalization ("predispositions to behavior") were stressed, the easier it became to explain the depths of feeling that got expressed in the event of perceived transgression, but the harder it became to explain why transgression occurred in the first place. The one possibly important answer to this question, suggested by Tocqueville, the intended or unintended violation by authoritative leaders of ideological or moral commitments, the standards and expectations that oriented "masters" and "servants" to each other, an answer that is related heuristically to psychoanalytic notions of loss and recovery, was precisely the kind of answer that professional social scientists tried to avoid because they could not approach it numerately or in terms of the familiar categories.[75]

Addressing the Question of Interpretation

The emphasis on perception, feelings, ideology, and authority, particularly in terms of such noncognitive factors as moral and wishful thinking, those things that foster emotional commitments to cultural goals, heighten the significance of everyday tasks, and permit the matching of perception and conception to continue, raises all the questions raised earlier about verification or assessment. At one level, it is possible to discriminate historical instances in terms of perception and feeling or in terms of sheer logic and routine notions of "cause and effect" (considering, e.g., the use of the language of safe and dangerous as distinct from the language of good and evil, and the feelings that might occur in either case, or the ability of people to live with contradictory beliefs).

At another level, however, not only are societies able to absorb this kind of variety (so that instances are always complex and analysis problematic), but historical subjects, the people who responded continuously to events, did not themselves have an adequate conception of the significance of events as they occurred, so that the reasons they gave at the time for the ways that they felt about and acted on things are insufficient or incomplete from the standpoint of the observer. Still, there are criteria that take these problems into account, allowing us to distinguish to a useful degree better interpretations from worse ones. Moreover, without such criteria as these, there is no way to talk about history as a discipline. Their importance, in other words, is not only historiographical as such, but they also serve as a constraint on the political-ideological aspects of the interpretive process.

1. The interpretation of people's actions must be rendered in two languages, the language of the people themselves (because that is one of the really crucial sources for their subjective sense of things and still the most important source for understanding what they have done) and the language of the observer (because people were not aware of different significant reasons for their action, which may be better specified in retrospect, and because their world is being ordered for them in a way, finally, that they did not experience). Choosing only one of the two languages distorts the experience of one of the two groups of people involved, a situation that must lead to ideologically contaminated conclusions.

2. The interpretation of the action that people engaged in must be formulated in a manner consistent with what is actually known to have occurred. It is not reasonable to argue, given the religious concerns of Protestant activists during the Reformation, that they were really fulfilling capitalist requirements. Such an argument, which does not rely on data, denies the authenticity of the religious experience of the people involved, falsifying the world that they lived in by denying the reality of the problems of the world as they perceived them. In other words, the observer's interpretive stance must include the perspectives of the people who lived through events so that the observer's abstract, ordered, unifying version of events could arguably or conceivably have made sense to them. At least, an observer must be able to imagine that, if he or she explained an interpretation of events to the people who participated in them, they could have acknowledged the truthfulness of it.*

* Of course, it may also prove necessary to impose an interpretation, e.g., when events contradict expectations and beliefs. The language of the subjects would then still be used, but in a different way, to make a different kind of case. There is at least one instance of this approach below, although what follows is characterized for the most part

Structuralist arguments of any sort are therefore no solution to the problem. Any claim that people are merely the effects of structural arrangements, that their individuality or their group loyalties are a matter of structural determinants, that people have no place in theory except as examples of structural relationships, is constantly belied by the data. If this kind of theory described reality with any degree of precision, the variations in practice would not exist.

3. Any interpretation of the behavior and beliefs of people must be rendered so that it can, in relation to interpretations of different aspects of behavior and belief, account for heterogeneous participation. The tendency in history to focus on unique instances, or in sociology to focus on middle-range theory or on a discrete segment of population as a means of making the study of society more manageable, means that there will likely be multiple interpretations of the behavior of the different segments, with no sense of how they might be linked to each other. There is no social or cultural movement or group of any size that does not have represented in it more than one mentality or perspective or class (or similar kind of group), so that interpreting the behavior of any one segment without suggesting at the same time how that one might be linked to others is not a useful approach.[76]

4. There should be, as part of any interpretive stance, a discussion of the process by which conclusions about the intentions of people were arrived at. This attention to content and process is a package deal; it is not really useful to have one without the other. Social scientists take the issue of process more or less for granted, but historians also choose, exclude, and abstract, and they are obliged as a result to define the process by which they perform this operation. The traditional requirement that the basis for the exclusion of data must be specified is mostly honored in the breach. Moreover, the discussion of process should also be related to some empirical or experimental tradition or prospect in social psychology (understood more broadly than is currently the case). The emphasis in psychoanalysis on emotions that emerged in the 1970s, and a similar, more recent emphasis in history and sociology, is an interesting case in point.[77]

It must be emphasized that the suggestions outlined here are not

---

by an interpretive stance that is imaginatively consistent with the capacity of the subject to accept. There is one other point that needs to be made: if a historical study is completely dependent on an imposed interpretation in the sense that data are irrelevant and no real reference to human subjects is required, as sometimes happens, then we have an example of a "dead text," a pointless and typically giftless exercise. The best example for historians of such a "dead text" is Rudolph Binion, *Hitler among the Germans* (New York, 1976).

intended in a concrete sense to lock anyone into a "system." Rather, they represent a way of examining one kind of response that is possible in the light of the indisputable sense of crisis that currently pervades history and the social sciences, very largely focused on issues of heterogeneity and discontinuity. The point is that it is necessary to accept the implied challenge, just as it is possible to approach these very real issues in interesting ways, as I hope to show, and therefore to address the problems of history and the social sciences still with some sense of prospective achievement.

3

The Role of Ideology in a Heterogeneous World

Perspectives on Ideology

The most obvious answer to the question of how the heterogeneity problem is contained within social order is ideology (conceived of as symbolic structures, directive and defensive systems, cultural cues, or whatever such words or phrases one chooses to employ).[1] There is no social order that is not hierarchically organized, that does not justify unequal access to power and resources and to unequal shares of goods, and there is none that can survive for long unless it can evoke a sense of loyalty across such divisions. If there were no other issues involved, the rational pursuit of interest alone would lead to endless conflict unless ideology proved effective in keeping heterogeneous groups oriented to a common goal or to one that can be so perceived.

Perhaps the most important aspect of the process in these terms—how it works and why it sometimes fails to work, leading to revolt or to others forms of conflict and breakdown—is contained in Frank O'Connor's passing observation that "we like our storytellers to come from a far place." This phrase could be understood as a metaphoric expression of the capacity of storytellers to make the unconscious conscious, to traffic in this sense with "a far place." But O'Connor's phrase could also be understood in a more literal social sense, especially as the writers and theorists who provide the conceptions that serve to orient people to each other and to the social world are also in important ways storytellers who come from a far place: they are storytellers insofar as their conceptions of the world serve closure before they serve truth, and they come from a far place not only in the sense that they are marginal in different respects relative to the general run of the population but also in that they are segregated or they choose to segregate themselves in special communities, in "bohemia," or in salons or universities, any of these communities being, from the standpoint of everyday circumstances, such a far place. Moreover, with whatever ambivalence, suspicion, and hostility, societies continue to permit the organization of special communities, often specifically setting aside a share of the social product for people whose task it is to create and elaborate the symbolic structures, the directive and defensive systems, the ideology that makes life appear coherent and comprehensible to people.[2]

The truest and most general thing that we can say about the organized, governed social world with respect to process is that people do not and will not live in the absence of such ideological conceptions or a codified network of ideas expressed in theoretical, religious, scientific, or legal language. They may have a commonsense, everyday language of their own, but it is the more remote and elevated conceptions that allow them to sustain a sense of continuity and adequacy, to identify with other individuals and groups, and to perceive and define a relationship to past, present, and future. However, just because ideological conceptions have such a paramount role in society, they must appear to people precisely to have originated in or come from a far place, designed or discovered by special individuals; these contents must appear to be different from and better than the commonsense thinking that ordinary people can themselves manage.

The hopeful Bertolt Brecht once wrote in this vein that, "even in the panoramas of the side shows and in folk ballads, the simple people, who are hardly simple at all, love the stories of the rise and fall of great men, of eternal change, of the cunning of the oppressed, of the potentialities of mankind. And they look for truth, for 'what is behind it all.'" Michel Foucault, too, harking back to the events of May 1968, stated that "the intellectual discovered that the masses no longer need him to gain knowledge: they *know* perfectly well, without illusion; they know far better than he and they are certainly capable of expressing themselves." Foucault went on to say that there is nevertheless a system of power that blocks expression of this discourse and knowledge, a power that resides less in overt censorship than in the way that elite conceptions "profoundly and subtly penetrate an entire social network. Intellectuals are themselves agents of this system of power—the idea of their responsibility for 'consciousness' and discourse forms part of the system." Foucault concluded that intellectuals should no longer take on the task of expressing "the stifled truth of the collectivity." Rather, they should struggle against the forms of power that make use of them as instruments "in the sphere of 'knowledge,' 'truth,' 'consciousness,' and 'discourse.'"[3]

But just as it is not enough and has never been enough for "the simple people" to think or to say to each other that the rich have it better than the poor and they work hard to keep it that way, that from time to time the high and mighty overreach themselves, stumble and fall, or are cast down by their exploited and exasperated subjects, some of whom rise to take their place, so too it is not enough to say that the intellectuals are part of a system that penetrates society and blocks, inhibits, or invalidates the insightful discourse of ordinary people. On the contrary, this is a two-way street; the manipulations occur on both sides of the line: people use the language that intellectuals develop; indeed, it is no exaggeration to say that people are hungry for language that they can borrow and use because they perceive it to be better, that is, more important, more acute, than their own. It does not matter how impoverished people are or how oppressed they feel or know themselves to be; systematic organization or revolt does not occur until an appropriate language offered by authoritative figures becomes available, the language of feudalism, imperialism, bureaucratic capitalism, and socialism being the most notable contemporary example, at least as far as the West is concerned.[4] People may accommodate such language to their own situation or use it in their own interests, as this language of Marxism is currently used—but they are nevertheless looking for it. Or, to paraphrase a comment of Freud's in a different but related context, it does not matter how writers like Brecht or Foucault treat people; people treat themselves therapeutically.[5]

Obviously, the clergy of every denomination have always understood that the force of religion stems from a need that people have for words from above, and many a secular master has come to the same conclusion.[6] V. I. Lenin, as we know, claimed that the workers cannot produce the ideological language that must serve to liberate them; rather, this language must be brought to them from the outside by bourgeois intellectuals who identify with their interests. There may appear what Antonio Gramsci called "organic intellectuals," capable leading individuals from among working people; but these individuals too become effective only as they can distinguish themselves from or elevate themselves above their peers. The cunning of "the simple people" becomes significant only when it is connected by such elevated people to the cunning of history, the lawfulness of nature, or the mechanisms of social "structure."

Concepts of ideology and culture are not easy ones to pin down. As Raymond Williams pointed out, the concept of ideology is indis-

pensable to Marxist thinking on the subject of culture, especially literature and ideas, but it is also problematic because Marx used it in three
different ways, to refer to the beliefs characteristic of a particular class,
to a more general process of the production of meaning and ideas, and
to a system of illusory beliefs that can be contrasted with scientifically
derived beliefs.[7] Of course, the usage typically identified with Marx is
the last, ideology as illusory belief, a system of thought that fosters
distorted perceptions of reality, characterized also as "false consciousness."[8] Thus, Marx viewed the justifications of the contemporary bourgeois cultural arrangements as ideological, obstructing accurate perceptions of reality, conceiving of future proletarian arrangements as
objective, the source of unobstructed perceptions of reality.[9] By contrast, however, Lenin conceived of ideology as a mobilizing instrument
indispensable to the organization of the working class and to the ability
of workers to sustain the revolutionary struggle.[10] In addition, as Williams pointed out, the concept did not originate with Marx, and its use
is not confined to Marxists; there are still other perspectives on the
problem.[11]

The concept of ideology is difficult to use, then, but it is also
difficult to give up. It seems that logical problems arise no matter how
the concept is used: there is always something arbitrary about what is
included and what is left out of discussions of it. On the other hand,
whatever the logical difficulties, the concept continues to have value
because it addresses something real, namely, the process involved in the
ongoing struggle of people to maintain themselves as separate individuals, to control the impact of social and dynamic events, especially
events that are unanticipated from the standpoint of conscious expectations.[12] As Nietzsche once put it, this "compulsion" to generate ideology, "to form concepts, genera, forms, ends, and laws . . . should not
be understood as though we were capable through them of ascertaining
the true world, but rather as the compulsion to adapt to ourselves a
world in which our existence is made possible."[13] On this view, cognitive capacities are directed not at knowledge but at the control of
things, a reference to the need and ability of people to establish connections instantly and constantly, including false connections when true
ones are not possible, guaranteeing that there are no gaps or lapses in
the scheme of explanations and legitimations that they must rely on in
order to assimilate and absorb the impact of events.

Ideology orients people cognitively, particularly to the social
world and the means of acquiring a livelihood, and people do strive in
these terms to remain cognitively adequate. But what makes the cognitive orientation "ideological" is that the cognitive part of the story is

not the only important one. There are two other spheres or realms of mental activity to consider, the moral and the wishful, as well as the forms of emotional expression and experience associated with them. Even though the development and use of cognitive capacities may be systematically encouraged by parents and the wider society, not only are they bound by moral mandates and affected by wishfulness, but their primacy can be legitimately suspended among individuals and groups in the course of a day (in religious, artistic, or even sporting events and in sexual activity), just as their primacy can be compromised outright by threatening or disruptive events.

Bourgeois ideologists have consistently claimed that cognitive capacity or perceptual accuracy is tied to practical activity and real contacts in everyday life, that manufacturers, merchants, artisans, those people who deal concretely with the manufacture and trade of things, with productivity, the generation of wealth, could see the world's affairs more clearly and correctly than academics or philosophers, who are remote from "the objects of knowledge" and from "the common scene of occupation" and who deal only with ideas. This is a point that Rousseau made for his own purposes in *Emile:* one hour of manual work provides more learning than a day's worth of verbal instruction, and it is a habit of mind that persisted in the commonsense notion that book learning is inferior to practical experience and the school of hard knocks is a more instructive one than any school devoted merely to formal education.[14]

However, as Marx argued, working actively with concrete affairs in the everyday world is not sufficient to promote the accurate perception of reality; on the contrary, the pursuit of personal gain and the need to acquire and defend private property preclude such a result. Bourgeois perception is distorted, characterized by moralizing justifications of their particular interests. The bourgeoisie justify their exploitation of workers by reference to human nature, missing or misperceiving the real social relationships involved; they claim universal validity for standards that serve only their particular interests, and they manage somehow to desensitize themselves to the effects of their activity by imagining that relationships between people are relationships between things. By contrast, however, the workers, who have no property to defend, who are already reduced in bourgeois society to the status of commodities, having nothing but their own labor to sell, are nevertheless in a position to see things clearly: their social location and practical activities are so threatening and damaging to themselves that they are compelled finally to achieve insight and act.

But, as it turned out, threatening social location and practical activities are not a sufficient basis for insight into social reality either. It was precisely Lenin's point that the experiences of workers are too narrow, confined, and limited to permit them to gauge reality accurately. On the contrary, their social location and activities lead only to yet another type of false consciousness, economism. However, bourgeois intellectuals and activists who have repudiated their class interests, acquired Marxism as a worldview, and elevated themselves above the desire for personal gain and private property, identifying with the workers' cause—without themselves engaging in productive labor or becoming enmeshed in the workaday world—are able to perceive reality accurately, a standpoint already deemed bourgeois, revisionist, and idealist by certain of Lenin's contemporaries.[15]

These views do not encompass all the different, contradictory views of the "real" basis for the accurate or distorted perception of reality. But, in a sense that we may deem ideological, in the sense of a systematically conceived mobilizing public standpoint capable of justifying familiar or novel actions or novel interpretations of familiar actions, legitimating commitments to stability or change, constraining or otherwise shaping emotional responses, focusing attention on particular problems by necessarily and usefully narrowing the perceptual field, not only are they the most important ones in the Western world, but, as opposed as they are to each other, they all nevertheless share one crucial characteristic: they are all rooted in a conception of the unobstructed perception of reality resulting from the social location of the perceiving, interpreting subject. They all acknowledge and insist on the primacy of cognitive activity, rationalizing a sense of cognitive enhancement that is typically directed at the mastery of the external natural and social world, at the expense of any systematic awareness of the equally complex though not equally accessible dynamic world, particularly in terms of the moral and wishful strivings of people. Characteristically, if Marx, for example, wanted to stress ceaseless change as a condition of life, to distinguish his viewpoint from a static one, he might invoke the saw about no person being able to step into the same river twice. But that always says more about the river than about the person, who may also not be the same.

Of course, Marx is particularly vulnerable to this kind of criticism, considering especially that he thought that he had discovered and elaborated an objective construction of social process, one that could serve as a fixed standard of analysis, technically correct on principle, needing only to be amplified in detail or in relation to specific historical instances. One might well ask how Marx could have escaped unaffected from his own contacts with a hegemonic culture to achieve such a level of insight, or who he thought he was writing for, if, as he claimed, the traditions of all the dead generations weigh like a nightmare on the brain of the living and no man can be detached from his social being and judged in the abstract, except on the basis of an ideologically distorted theory of individuation or as an idiosyncratic case.[16] Marx's own explanation offered in *The Communist Manifesto,* that some bourgeois intellectuals can surrender their own class standpoint and identify with that of the working class because they are able to comprehend theoretically "the historical movement as a whole," in the absence of any empirically viable conception of the process by which this occurs, is merely an evasive, self-serving gesture, precisely the kind of ideological gesture that serves closure before it serves truth.[17]

The point is, however, that all these views that direct attention primarily to practical activity in the external world, Marxist or bourgeois, obscure the other side of things. Whether we think of property in Locke's terms, as a product of the "industrious and rational" activity of autonomous individuals that it is society's business to defend, or in Marx's terms, as the product of exploited labor that is more rationally employed to achieve communal as opposed to individual goals, the possession of property, especially in the means of production, historically made the bourgeoisie the dominant force in society. But this was not only a matter of income or even of power. Rather, property also served to define and enhance their personal integrity and sustain their individuality as self-disciplined, self-controlled autonomous actors against the power of wishful strivings on one side and the power of the social world on the other. Property served in both a directive and a protective way to establish and confirm their sense of what was good, worthy, and admirable about themselves and their class.[18] The bourgeoisie have therefore not feared the loss of property per se so much as they have feared an assault on their integrity and esteem, and this is why they are so emotionally affected when their rights to property are challenged or threatened and why they so readily express anger, alarm, anxiety, frustration, and so on in the face of social change; this is also why they so typically claim and feel that they are defending a moral position rather than an interested stake in property as such.

At the same time, given the heterogeneous composition of the social world, there have been and are bourgeois individuals whose personal integrity or sense of worth has required the sacrifice of their property or the repudiation of the desire to acquire property, and they have willingly complied. Friedrich Engels was not the first or the last bourgeois entrepreneur who was prepared to sacrifice his so-called objective interests on behalf of his conception of what he thought was just or right. As Eugene Genovese noted, for example, Southern industrialists during the Civil War, "whatever their extenuating circumstances, repudiated their class interest, which they too identified with Southern civilization, when they joined, however reluctantly, in a crusade on behalf of a social system they had every reason to abhor."[19]

In short, as especially Durkheim and Freud tried to explain in their different ways, it is the representations of self and group that become the primary interest to defend and not property as such. This is why monks and Bolsheviks have run just as scared and reacted just as violently as any bourgeois when their vision of the world, which does not include the private acquisition of property or personal gain, was threatened or attacked. What people share first of all, regardless of class background, is an interest in their self-regard as defined by their self-conceptions and conceptions of the world, which they seek to enhance and will, if need be, even die to defend.

The belief in the possibility of cognitive mastery of the social world based on practical activity, whether in Locke's terms (the acquisition of property) or in Marx's terms (the conscious repudiation of any interest in property), is revealed as ideological in at least one of the senses that Marx and Engels intended: the unobserved or unconscious moral and wishful rationalization of interest based on a thoroughgoing abstraction from social process. Such unobserved aspects of mental activity are useful for freeing bourgeois entrepreneurs or radical activists for certain kinds of action in or against the world, but they are left vulnerable to threats of loss and disruption and to the feelings that arise with such vulnerability, the "objective" perception of the world becoming as problematic for them as for anyone else.

It is not hard to demonstrate that bourgeois and Marxist notions are permeated with this kind of ideological expression and that they are especially permeated with the kind of moralizing that Freud characterized in terms of "superego," which implies a punitive capacity and also the elevation and self-satisfaction that comes from loyalty to ideals or successfully realized ambitions consistent with cultural expectations.[20] But then so is every orientation to the world whether borrowed from or formally cast in theoretical terms or in religious or some other set of terms.[21] We can determine this from the uses of language (the language of good and evil as distinct from the language of safe and dangerous), from the lapses in logic that are characteristic of any or all of these orientations, as well as from the feelings of anger, alarm, anxiety, disappointment, resentment, frustration, sadness, and so forth aroused by perceived threats, betrayals, failures, or lacks or from the feelings of certainty, conviction, virtue, and rectitude (which may well appear to outsiders to be arrogance, smug self-righteousness, and intolerance) that follow from attempts to set things right. Insofar as all ideological orientations may be characterized in these terms, they are all equally valid; we may have our own standards, expectations, perceptions, feelings, and wishes that we want to promote or defend and that we are prepared to struggle for, but we cannot do so in the name of some nonevaluative standpoint (e.g., "value-free science").[22] However, insofar as all such orientations try to base themselves in evidence, to adduce proofs and use "facts" to demonstrate their validity, necessity, and superiority, insofar as there are criteria for logical expression and for defining cause-and-effect relationships (any orientation to the world has evidential value for people if they define things that way, including religious orientations, and they all make claims to be able to judge the relative worth of their own position against that of others on this basis, but they also strive for consistency of argument as a sign of their rigor), not only does it become possible to weigh them hierarchically in the light of what can actually be established (we learn more about the social world from Marx's conception of class than we do from Hitler's conception of race, whether we are for or against either or both), but we can also begin to " read" these orientations, to determine what people seek, intend, expect, and wish to achieve or what their world is about.

The problem with the concept of ideology has always been getting a nonevaluative, discriminable definition of it, being able to discriminate ideological from nonideological thought (and from other forms of thought, e.g., myth). Marx's solution was to declare his own position to be objectively correct and any other to be ideological, meaning contaminated, infiltrated, or distorted by class-interested moral and wishful thinking. The logical dilemma raised for Marx by his position—taking for granted what he had to prove and exempting himself on that basis from the criteria that he established for everyone else—has been identified many times.[23] But the response to Marx's failed logic is not to abandon his observation of the moral and wishful contents in social thought but to make him an object of his own theory. If we think of this somehow as closing a circle, as Mannheim's paradox, the absence of any position from which to interpret reality on any grounds other than ideological, leading to an intolerable ethical or epistemological relativism, then we are in trouble.[24] For this reason, it is perhaps better to think of the problem as "Freud's paradox," in the sense that the ability to think objectively about the social world at all is based on a compromise, the result of a struggle to maintain the primacy of cognitive capacities, because thought is in any case admixed with moral and wishful elements. The point is that, as long as cognitive mastery occurs, which Freud had necessarily to affirm, and as long as moral and wishful thinking occur and can undermine and dominate cognitive capacities, which Freud also affirmed, then we can discriminate ideological from nonideological interpretations of the world, providing that we can agree on the criteria for identifying the different elements of which thought is composed.*

This approach, which holds that thought (perceptions and feelings) has meaning at different levels, has two virtues. First, it directs attention to the fact not only that cognitive controls can be dominated by moral and wishful strivings but that such controls are not socially obligated in all or even most situations. The reasons for this are that all social relationships must be directed to a collective goal and all people insofar as possible imbued with a sense of commitment and the desire to develop and use their capacities to achieve this goal; that all societies, capitalist, socialist, or other, are obligated to justify hierarchy, subordination, and the necessity for the unequal distribution of goods at the same time that they must be in a position to mobilize even those who have the least advantage in these terms for large-scale tasks, including production and warfare; that people must be provided with a communal conception of the right way to do things so that the social world is or can be perceived as a safe arena for them to live and work in despite the fact that the rational pursuit of interest must produce conflict in a heterogeneous population and that a single interpretation of the world by all the "normal and realistic" people who perceive the things that occur is not possible; and that people must be provided with the materials, the language and symbols, for making connections instantly, including false connections, so that they can maintain a sense of continuity and adequacy, precluding the need for them to fall back on a version of the world that emerges from their own personal history, which in large part is not usable history.[25]

Second, however, the approach directs attention not only to the possible primacy of cognitive control in different situations but also to the fact that societies can foster the development of such control, encouraging people to learn about and to come to disciplined conclusions about the physical and social world. One of the things that follows as a result is the ability to discriminate criteria by which to establish the

---

*I have employed a familiar tripartite division of mind, although such a division, especially as Freud had elaborated it in the structural theory, is anachronistic in important ways. This is particularly so with respect to the discussion of fantasy thinking as I will develop it in this chapter. I will not attempt to reconcile the discussion of fantasy thinking with the structural theory or suggest any alternative here, though it is important to be alert to the problem.

moral and wishful aspects of any point of view. The kind of cognitive control that Marx thought would become a generalized phenomenon leading to the self-emancipation of the working class, or that Lenin and Freud thought possible for certain elites, has not occurred. But this does not mean that on principle cognitive control cannot occur, or that the cognitive aspect of thought cannot dominate the moral and wishful aspects, or that we cannot discriminate among instances. The problem is to find a way to talk about the relationship of moral and wishful strivings to cognitive control as well as the relationship of "internal" to "external" worlds without stumbling again on the heterogeneity problem. The ideology concept is one way of talking about these relationships, despite all the difficulties it harbors, because ideology is acquired by people from the social world; it is capable of guiding and orienting heterogeneously motivated people to a common goal while systematically absorbing and integrating recognizable elements of the private world as well.

The Social Significance of Fantasy Thinking

The importance, even the primacy, of the moral sphere of mental activity in the social world has often been addressed. Talcott Parsons stated at one point that the confluence of Durkheim's and Freud's thought on the issue of internalized morality represented the most important contribution to the social sciences in this century. The moral sphere was obviously of great importance to these writers as it was also to Tocqueville at an earlier time or to Mary Douglas and Lawrence Kohlberg at a later one. Marxists too currently make their concessions to the role of morality, as well they might, for it is hard to imagine anyone recognizing material interests, let alone pursuing them, in the absence of a moral orientation.[26] Even if one does not conceive of morality in terms of superego, which is useful to do, as I have suggested, because it addresses specific expressions of punitive and ideal strivings and of the emotional responses that simultaneously occur, it is not hard to imagine the significance of the moral sphere to the social world in some sense.

The relationship of fantasy, the sphere of wishful thinking, to the social world is more difficult to conceive and much more rarely discussed in systematic terms, though it is no less important than the moral sphere. Disparaged long ago by various classical theorists and philosophers (e.g., Hobbes, Locke, and Descartes) because such thinking seemed too idiosyncratic, too readily linked to the bizarre, extravagant, or merely frivolous, and too remote from disciplined thinking or from the serious issues of life, the status of wishful or fantasy thinking as a concept is hardly improved because of its nearly exclusive current identification with psychoanalysis or psychohistory.[27] However, the concept persists outside the realm of systematic social thinking, all but illegitimately in an academic sense, very often employed but typically unexplained and unexplored; it is evidently too useful to be dispensed with, even if it is also too problematic to become the focus of systematic attention. The idea of wishful or fantasy thinking recurs constantly in the professional and popular literature, presented to readers tachisto-scopically as it were, a word or thought that flashes by, engaging the readers' attention in a fleeting, momentary way, establishing the briefest kind of mental contact, of necessity implying that this richly connota-tive and complex concept has value somehow but is not worth dwelling on. The use of the word is meant to convey an impression or hint at a possibility, to serve as a culturally shared cue, orienting the audience to a largely unexamined experience or mode of expression, addressing something that the audience must recognize as real in themselves so it can hardly be as casually received by them or intended by any author as may be implied by the way in which it ordinarily appears. The word or concept *fantasy* turns up in general historical discourse—apart, that is, from whatever might happen in the psychohistorical literature—in the *American Historical Review,* for example, as well as in a lot of other professional literature that historians are likely to read, and in the pop-ular review literature, too, just in the manner I have described, brief, throwaway references to "violent fantasy," "collective fantasy," or "fan-tasies of ritual," to "the erotic, fantastic components of human life," to Rousseau's "fantasy of a perfectly autonomous, fulfilled 'I,'" or to cap-italists "engaged in the process of reifying the exchange of fantasies" (or the governing or future-oriented fantasies of capitalists who gamble on their own wish fulfillments or, in another version, who stimulate and encourage people to become "creatures of fantasy rather than rea-son"), to "the prevalent fantasy of electoral sway," or to "women's dif-ferent fantasies about language," and much more.[28] There is a book entitled *The Fantasy of Reason,* a biography of William Godwin, and, when the author cites Godwin's conception of the harmonious com-munity (in which there will be "no war, no crimes, no administration of justice, as it is called, and no government . . . no disease, no anguish, no melancholy, and no resentment," as each man will seek, "with inef-fable ardour, the good of all"), then we have a fair idea of what he means by his title, although there is no discussion of the process by which fantasy comes to dominate systematic thought.[29]

However, any concept that is used so often and has so much sig-nificance attached to it in our cultural context ought to be considered systematically in terms of process or at least in terms other than the bizarre and the frivolous. The point of such systematic consideration, moreover, is quickly revealed by reference to Georg Lukacs's classic depiction of what was truly distinctive about the work of Karl Marx: "The primacy of the totality in historical explanation, not of economic motives, is the decisive difference between Marxism and bourgeois science. The category of the totality, the all-pervading supremacy of the whole over the parts is the essence of the method which Marx took from Hegel and transformed into the basis of a wholly new science. . . . *The primacy of the category of the totality is the bearer of the revolutionary principle in science.*"[30]

Lukacs meant to emphasize with this notion of "totality" that the internally heterogeneous parts or elements that compose a society take the shape they do because of their relationship to a forming "whole," and they have no prior existence as elements independent of that "whole." However, this is never entirely true because of the human capacity for fantasy thinking, which, even if the language and images are borrowed from the extant culture, still eludes the forming power of that culture. Any suggestion that language determines our conceptions of reality must be modified to account for the ability of people to recombine language in novel formulations. Human thought in this sense is constantly transcending its frame, initially perhaps in a manner that is not bound by the conventions of logic and causality. This can prove to be dangerous, of course, and fantasy thinking is often threatening to people, though it also provides them with imaginative latitude. The inevitable discrepancies and disparities in any society, the inability of any society to integrate everyone equally or even just favorably in its arrangements, permitting people to match ideals and reality to some acceptable if imperfect degree, in addition to the struggle that they must wage to maintain a sense of adequacy in the face of events, provide a constant stimulus to repair reality in imagination.[31] Normatively perceived injustice or loss, or the failure or absence of a standpoint that can make sense especially of unexpected events, invite fantasy thinking, which has always provided the occasion for some individuals to explore, elaborate, refine, and, finally, promote an alternative standpoint, reorienting people to the social world, often in unexpected ways.

The intellectuals with whom we are most familiar in this context, Hobbes, Locke, Smith, Rousseau, Hegel, Marx, Freud, and many others besides, who have organized or crystallized and developed novel perceptions of reality, reveal thereby a particular talent for resolving in some way their own unique conflicts, subordinating fantasy expectations to the cognitive and moral requirements of their time, interpreting these requirements first for themselves and then for others. Scanning various bodies of information for connections among the different dimensions of social life, such intellectuals are able to foster concerted action, providing people with the opportunity they need to construct a sense of life as continuous and their own task-oriented and moral behavior as adequate and appropriate. The need to repair a reality that always appears in some measure as failed, insufficient, or threatening to someone (or some group) is an important source of reparative forms of thinking as well as of competing and multiple perspectives. There is no way to forestall imaginative attempts "to make things better," just as there is no basis in current social arrangements for imagining "an end to ideology."

If this were not true, there would never be any novel language, innovative challenges, radical departures, unanticipated syntheses, or great conceptual leaps, such as the one that Marx himself attempted. As long as this is true, the sum of the parts is greater than the whole, which can never achieve the kind of preeminence that Lukacs ascribed to it. In fact, the Marxist fantast, Ernst Bloch, used precisely this logic against Lukacs to get around the notion of totality, or the hegemonic power of culture, and to offer "a principle of hope," to urge in his own fantastic terms that mankind indulge in "forward dreaming," about the "Not Yet Conscious" and the "Not Yet Become."[32] He did so, moreover, by referring at one point to some ruminations on fantasy of an individual who absolutely prided himself on his tough-minded realism, V. I. Lenin, literally taking a page on the subject of fantasy from Lenin's classic *What's to Be Done?* Lenin admitted in that text that his plans and expectations were as yet only a dream, but he defended his right to dream by "hiding behind" some thoughts of Dmitri Pisarev on the subject of dreaming:

> My dreams can overtake the natural course of events, or they can go off at a complete tangent, down paths that the natural course of events can never tread. In the first case dreaming is totally harmless; it can even encourage and strengthen the working man's power to act. . . . There is nothing about such dreams which impairs or cripples creativity. . . . If a person were completely devoid of all capability of dreaming in this way . . . then I find it absolutely impossible to imagine what would motivate the person to tackle and to complete extensive and strenuous pieces of work in the fields of art, science, and practical life. . . . The gulf between dream and reality is not harmful if only the dreamer seriously believes in his dream, if he observes life attentively, compares his observations with his castles in the air and generally works towards the realization of his dream-construct conscientiously.[33]

Lenin referred again to fantasy on several occasions, noting in his "Philosophical Notebooks" that

> the approach of the (human) mind to a particular thing . . . is complex, split into two, zig-zag like, which *includes in it* the possibility of the flight of fantasy from life; more than that: the possibility of the *transformation* (moreover, an unnoticeable transformation, of which man is unaware) of the abstract concept, idea, into a *fantasy.* . . . For even in the simplest generalization, in the most elementary general idea . . . *there is* a certain bit of fantasy. (Vice versa: it would be stupid to deny the role of fantasy, even in the strictest science: cf. Pisarev on useful dreaming, as an impulse *to* work, and on empty day-dreaming).[34]

These thoughts of Lenin's on fantasy are interesting because, as his revolutionary colleague, Leon Trotsky, explained, he was free of all formalistic prejudice; formulas never took precedence over concrete experience or the demands of immediate situations. Leninism on this view was a policy of swift tactical shifts, abrupt turns, a search for concrete alternatives that reduce routine formulations and excuses for inaction to a minimum, diminishing the tendency of Marxism to appear as a fixed, unchallengeable complex of ideas closed to the possibility of practical revisions. According to Trotsky, Lenin was the most extreme pragmatist who also always thought in the broadest terms.[35] Thus, Lenin explained about the revolution, "We had to feel our way all the time. . . . But that necessity never made us hesitate, even on October 10, 1917, when the question of the seizure of power was decided. We had no doubt that, to use Trotsky's expression, we had to experiment, to make experience."[36] All this is consistent with Lenin's references in the matter of the revolution to Napoléon, the soldier-adventurer, and to Goethe, the poet, which are better known than his references on the occasion to Marx: "Napoleon, I think, wrote, 'On s'engage et puis . . . on voit.' Rendered freely this means 'first engage in serious battle and then see what happens.' Well, we did."[37] For as Lenin also said, every step in a chosen direction is worth a dozen abstract statements: theory is gray; green is the eternal tree of life.[38]

The point for Lenin was that the social world is embedded in an overarching design that is nevertheless capable of many surface variations; in the short or even in the middle run, events do not appear to follow a predictable course and may well appear to be unrelated to any design. The ultimate direction of change is unalterable, but the rate, timing, and contents are not unalterable, nor is the character of those who step forward as the representatives of revolutionary change. On the contrary, it is necessary to expect failures, errors, miscalculations, betrayals, opportunism, backsliding, and personal and structural deficiencies of all kinds. Therefore, "every attempt to establish stereotyped forms and to impose uniformity from above, as intellectuals are so inclined to do, must be combatted. . . . The unity of essentials, of fundamentals, of the substance, is not disturbed but ensured by *variety* in details, in specific local features, in methods of *approach,* in *methods* of exercising control."[39]

The world, reality, "life itself," is not fixed and patterned precisely so that people can know immediately and for their convenience how to respond. There are situations that are consistent with theory, but there are also ambiguous, contradictory situations and accidental situations, and, when one is in the middle of things, it is often hard to tell which is which. Hence, no fact or event could embarrass Lenin, who never thought for a moment, regardless of circumstances, of changing his theoretical position. Rather, he responded to conflicts, dilemmas, and setbacks by imperative revisions of his tactical and strategic positions, doing whatever he thought necessary at the time, justifying it retrospectively.

Theory does not furnish guidelines for specific instances; it furnishes only a general line, and activists must adapt to instances as best they can. Of course, Lenin constantly invoked the language of the theory, as ready to fight for control over the nouns as for control over the means of production. At the same time, he was often deliberately manipulative, as a way of rallying or encouraging people to continue the struggle. That is, Lenin was no Sorelian, using Marx's work as a mobilizing myth that he did not himself believe to be objectively correct; much less would he have agreed with another contemporary activist, Benito Mussolini, who claimed that every system is an error, every theory a prison, and that leaders must be free to act because there are still national—or, in Lenin's case, class—interests to defend. Rather, this was the position that Lenin evolved that, he hoped, would allow him to remain cognitively or empirically adequate in response to unanticipated situations.

The phrase that Lenin used to explain this posture is "history moves in zig-zags," which means that we often do not know where we are or what is going on, but that does not matter because we know how things must turn out in the end:

> Commodity production begot capitalism and capitalism led to imperialism. Such is the general historical perspective. . . . No matter what the further complications of the struggle may be, no matter what occasional zig-zags we may have to contend with (there will

be very many of them . . .) in order not to lose our way in these
zig-zags . . . to be able to see the scarlet thread that joins up the
entire development of capitalism and the entire road to Socialism
. . . it is . . . important not to discard our old basic program.[40]

Practice as Lenin understood it is a response to experience and is
guided only in the loosest sense by the "essentials" of theory. Thus,
Lenin believed in the inevitable effects of structural arrangements in a
developmental scheme, but he always acted as if the interim process is
a subjective one, involving meanings, character, and values. He never
thought it important to get caught up in phrases or persist in courses
of action that promised to end badly, no matter how principled they
may have been from the standpoint of theory. As a result, nothing is
easier than to oppose an earlier statement of Lenin's in the wake of the
revolution to a later one. He contradicted himself so often and absorbed or brushed aside the contradictions so quickly that to conceive
of him as guided by theory in any sense but the one that he indicated,
or to imagine that his thinking was structured except in "the essentials"
that he specified—keeping in mind his undeviating belief in the necessity of class struggle and the inevitable direction of history—is a mistake.

　　Lenin dreamed of the final result, and he also acted with great
energy in the world: by his own standards, he was entitled to dream
provided he worked hard to achieve practical results, pursuing steadily
a course of action that would turn the dream into reality. By the same
token, he could also recognize failed action, and, while he used a variety
of terms in which to express failure, *fantasy* was certainly one of them.
At the Tenth Party Congress in 1921, introducing the New Economic
Policy, Lenin declared that "any Communist who dreamed that the
small scale agricultural basis of the economy could be changed in three
years was just fantasizing. And—let us confess—there were many such
fantasts among us."[41] It was one thing for an activist to imagine prospectively what things could be like, but activists can evidently get carried away by their imagination and misperceive the true situation.

　　Lenin, however, did not dwell on the negative prospect, though
with hindsight it is not difficult for a critic to claim that the expected
unity of theory and practice never existed; that none of the prospective
relationships established by even the very loose theory that guided Lenin's actions in Soviet society, the relationships of workers to peasants,
of masses to party, of party to productive and ideological processes,
existed anywhere but in his imagination; that Lenin's concern for the
harshness of life experienced by the working poor and the vision of

things to come inspired by Marx were more readily rendered effective by his efforts as a leader than by Marxism as an objective description of structural arrangements; and, finally, that, intent on realizing a moral ambition, to secure a qualitatively different kind of life for people, not only did he misperceive the effects of his own role as a leader and the different effects on colleagues of being leaders, but he confused cognitive and moral standpoints in the process, however justified such a confusion might be for a revolutionary who had witnessed the First World War. For, whether one interprets events in the language of "safe and dangerous" or of "good and evil," considering the feelings that attend the different interpretations, makes a lot of difference to the outcome, as would any confusion about the role of leadership and ideology as distinct from structures. The particular questions raised by such claims here are the extent to which Lenin, alert to the influence of fantasy thinking on practical activity, was nevertheless affected by it in ways that he did not observe and what the criteria for making judgments of this sort are.

Similar questions are raised by Godwin's "fantasy or reason" or, according to Leszek Kolakowski, about Marx and Freud, whose work Kolakowski argued, had a rational content but lacked the restrictions and reservations characteristic of systematic bodies of "rational" thought. The fantasy content (Kolakowski stated that Marxism "has been the greatest fantasy of our century") is identified by exaggerated claims and expectations, an absence of restraint in intended applications, an "element of absurdity," which was, on Kolakowski's view, the effective basis for transmitting their rational content.[42] This view, however, says more about the audience than it does about Marx and Freud, whose work is not really without restrictions and reservations for anyone who wants to find and use them. Marx and Freud both insist that the claims that people make for themselves cannot be taken at face value, and they both attempt to explain why this is the case. Marx and Freud are also contradictory, both of them holding and offering opposed views of reality. This is, paradoxically, one of the main sources of their universal appeal; they attract a wider audience by promoting opposed points of view (it is well known, e.g., that conservatives, moderates, and radicals have all justified particular points of view in psychoanalytic terms).[43] But this also means that they provide the audience with the means to use one part of their work against another part or to impeach the work altogether. Besides, Kolakowski's view is not yet a sufficient basis for "operationalizing" a concept of fantasy, for accommodating it to the many and varied uses noted above, making it systematically available to anyone interested in distinguishing fantasy thinking from other kinds of thinking. Exaggerated claims and expectations, an absence of restraint in thinking, or future-oriented thinking can nevertheless prove to be the basis of realistic attainment and effective actions, as many a successful scientist has explained, so there must be something more to fantasy thinking than that.[44]

We should think of wishful or fantasy thinking, then, as running the gamut from peremptory, impulsive, irruptive, fleeting thoughts to the kind of thoughts that Lenin had in mind, following Pisarev, which involve an elaborate, complex mental picture of a completed event that one's actions are only beginning to shape, an imaginative construction embedded in a cognitive scheme or matrix, a highly developed, organized, self-initiated orderly narrative cast in language and images provided by one's culture—which must still be characterized as lacking from the standpoint of logic and causality. (Even in Freud's original conception of fantasy, in which the "component instincts" of the sexual drive unfold in a sequence of aims based on bodily tensions, the component instincts could never become the object of consciousness; only an idea that represented them could.[45] Even unconsciously, i.e., and granting for the sake of argument the ultimately wishful nature of thinking, a component instinct could not be represented other than by an idea framed in language and images that must have had a cultural source.)

Although fantasy thinking is characterized even in its elaborated, complex form by its segregation from realistic limitations or obstacles, it cannot, because of its cultural context, be infinite or unlimited in its variety.[46] Sexual and aggressive fantasies, or fantasies of triumph, revenge, rescue, vindication, mastery, domination, of sacrifice or punishment, or of helplessness, hopelessness, imprisonment, or abandonment, or, if people like Marx and Freud are the subjects, of chosenness and special favor, of accomplishment, productivity, problem solving and breakthrough, all occur in a cultural context, as people make their way over what has become for them familiar mental terrain. In these terms, fantasy has a history; contents, language, and images change over time, and fantasy thinking and its effects can be studied as much as the history of any subject can, for fantasy thinking has infiltrated and in certain instances shaped or dominated political action as well, obviously, as the conceptions of even the ablest and most cognitively disciplined thinkers.

This wishful or fantasy thinking, which emerges from a current sense of loss, failure, or lack, whether perceived as an opportunity or as a threat, is meant to rearrange events in the mind, imaginatively transforming potential or actual outcomes, to see things another way, the need for which arises from the inability to solve a real problem immediately or to tolerate the significance of important or affecting social events that appear not to be directly within the sphere of one's personal control. In wishful or fantasy thinking, things work out the way one wants them to because the demands of reality, as exemplified by routine notions of logic and causality, are wholly or partially ignored, *reality* defined here as the world outside one's omnipotent control (i.e., the source or location of obstacles and limits, including other people's interests, moral perspectives, or wishful strivings, objective inadequacies, in brief, those things that caused problems in the first place and that would prevent fantasy solutions from being achieved in the event one tried to do so).[47]

Still, fantasy thinking is in all cases preliminary to real action in the world, establishing the initial basis for solutions to problems, including withdrawing from them. The rather too familiar notion that first we eat and then we moralize is not quite correct: first we think about eating, and in the process there is always more or less a residue of fantasy no matter how refined one's thinking may ultimately get in the light of real contacts and effective action. It is easy to be deceived about the extent of fantasy thinking in routine social contacts, especially because of the way that language works in everyday life: people are not inclined to plumb meaning in routine exchanges, and all that is really required is that behavior remain appropriate to context. But even the most casual, ordinary offhand phrase, such as "Let's eat" or "Let's go to the game," harbors much more content than one wants or needs to know about. We may offer preoccupied people a penny for their thoughts, and pretty much that is what we get, about a penny's worth, a muted, socially acceptable, appropriate but diminished expression related to but hardly equal to the initial, unspoken thoughts.

There is (as Lenin noted) a positive side to wishful or fantasy thinking that has the capacity not only to release people from oppressive, threatening, or ordinary, unexciting situations but also to promote the elaboration of possibilities, a segregated arena in which relationships can be explored in exaggerated but also novel ways, providing a subsequent basis for realistic thinking. It is interesting to note, for example, that the abstract, symbolic, mathematized language of science, being immediately unrelated in visual and other ways to larger social questions or moral conflicts, allows mathematicians and scientists to be freer to combine and recombine the language and symbols in novel and unexpected ways. This capacity for the freer use of fantasy thinking is supported by the subject matter itself, which is remote from the understanding of the overwhelming part of the population and is capable of being judged only by other professionals who are supposed to value innovation on principle. It is supported by the culture of the discipline as well: the main limitation of fantasy thinking in cultural terms involves professional standards (including moral standards): the results of scientific work must be seen to constitute a realistic attempt to solve an outstanding problem. To be sure, there are many other personal, social, and institutional limits even on scientific thinking, including the extent of any individual's talent, or of idiosyncratic "neurotic" dilemmas, and the actual arrangements of the scientific community itself, which involve hierarchies, professional jealousies and rivalries, and struggles over resources and strategies. There is also a problem with respect to practical applications, that is, the extent to which the wider society is prepared to use innovative thinking and novel technique. These limits clearly prevent scientists from being as free as they might otherwise be to conjure alternatives. Nevertheless they are freer than social scientists to do so because the language and images of social science are more clearly tied to real interests and moral perspectives and appear as well to be more accessible to a public that is always ready to judge such things. Social scientists have evidently always been more exposed and vulnerable to censorship and self-censorship, and this has affected both their ability to think and what their audience does with the results of their thinking.

By the same token, there is also a negative side to fantasy thinking in the sense that especially peremptory, impulsive, irruptive, and fleeting thoughts are worrisome and even frightening, compelling a constant search for people and things to remain connected to, but also in the sense that even cognitively disciplined thinkers can in their desire to achieve or succeed or for some other reason fail to control the degree to which fantasy thinking continues to affect even their systematically elaborated work. To recall one famous instance, Freud had trouble explaining what he perceived to be the recurrent contents of mental life, either in terms of what he deemed accidental factors (e.g., the vicissitudes of life in society, including family life) or in terms of instincts or drives. The concept of instincts or drives may refer to somatic or to psychic processes, but Freud could not infer and then insist on an exclusive, universal mental content, a story in effect told more or less the same way around the world, on the basis of such processes. Drives, as he pointed out, are without quality: somatic tensions may provoke activity and a search for content to justify it, but drives cannot themselves be the source of any content.[48]

Still, Freud wanted very much to say that drives, somatic tensions, could in fact acquire psychical representation as wishes or fantasies independent of any real, external event, for this was the parsimonious solution: he could have explained everything about the origin and power of social order, morality, religion, and law, without reference to the social world. If wishful thinking ever threatened to overcome Freud's attachment to science, and did overcome it in a way, this was the occasion. For Freud actually suggested in *Totem and Taboo* that one aspect of the narcissistic organization of primitive people was the overevaluation of their psychical acts to an extraordinary degree. Accordingly, "the mere hostile *impulse* against the father, the mere existence of a wishful *fantasy* of killing and devouring him, would have been enough to produce the moral reaction that created totemism and taboo."[49] If that were so, Freud continued, we would not have to think of our cultural legacy as stemming from a "hideous crime," the totem murder; we could think of it instead as stemming from innate drive activity with no damage to the explanatory network linking earliest times to the present—because, as Freud wrote, "psychical reality" is "strong enough to bear the weight of these consequences."[50]

But this formulation begs the question of content. Where does the (father-son) content come from? In his initial psychoanalytic efforts, the content that Freud reported came from the culture around him, from the real experience of people who, if it was traumatic enough, would have repressed it because it was so radically incompatible with their self-image. As Freud explained matters then, affect is produced by traumatic experience, and, if it cannot be "discharged," it produces a pathological result. Illness arises from the persistent memory of a real event, or, as Freud initially put it, "hysterics suffer from their reminiscences."[51] Cäcilie M., who suffered from "an extremely violent facial neuralgia," had had a quarrel with her husband, whose insulting response she felt as "a slap in the face," though, once Freud called up the traumatic scene, "her pain and her attack were both at an end."[52] But the content that this woman reported came from a real, unequal, culturally legitimated, commonly experienced social relationship.

Freud, however, was not satisfied with this social source of mental content and not only, or even primarily, because he concluded that the events reported by patients were fantasies and had not really occurred. For, even if the reports were fantasies (he never believed that all of them were), the content was still derived from and descriptive of real current relationships. Rather, Freud was after a grander solution to what he perceived, rightly or wrongly, as a puzzling phenomenon, the fact that the fantasies that people related were so much alike and included events that he thought they could not themselves so consistently have experienced or would not themselves have had such knowledge of, concluding that certain responses were apparently being transmitted from one generation to the next in ways that could not be accounted for by what he considered the accidental circumstances of the everyday social world. At the same time, because the recurrent fantasies entailed a particular content, he could not continue to claim logically that it did not matter whether something had actually occurred or not. Of course it mattered: where else could the content have come from except an external event of some sort? Freud therefore accounted for the recurrent content by assuming a real event, a shared historical trauma, the totem murder, which he claimed had genetic effects transmitted to succeeding generations.[53]

The fate of this notion of phylogenetic endowment, Freud's commitment to the Lamarckian proposition and to the related premise that ontogeny recapitulates phylogeny, is well known: it proved to be an embarrassment to those who followed and it was dropped; Freud's primary, preferred solution to the question of content could not be maintained.[54] At the same time, Freud did express briefly this other illogical notion that it did not matter whether the totem murder had actually occurred or not in the sense that the life we are compelled to live in the body is sufficient by itself to account for content. This last thought is so errant and in terms of Freud's own beliefs so unfounded that it cannot be viewed as merely an error in logic; it was rather a result of a momentary failure to control an unexpected degree of fantasy thinking. Freud, bitterly disappointed over the loss of C. G. Jung to psychoanalysis, and anxious to realize the expectations that he had for his discipline, to make it universally applicable, was struggling to solve an awkward problem. It is important to observe that in this instance he did not lose sight of the problem, that he realized and explained how tenuous his preferred solution was, and that, in this text at least, his claims for it were finally very modest. But if, as he said, scientific creativity is a combination of daring fantasy and relentlessly realistic criticism, then the critical capacity in this instance came very close to being compromised.*

*"It must be admitted that these are grave difficulties; and any explanation that could avoid presumptions of such a kind would seem to be preferable. Further reflection, however, will show that I am not alone in the responsibility for this bold procedure. Without the assumption of a collective mind, which makes it possible to neglect the interruptions of mental acts caused by the extinction of the individual, social psychology in general cannot exist. Unless psychical processes were continued from one generation to another, if each generation were obliged to acquire its attitude to life anew, there would be no progress in this field and next to no development. This gives rise to two further

Thus, although fantasy thinking is couched in language and images derived from the common culture and is always enmeshed with cognitive and moral thinking directed to the solution of real problems in the world, it is possible to discriminate and identify such thinking even in the efforts of theorists as fiercely committed to science as a discipline and an outlook as Marx and Freud. T. B. Bottomore wrote of Marx that his cast of mind "was fundamentally scientific. His whole life and work reveal not only a moral passion, but more strikingly a passion for empirical inquiry and factual knowledge."[55] However, as Erich Fromm could have told him (Fromm happened to have written the foreword to this particular volume of Bottomore's), sometimes the wish to achieve a solution, not only to see an end to a pervasive problem but to be the one who discovered how to end it, overrides the commitment to logical rigor and discipline. Keeping in mind that fantasy thinking is constant but not necessarily dominant and that there are both positive and negative aspects involved that foster as well as inhibit insight and action, there are several specific criteria by which we can identify occasions in the work of Marx and Freud (and some notable loyalists of theirs) when this occurred, as Kolakowski raised the issue, distinguishing fantasy thinking from cognitively controlled thinking in their work and in general terms as well, linking it back to the problem of ideology.

First, fantasy thinking is affected by but cannot be inferred from current social relationships, the equivalent of what Marx referred to as utopian thinking or bourgeois idealism. It is not the future-oriented nature of the thought per se that distinguishes it as fantasy since it is possible to project into the future with some degree of realism on the basis of experience and commitments to cultural standards and expectations, especially if the problem is simple enough; and it is not that the conclusions that people arrive at cannot or do not at some point

---

questions: how much can we attribute to psychical continuity in the sequence of generations? and what are the ways and means employed by one generation in order to hand on its mental states to the next one? I shall not pretend that these problems are sufficiently explained or that direct communication and tradition—which are the first things that occur to one—are enough to account for the process. Social psychology shows very little interest, on the whole, in the manner in which the required continuity in the mental life of successive generations is established." (Sigmund Freud, *Totem and Taboo*, in *The Standard Edition of the Complete Psychological Works of Sigmund Freud*, ed. James Strachey, 24 vols. [London, 1953–74], 13:158. I have collapsed two paragraphs into one here. See also the discussion in Robert A. Paul, "Did the Primal Crime Take Place?" *Ethos* 4, no. 3 [1976]: 311–52. Freud's remark about scientific creativity is quoted in Stephen Jay Gould, "Freud's Phylogenetic Fantasy," *Natural History* 12 [1987]: 19.)

come true. It is rather that, in the current social context, there was no way for them to have known or even reasonably guessed how they might come true. Leon Trotsky's musings on man's future, so reminiscent of Godwin's on the same subject, provide an excellent example of fantasy thinking in these terms:

> Man will learn to move rivers and mountains, to build peoples' palaces on the peaks of Mont Blanc and at the bottom of the Atlantic. . . . Man at last will begin to harmonize himself in earnest. He will make it his business to achieve beauty by giving the movement of his own limbs the utmost precision, purposefulness, and economy in his work, his walk and his play. . . . The human species . . . will once more enter into a state of radical transformation and will become an object, in his own hands, of the most complicated methods of artificial selection and psycho-physical training. . . . Man will make it his purpose to master his own feelings, to raise his instincts to the heights of his consciousness, to make them transparent, to extend the wires of his will into the hidden recesses of his personality, and thereby . . . to create a higher social-biological type, or, if you please, a superman.[56]

More to the point, however, given Kolakowski's claim, are Marx's judgments, philosophical or social, involving the organization of life after the abolition of private property, his perception of the bourgeois mode of production as the last antagonistic mode, and communism, as "the *definitive* resolution of the antagonism between man and nature, and between man and man."[57] There was no realistic way by Marx's own standards, no way based in evidence revealed by current social relationships, that could have allowed Marx even so much as to guess reasonably about these matters. His notion of the direct relationship of the social organization of production to perception and outlook, and hence the prospect of a single interest beyond class struggle, was an invention unrelated to evidence.

Second, fantasy thinking is characterized by an omnipotent quality, a confusion over what is in one's control and what is beyond it, what is in one's mind and what the world beyond might allow, as ideal aims and expectations are expressed in a measure of concrete detail unjustified by what anyone actually knows or by events that follow. Consider, for example, Marx's belief that his categories permitted prediction or that his insight with respect to Hegel's method had provided him with knowledge of the main tendencies in history, or Freud's claim for psychoanalysis:

In point of fact I believe that a large part of the mythological view of the world . . . *is nothing but psychology projected into the external world.* The obscure recognition of psychical factors and the relations in the unconscious is mirrored . . . in the construction of a *supernatural reality,* which is destined to be changed back once more by science into the *psychology of the unconscious.* One could venture to explain in this way the myths of paradise and the fall of man, of God, of good and evil, of immortality, and so on, and to transform *metaphysics* into *metapsychology.*[58]

Third, fantasy thinking is characterized also by the appearance of unexpected or unwarranted gaps in logic or in the explanatory network of an argument that have occurred because a connection was missed that it is reasonable to expect should not have been missed, or by the appearance of contradictions in different texts or between texts and practice, that are disavowed or by some rationalization made to appear logically consistent. The most immediate and obvious kind of logical gap or contradiction is the refusal of Marx and Freud to become objects of their own theory, the ease with which they exist as exceptions to the rules that they have established for everyone else.[59] Marx's linkage of ideological (distorted) thinking to material interests as a way of separating and elevating his own thinking, being able thereby to define it as objective, has always been a remarkably effective rationalization. Even more interesting in these terms is the persistent, long-term absence in psychoanalysis of a systematic theory of affects and a noticeable lack of awareness of the significance of such an absence, reflected in discussions in the professional psychoanalytic literature itself. Apart from an occasional reference, it was not until approximately the early and mid-1970s that psychoanalysts began to consider the situation systematically with the intention of changing it, and changing also a related and equally puzzling imbalance as reflected in the literature between discussions of transference and countertransference (papers on transference outnumbering papers on countertransference by about eight to one).

The countertransference issue is an interesting one, no doubt. But the absence of a systematic, ongoing discussion of affect is astonishing, considering that Freud's last major suggestion on the revision of theory involved the problem of anxiety, which he claimed occupied a unique position in the mental economy (though without the kind of elaboration devoted to libido or even to aggression); that the implications in cultural terms of affective bonds and expression in religion, art, politics, the family, and, not least for what it might reveal, sports are so readily taken for granted by psychoanalysts; and that the very organization of psychoanalytic therapy is so bound up with affective expression (Freud had described early on, e.g., how in the process of recovering memories patients became "prey to an emotion it would be hard to counter-feit").[60] It is really difficult to understand, given these issues, how the systematic discussion of affect was avoided for so long.[61]

The contradictions and logical gaps in these bodies of thought, the omnipotent expression and expectations that were offered apart from the evidential basis claimed for them, are historically important because they became the source of bitter splits and divisions, of multiple views of subjects that in the minds of the founders should never have occurred and could not have occurred except as a result of maliciously inspired symptomatic error, the reverse side of their belief that they offered their work in the spirit of reason and science and that their audience would have no motive for treating it otherwise. They found it hard to accept that the audience could with any sense of legitimacy bring their own wishes and expectations to the work, turning it into something they never intended. Indeed, the destructive struggles that occurred continue to mystify sympathetic adherents of these doctrines. As one observer of the contending factions identified with Anna Freud and Melanie Klein in English psychoanalysis put it, "What one group felt to be a legitimate development of Freudian doctrines, the other group felt to be flagrantly illicit—how could a single institution embrace such antagonistic positions?"[62]

On the one hand, I have spent as much time with Marx and Freud as I have in order to demonstrate that it is possible to establish criteria for discriminating better from worse interpretations of reality—it is not just a matter of moral or ideological preference. On the other hand, the discussion also provides the opportunity to explain that the things that can be said about Marx and Freud (or about Godwin or Lenin), with respect to unwarranted inferences, logical lapses, contradictions, exaggerations, and so on, can also be said about the way people have used the efforts of any social theorist or activist to bring order to a heterogeneous and conflicted world. The criteria established to define fantasy thinking in these particular instances are intended to illuminate one of the important ways in which people generally remain connected to the social world. This kind of thinking facilitates belief and action across class and other lines because the sense of stability, distinctiveness, moral elevation, and superiority that it provides in the face of social conflict is for most people most of the time more important than the differences it may also justify. If some of these authors and activists inspired greater or more disastrous struggles, that was because the universality of their claims roused people against them in ways that they perceived to be immediately dangerous and threatening, not because the reparative, facilitating function of their views is different from the function of other views. The heterogeneity problem affects everyone, and there is no standpoint serving as a mobilizing public code anywhere that is not similarly founded or does not similarly employ unwarranted inferences, logical lapses, contradictions, and exaggerations.

That is to say, people use ideological language situationally as they must. Americans pride themselves on their competitive spirit, but, apart from the difficulty of deciding what they mean by this, the following is also true: the New York dairy industry for years accepted a law that barred "destructive competition," a principle that the industry carried to a logical conclusion, as twenty-three companies were convicted of conspiring to fix prices in 1982–83; twenty-five of twenty-eight billion dollars of agricultural profits in 1986 were a result of government subsidies (export subsidies and direct payments to farmers amounted to forty-nine billion dollars over the two-year period 1986–87); the American Medical Association, faced with declining physician incomes, announced in 1986 that market forces were an unreliable regulator of demand for medical services, recommending that medical schools take action to limit access and reduce the number of entering students.[63] Nor is this all that can be said on the subject of competition in the market-place: the so-called free market is heavily managed, there is unequal access to resources on all levels, there are protectionist sentiments and protectionist lobbies, the government acts to bail out failed corporations, and so on and on.[64] It is all very contradictory, and it all washes (the Reagan administration said that it had no official policy on the American Medical Association's proposals, although it continues to believe that the marketplace is the best regulator of supply; and some few journalists complained about the proposals, one of them pointing out that they were "a blueprint for anti-competitive action," clearly with no effect).[65] I have chosen these few examples because they are not in any way hidden, masked, or obscure. There are many more serious examples of contradictory belief and behavior that can be adduced, but there is no need to do so—every reader can suggest such a list, which is easily extended. We can just take it for granted that any society that holds fast at the same time to a belief in the moral legitimacy of inheritance and to a belief in the moral legitimacy of equal opportunity does not have its collective thinking cap on straight.

These several examples of contradictory belief and behavior in one sphere of activity do not constitute an exceptional circumstance. People in their everyday lives struggle in this way to remain cognitively adequate whatever the task, simple or complex. They know where their jobs are and what it means to be paid for their labor. They try to improve their position, to secure a future for themselves and their families, and in any number of ways to see to their interests. However, in order to preserve the sense that current social arrangements constitute (or organized challenges to these arrangements could constitute) a sufficient background of safety, an orderly arena in which interests can continue to be pursued, and in order to have an animating conception of the future, to be able to elaborate a notion of "someday" (right now things are hard, but "someday . . ."), to feel that society is working for them or represents them in these respects, interpretations or perceptions of current conditions, of official policies such as the ones that I have noted, utterances of authoritative figures on the subject of friends and enemies or past and future and the like, are characterized by different aspects of fantasy thinking as I have outlined them.

Such fantasy thinking does not necessarily dominate thinking about or behavior in the world (although historically this has happened, and, in certain segregated social situations, religious, artistic, sexual, and sporting, it is expected to happen). Nor does it inhibit the ability to function: on the contrary, such thinking is one of the conditions on which people can continue to function, to remain effective in their own immediate domain as parents, workers, neighbors, churchgoers. Moreover, if people are given information, they can understand decisions that are made, and they can make decisions of their own; they are not in this sense impaired. Still, not only are people everywhere uninformed, ill informed, misinformed, and disinformed, but the need of people to sustain the tie to the protective and facilitating environment, to live with a sense of adequacy, stability and worthiness, to continue to believe especially that the ideas that legitimate social practices, that explain the conflicts and dilemmas arising from multiple and competing interests and perspectives, do come from "a far place," compels the constant resort to one or another aspect of fantasy thinking. In these terms, it should be noted, the most problematic of Marx's uses of the concept of ideology is still worth thinking about, providing of course that we submit Marx to these same criteria.

"Transitional Phenomena, Transitional Objects, Transitional Space"

The pluralization or fragmentation of psychoanalysis referred to earlier has enhanced the reputation of a number of writers whose work might not otherwise have come to be appreciated to the extent that is currently the case. Prominent among these writers, as I have already noted, is D. W. Winnicott. Winnicott was a pediatrician with psychoanalytic developmental concerns, which seems remote from historical and social concerns except that his work is addressed to the need of children to relate to real people in the social world and to symbolization, the imaginative capacity people have for constructing versions of the world. His work in a quiet way has therefore begun to affect religious studies, artistic and literary criticism, sociology, and history.[66]

Winnicott's main contribution to psychoanalysis was the invention and elaboration of the concepts of transitional object, transitional phenomena, and transitional space, concepts that—it cannot be emphasized too strongly—had developmental, not historical, significance for him. By *transitional object,* then, Winnicott meant the "first not-me possession" of the child, the first step in discriminating self from others, inside from outside, fantasy from reality. Children use things they find, a toy, a shred of blanket, a teddy bear, to facilitate the process of separation from parents, adapting in this way a part of the world they find to conform to their own needs and wishes. They endow these things with special meaning, which allows them to develop a sense of the capacity to be "on their own," allowing them also, to use Winnicott's phrase, a "transitional (or intermediate) space" between fantasy and objective reality, in which they can begin to explore unfamiliar territory in an imaginative way.

According to Winnicott, the extent to which the illusion of invention and mastery in this transitional space is maintained by the mother will determine the child's ability to feel at home in the world and have a creative relationship with it. In this process, children develop a more objective conception of what their parents are like, in terms of absences, preoccupations, different vulnerabilities and interests, while expanding as separate individuals their own capacity to imagine, pretend, and play. The transitional objects, which afford children a sense of remaining connected even as they recognize their separateness, are dispensed with or abandoned as soon as the fact of separation is no longer threatening, implying, if the process is handled well by a caring parent, a shift from the experience of themselves as the center of a totally subjective world to a sense of themselves as one person among others, the ability to be separate in the presence of others, to take a step away from people and things to pursue a more autonomous course of action.[67]

Winnicott's genius as a therapist, observer, and communicator are well known and require no comment. A critical approach to his work is not likely to affect the esteem in which he is held. On the other hand, a sense of what such criticism might entail is useful here and mandates some comment. Apart from the fact that any developmental psychology that ascribes specific mental contents to children who do not themselves report must be problematic, whether it is Sigmund or Anna Freud's, or Melanie Klein's, or Winnicott's, the last named is particularly well known for having maintained an optimistic outlook that a British colleague, Charles Rycroft, himself a veteran of the British Psychoanalytic Society's wars, called "soppy" and otherwise treated with not a little sarcasm.[68]

One of the things that Winnicott's developmental stress led him to be "soppy" about was the degree to which parents could be effective in fostering the creative capacities of their children or, to put it the other way, failing to observe the degree to which society can adversely affect the capacities of children regardless of how able and interested parents are.[69] It is not clear in his work the extent to which there are class, gender, racial, ethnic, religious, and regional bases on which societies have historically encouraged or discouraged creative capacities regardless of the intentions of parents. Anyone who grew up in a ghetto anywhere recognizes that one of the really damaging aspects of life in such a place is the information deprivation that people are subjected to and the tremendous effort that is required to recover a portion of the ground. More broadly, children give up specific people and things ("objects") as the precondition of greater degrees of separation and autonomy, but there are limits to the effectiveness of the process. The heterogeneous reality of competing interests and perspectives makes the sense of threat and loss so real that ideology must remain available as a "transitional phenomenon," just as the physical presence of authoritative figures remains necessary as "transitional objects," to provide a morally legitimate sense of how "social space" can be used. Because, as Winnicott himself observed, no one is ever free of the strain of relating inner to outer reality, attachments to transitional phenomena and objects persist through life, and there is a social and historical sense as distinct from a developmental one, in which these concepts can be heuristically conceived. Transitional phenomena and objects are used by perceiving, interpreting individuals in terms that are important to them, for the sake of maintaining a personal sense of stability and adequacy and a sense of the social world as a background of safety within which they can legitimately pursue personal and group interests.[70] This interpretive elaboration of the world, this "social construction of reality," is an active process that, considering the vicissitudes of personal development and the variety of social locations, helps account for the persistence of competing interests and perspectives.[71]

These phenomena and objects at the social level are correctly identified as transitional to the extent that people both find them in the world and construct versions of their significance in terms of their own needs and interests. But they are transitional also in the more common sense that other potentialities, greater degrees of autonomy and independence or of creative capacity, are possible given other forms—or even the absence—of such phenomena and objects, which are, after all, historically derived and have not remained the same over time. Where or how these potentialities can be realized, or what they might entail, are subjects for discussion, but the sheer fact of them is not.

At the same time, however, these phenomena and objects are also different from those described by Winnicott in at least one important respect: being social and historical rather than developmental and individual, they do persist whatever the form (including especially for our purposes money and property), and there has been no occasion yet when they have been dispensed with or abandoned. Of course, specific transitional phenomena or objects have failed historically, but they have been replaced again in other forms, the point being not that the differences are unimportant—an inconceivable proposition—but that society is not simply the family "writ large"; it is a much tougher, more problematic arena for people. As the great English political theorist Sir Henry Maine once observed, people like to think that those who die young are favored by God, but they never think that way about governments. Societies provide various kinds of mourning rituals to help people overcome the sense of loss that attends the death of parents or other loved people, but no society ever instructs its citizens in the possibility of its own demise.[72]

The larger, more remote social world exists for people in ways quite different from the intimate family. The element of illusion that is lost to some degree with respect to parents, allowing children to move away and be on their own, has not yet been so effectively lost with respect to the larger society, and no organized society anywhere has demonstrated the ability or willingness to continue without the presence of such phenomena and objects as I have discussed. However, one of the reasons that I chose to use the language of transitional phenomena and objects is that it allows us to underscore the tension that persists in every society, although significantly to greater or lesser degrees, between dependence, as revealed by the need for beliefs, leaders, and things on the one hand, and independence, as revealed by the capacity for imaginative solutions to social, scientific, and artistic problems based on the presence of beliefs, leaders, and things on the other. Either this world of transitional phenomena and objects can appear discouraging, too powerful against people, requiring their passivity and subordination and the exclusion and manipulation of others, or it can appear encouraging, a safe arena in which people can develop different perspectives on the world or even begin to think that they can master the problems presented by it.

The reason that transitional phenomena and objects persist in this social sense, why people need them to, and why they cannot decisively resolve the tension that follows in the direction of greater degrees of independence is that the struggle for individuation continues beyond the world that parents initially establish for children, a struggle that people must engage in to sustain themselves as perceiving, interpreting individuals, as a triangular point, so to speak, against the power of fantasy to disrupt or control on one side (peremptory, impulsive, irruptive sexual and hostile thoughts being one obvious example of the power of fantasy to affect how people think and feel) and against the power of the social world to disrupt and control on the other. The continued presence of transitional phenomena and objects (ideology, leadership, property, money) establishes for people the opportunity to invent a "space" between fantasy and the heterogeneous world, to imagine an approach to the world in which they can act effectively or excuse themselves when they cannot. These phenomena and objects to which people remain intensely loyal and attached or in which they remain intensely interested are the condition on which any degree of autonomous behavior is possible at all, as far as people have been able to master the problems and conflicts that they have had to face.

As I noted earlier, fantasy thinking is indispensable to the development of realistic thinking, including scientific thinking, allowing people and events to be conceived of and dealt with in imagination before any action is undertaken. But fantasy thinking can also undermine realistic thinking; fantasy can threaten people, deflect attention from the solution of current problems, hamper the ability to deal effectively with solutions, and it may even suggest solutions or possibilities where none exist or that would be dangerous to implement (Nazi strivings for economic autarchy being a case in point). Moreover, the social world has a similar dual potential. The ability to be an independent interpreting individual is made possible by life in society, which people must be able to imagine as a safe arena for personal and group development and for the accomplishment of goals. But society can also fail as a safe arena, becoming either too disruptive or too controlling to permit interpreting individuals to occupy that triangular point, to use "transitional space" to mediate between fantasy and the social world. The awesome singularity of the concentration camp experience derives from the juncture of these two possibilities. For the camps were a place where a community, too weak to be protective of its members, who were demoralized as a result, was destroyed by another community, animated by fantasies of omnipotence and unlimited accomplishment, unhampered in the domain of the camps by any opposing force and thus too strong against them.

In Freud's version of the world, it will be recalled, man's antagonistic feelings cannot be resolved because of the renunciatory demands made by society on him. Man remains discontented with life in society because his most fundamental sexual and aggressive wishes are frustrated, the cost of sustaining any civilized life at all. But Freud had no particular empirical basis for this conclusion or for his notions about the origins and uses of social order, law, morality, and religion. These were inferences based on his clinical experience, his knowledge of literature and the contemporary anthropology, and his own observations of the world around him, especially the propensity of Europeans, organized in competing and hostile nation-states, to enhance their own ethnic, religious, national, class, and racial particularities at the expense of others.

Based on what he knew, in other words, Freud could just as easily have come to the opposite conclusion about society: the role played by authoritative figures in suppressing sexual and aggressive wishes is indispensable and justified because acting on such wishes would lead only to frustration and bitter disappointment while merely perseverating on them would lead in turn to other kinds of failed actions or to inaction. It is just as reasonable to suppose that society exists to encourage activity, to keep people from falling prey to the consolations of a predominantly fantasy world (except under specific, segregated cultural conditions such as religion, sex, sleep, and play), as a way of providing them with a source of support while mobilizing them for socially necessary tasks that individuals and families could not accomplish on their own. Man's alienation from some supposed preoedipal or oedipal ties to parental figures can be viewed as a source of unity and cohesion as readily as a source of division and conflict, and usefully so because real social relationships beyond the family provide a more substantial basis for the recovery from the loss of these family ties than fantasy.

Both fantasy thinking and social relationships can be used productively by people, but they can also become destructive as more or less exclusive poles or entities, a possibility defined by the characteristically unrestrained expression of life at the poles, by the dominance of fantasy thinking on one side (the failure to constrain the sense of entitlement or omnipotence, to recognize the inevitability of opposition to claims for an exclusive set of ambitions, the failure to be alert to the interests and moral perspectives of others and to the sanctions that they may be able to impose), and by the demands of authoritative figures on the other side (for the exclusive right to make decisions regarding social problems, preventing people from exercising their capacities as perceiving, interpreting individuals).

This is the second reason that I chose to use the notions of transitional phenomena and objects: it is possible to see in these terms how fantasy thinking is constrained among both authoritative figures and the people. The transitional role of authoritative figures is revealed particularly by their invariable public use of a codified, "civic" language, the purpose of which is never to foster an objective version of the world but rather to exhort people to sustain a social position or to preserve the given sense of how space should be organized and used. Even the most commonplace figures use this civic language, not because of any loyalty to the class that originated it or because of any loyalty to mannerliness, which such figures could not persuade anyone they knew or cared anything about, but because the language embodies a common repertory of inherited phrases that people can in turn use transitionally to sustain a sense of space. The colloquial, improvisational language of people, which is not only constantly changing but different from one social location to another, allows them to express themselves in various ways. By contrast, the civic language allows them to interpret events in various ways while taking solace in a form of expression that is shared and venerable.

It is important to emphasize that all such civic language depends on so-called pragmatic contextual features to achieve a sense of shared meaning between authority and people, that is, on sociolinguistic features characteristic of a particular organization of social space and of relationships between authority and people that make effective conveyance of meaning possible. Among these "pragmatic contextual features" are shared background and memories, especially of the ways in which people had displayed themselves as good, worthy, admirable, and brave in the past, shared forms of knowledge, of standards and expectations, and of conceptions of social situations. These features provide authoritative figures and people with historical and communal information that allows the useful ambiguities inherent in natural language sentences to be "filled in" or that allows the manipulations to continue also on the side of the people, who need to maintain the link between "inside and outside," the sense of control over a heterogeneous reality, as they piece together a story from all their different points of view in terms of the statements that are made.[73] It is in this sense that we live continuously in a universe in which ideology functions as a transitional phenomenon, or, as Mikhail Bakhtin has written:

> Social man . . . is surrounded by ideological phenomena, by object-signs of various types and categories: by words in the mul-

tifarious forms of their realization . . . by scientific statements, religious symbols and beliefs, works of art, and so on. All of these things in their totality comprise the ideological environment, which forms a solid ring around man. And man's consciousness lives and develops in this environment. Human consciousness does not come into contact with existence directly, but through the medium of the surrounding ideological world. . . . In fact, the individual consciousness can only become a consciousness by being realized in the forms of the ideological environment proper to it: in language, in conventionalized gesture, in artistic image, in myth, and so on.[74]

Although Clifford Geertz would not use the concept of ideology in this sense, he has also written of "symbol systems" as "extrinsic sources of information in terms of which human life can be patterned— extrapersonal mechanisms for the perception, understanding, judgment, and manipulation of the world. Culture patterns—religious, philosophical, aesthetic, scientific, ideological—are 'programs'; they provide a template or blueprint for the organization of social and psychological processes, much as the genetic systems provide such a template for the organization of organic processes." The necessity for such "cultural templates," according to Geertz, stems from the extreme plasticity of human behavior, "the extreme generality, diffuseness, and variability of man's innate response capacities," which compels reliance on extrinsic programs for guidance and orientation.[75]

The problem, however, is that these "extrinsic programs" originated and were developed in unique historical contexts that cannot be repeated, and no such program has ever been flexible enough, at the outset or afterward, to preclude multiple and competing interpretations or extensive critique; there are unanticipated events that cannot be readily explained in terms of the available language but that must nevertheless be absorbed and accounted for, requiring novel elaborations that themselves become a source of dispute; there constantly occur felt discrepancies between ideal expectations and real actions; and any orientation that can serve to mobilize the conflicting interests, moral perspectives, and wishes of a heterogeneous population must be distinguished by a significant degree of ambiguity and contradiction and must therefore be open on these grounds as well to a variety of interpretations and uses. These different factors taken together (changing social conditions, unanticipated events from the standpoint of conscious expectations, multiple levels of appeal, and ambiguity and contradiction) account for the kind of wishful or fantasy thinking described earlier, for the constant proliferation of critical, antagonistic moral perspectives, and for the existence of oppositional groups of all kinds.

Thus, James Joyce compared the contemporary culture to the debris scattered on the battlefield at Waterloo, and W. B. Yeats exclaimed famously, "Mere anarchy is loosed upon the world." Joyce, Yeats, and the other writers referred to earlier perceived the world this way, absent a core, lacking a unifying center, because, even if life is scripted, there are many ways to read it. Indeed, the meaning of events to people, given their complex character and their multiple social locations, always threatens to exceed the codified language that they have in which to express it. The entry into language is supposed to make people more independent of the immediate environment, but the entry into history and the heterogeneous social world that occurs at the same time becomes a more generalized and threatening source of conflict, which is too great to be contained in a single framework conceived of as a program, template, or blueprint.[76] In order to maintain a sense of the world as a safe arena, people are compelled constantly to elaborate and expand on received versions of how the world works, to pick up, use, discard, and return to whatever versions work for them at any time; and the rationalizing strategies that are deployed in the matter of choice demonstrate how close to being unable to repair social situations people can get. This is the third reason I chose to use the transitional language, to think of ideology as a transitional phenomenon: people find the constructs there, but they also invent versions of them as they need to. The following statement by a member of San Francisco's gay community on the subject of AIDS, an extremely grave situation that must be imaginatively accounted for, is indicative of what occurs among people in a more general way all the time: "My own view is that AIDS is a terrible tragedy, and yet one that offers real opportunities for personal and collective growth. . . . Of course, large numbers will continue to die, but the threat of the disease has given us all a new perspective on life. It's growth-producing, and most people who have had it have grown into grace."[77]

The most significant results of this plasticity are the persistent occurrence of fantasy thinking, to foster connections where they do not exist or to miss connections as a way of avoiding an unacceptable degree of strain, the persistence of multiple perspectives and hence of social conflict, and the persistent reliance on authoritative leadership, political, religious, and other, which remains indispensable as a stabilizing social technique everywhere. Leadership, not in the sense of internalized moral representations, but as real, concrete, physically present individuals, the kind that used to appear on balconies in one guise and now appear on television in another, that goes on the stump and presses the flesh, that rules people and does not merely administer things, and whose absence, even in a metaphoric sense, causes distress, remains necessary to people as a means of assisting in the transformation of the fluid, indeterminate, and conflicted social reality into organized and usable forms. Forewarned in an ideological sense is not forearmed: the abstract, theoretical prospect of class, gender, or racial conflict, for example, never really prepares people for the kind of conflict that they are called on to participate in or to witness. Present situations are never like past ones; there is always some new and surprising challenge, an unexpected, unaccounted for opportunity or threat. For this reason, events that may well have been expected in the abstract cause more turmoil than individuals and groups are prepared to deal with, and leaders are still relied on for explanations and as examples of how to act.

In fact, the most interesting thing about the concept of ideology, considering everything that has been written about it, is that it can as yet be distinguished as an abstraction separate from authoritative leadership only for analytic purposes. This is the fourth reason that I chose to use the transitional language: ideology and authority, transitional phenomena and transitional object, are linked, continuing together to serve, to greater or lesser degrees but in practical fact, the needs of people with respect to dependence, constraints, and the construction of versions of reality. The problem of multiple and competing interests and perspectives, the heterogeneity problem, is too difficult for people to be contained by abstract systems even if they come from a far place and appear elevated and superior. Apart, perhaps, from idiosyncratic individuals, ideology has never yet been sufficient to sustain social relationships separate from authoritative leadership. To the extent that people have been able to distance themselves from leadership, to examine leaders critically, or to be able to replace them in a systematic way, they have done so only on the basis of other substituted concrete objects of support, notably money and property.[78] Virtue is not yet its own reward, or it is not a sufficient reward, and both rewards and supports remain extrinsic to people who still find it too difficult to cope with the conflicts of a heterogeneous world.

The resemblance of this situation to that of Franz Kafka's "Hunger Artist," who practiced his art of starvation in a cage for everyone to see but who would have filled himself up if he could have found the "right food" and left his cage, is not coincidental. Every now and again someone declares that the cage is man's fate, that there is no "right food"; and then someone else declares that the "right food" has been found and everyone will shortly be free to leave, pending a period of struggle and the urgent elimination of some interfering obstacle. But there is no social basis as yet for such definitive conceptions of how reality can be apprehended or life can be lived. The only thing that is evident is that people wish to continue as perceiving, interpreting individuals, to retain a measure of independence from the pressures of the inner and outer worlds, and that they must still use ideology, implying especially wishful or fantasy thinking, and authoritative leadership as the primary means of doing so.

4

The Persistence of Objects in a
Heterogeneous World

The Problem of Charismatic Leadership

How societies cope with the heterogeneity problem and how it must also be coped with in theory cannot be understood apart from how people are related and relate themselves to authoritative leaders and to those more tangible social objects that have served historically as emblematic replacements for the kind of support provided by authoritative leaders, most notably money and property. The ability to become independent of authority, to be self-directed and self-determining to any significant degree, to achieve the status that the Western world defines as "free," has depended less on "internalized morality" than it has on the continued attachment to such socially valued objects.

The best way to understand the role of authoritative leadership and to see how money and property figure in is to take yet another look at the problem of charismatic leadership. This approach is not without its difficulties precisely because few concepts produced by social theorists have penetrated both popular and scholarly imagination as widely, or have been used as loosely, as Max Weber's concept of charisma. In popular usage, the concept, having come to mean merely attractive, attention getting, having a certain charm, or (in Hollywood) "a unique rapport with the audience," has been emptied of significance;[1] even clothing is now described as having charisma.[2] But the concept has just about lost any technical specificity as well. There is little conceptual or empirical agreement in the professional literature on what constitutes charisma or who should or could be characterized as possessing it.[3]

If social theory has ended up imitating life in this instance, there is little to wonder about. For what can one do with a concept that

122

Weber himself treated ambiguously and that for some is still descriptive of the powerful, vital, and mysterious individuals, exceptional and anomalous, who appear in times of social crisis to rally people, mobilizing them for mass action, seeking to restore a past condition or to implement a novel one on the basis of their own personal authority (or appearing to people as personally authoritative whether they make such claims themselves or not), while for others it is descriptive of the sacred aura that surrounds those prominent people anywhere and at any time who are connected to the "animating centers of society," an aura that arises "in any realm of life that is sufficiently focused to seem vital—in science or art as readily as in religion or politics."[4]

Clearly, Weber's notion of the "routinization of charisma" favors the first description, implying that something vital and mysterious disappears from the world when crisis-ridden societies achieve again a measure of stability following the intervention of certain exceptional individuals. But the logic of social arrangements favors the second, the idea that something sacred is retained even in the process of routinization, that all leadership shares in this sacred quality in whatever sphere of life it becomes empowered, and that there is something necessitous about leadership that elevates it and segregates it from fundamental kinds of critical scrutiny or prevents leadership from becoming merely the administrative overseer of things. Marx and Weber both addressed the demystification of the world in the capitalist era, the erosion of the sacred, especially the desacralization of authority. But they need not have been so emphatic in their statements or so certain in their predictions, for even people in rationalized or bureaucratized societies, as systematically self-controlled and objective in their assessments as some of them may well be, still need a morally enhancing public story to share, and they still want to love the storyteller. Leadership in these societies, too, is still invested with moral and wishful significance, and the people who live in them still need to see their leaders as champions, moral exemplars, standards of behavior and belief, the source of virtue and stability.

The only imaginable situation in which this need would no longer obtain is the one that Jürgen Habermas characterized as an "ideal [or undistorted] speech situation," that is, a social situation in which individuals could live "in free, equal, and open communication with one another."[5] Psychoanalysis, rooted in communication, might seem to harbor a kind of practical emancipatory technique appropriate to the goal, considering the type of discourse that occurs in the therapeutic encounter (involving the exploration of motives, intentions, and reasons, a desire to see into and through one's assumptions about life, and a desire to arrive at a more objective, less conflicted assessment of abilities, prospects, and needs). However, any such expectation for psychoanalysis as an emancipatory type of communication in the sense that Habermas intended appears misplaced, primarily because analysis occurs almost exclusively in the presence of an authoritative figure who has the sole responsibility for establishing the rules in a segregated, hierarchical arrangement, and it is difficult to see how it could be otherwise. In this way (and in other ways, too), psychoanalysis mirrors and reproduces the society and is not in any large sense in advance of it.[6]

This expectation of an ideal speech situation is therefore still in the realm of fantasy in the sense that we have no knowledge of the social conditions that could give rise to it. Certainly, the effects of the communal ownership of the means of production, the removal of the economy from the sphere of competition, so far as we have historical experience of such efforts, do not encourage us to believe that such steps are sufficient to bring it about. Thus, authority everywhere retains its elevated and sacred status, establishing the conditions for hierarchy, distinction, access, and exclusion, if not passivity, dependence, and subordination, precluding the kind of speech situation that Habermas referred to.

All the different ways of organizing the everyday world of schools, shops, banks, churches, theaters, parties, prisons, corporations, and presses, of teachers, merchants, priests, politicians, police, and editors, are vulnerable to criticism on these grounds, even the most liberal and pluralized of them. Michel Foucault has emphasized that, under the conditions that currently prevail in the Western world, we are inclined to think of distinctive individuals only in terms of their pathology. Foucault also expressed his dislike of current forms of individualization, claiming that the contemporary problem is not the liberation of the individual from the state and its institutions but the liberation of people from the state and from the type of individualization linked to it. Foucault insisted on the refusal of this kind of individuality and the promotion of new forms of subjectivity.[7]

However, as long as people need extrinsic sources of support, claims for new forms of subjectivity are as suspect as claims for ideal speech situations—it is difficult to know in the sense of practice what these claims might even refer to. Moreover, a brief examination of any situation historically in which the ability of people to expect a favorable outcome based on continued confidence in the virtue and protectiveness of the group to which they belong is undermined, in which cultural standards and expectations are experienced by people as threatened or lost as a result of social change, in which events interfere with the ability to produce familiar behaviors, in which the past becomes an unreliable guide to the future, or in which the taken-for-granted features of everyday life are rendered dysfunctional, inapplicable, or unavailable so that people can no longer feel or believe that they are as good, worthy, admirable, and brave as they had been formerly led to believe, reveals why this need persists. The threatened or actual loss of familiar social arrangements as a safe arena in which to carry on promotes thinking away from the social world to a more private one, revealing to people in their thoughts, and especially in the unfamiliar and unexpected depths of their feelings, the actual precariousness of self and society.

The ability of people to recover in such situations (to avoid being demoralized or overwhelmed, to avoid being driven back into passive postures or into a spirit of helplessness or hopelessness, to avoid withdrawal into purely personal concerns or having to fall back on one's personal history, remaining connected to social concerns by accepting some workable, shared assumptions about the world as a means of sustaining a sense of continuity and adequacy in the face of events) has depended historically on the appearance or availability of authoritative individuals who bear witness to the morally compelling reasons for continued struggle and who organize and foster thinking about social concerns, narrowing and focusing attention on potential solutions to conflict that they insist are at hand if people could but muster the energy and the will. Such individuals have thus substituted temporarily for failed or failing "structures," warding off the need for people to retreat into their own minds, the contents of which, under these conditions, they must feel to be neither very heroic nor illuminating. It is the sense of conviction projected by these exceptional individuals, a consequence of their own stubborn, relentless pursuit of a particular vision of the world, that helps them rally others and makes them widely admired and even exalted by their contemporaries.

These exceptional, authoritative individuals are typically conceived as possessing charisma—in Max Weber's terms, "a certain quality of an individual personality by virtue of which he is considered extraordinary and treated as endowed with supernatural, superhuman, exceptional powers or qualities." As Weber further explained, men obey such an individual not because of tradition or statute but because they believe in him. If he is more than just a flash in the pan, the leader lives exclusively for his cause. The devotion of his followers is then oriented to his character, especially to his inner sense of having been called to this task and to his conviction and courage as reflected in deeds. For, as Weber also noted, "If those to whom he feels sent do not recognize him, his claim collapses; if they recognize him, he is their master as long as he 'proves' himself."[8] Adolf Hitler's declaration to the Reichstag by way of explanation of the Roehm purge in July 1934, taking for granted the sense of entitlement and the feeling that he could project on such occasions, is a classic expression of a charismatic leader, one who is both self-proclaimed and empowered by his community: "I was responsible for the fate of the German people, and so I became the supreme judge."[9]

Hitler also appears charismatic because of his peculiar emotional power, in his case a self-conscious, disciplined, rationalized awareness of the power that appeals to people at the level of feeling and wish have, an appreciation of the attractiveness of powerful individuals who make claims and appear able to solve their disruptive social problems. As Hitler explained in *Mein Kampf*, people who are weak and lacking will, who are feminine in spirit, and whose thought is determined by emotion and feeling are longing for a compelling, unifying force to appear, willful, determined, and intolerant, a leader capable of appealing to the "mysterious powers" of the emotions, an electrifying, magnetic force whose energies are focused on a single world-saving, world-destroying theme, and who is therefore capable of instilling in them a sense of absolute, fanatical belief.[10] On the basis of this insight and his manipulative capacities, Hitler was able to achieve a remarkable degree of compliance with his dictates.

But then what of a leader like V. I. Lenin, who neither sought nor wished for that kind of entitlement and acclaim. On the contrary, Lenin had clearly hoped to broaden people's field of vision, to foster a spirit of independent activity and to encourage them to think realistically and objectively, and, like any bourgeois rationalist or republican moralist, to be contemptuous of "enthusiasm" and to say, "Where feeling is, there reason shall be." In the early days of the revolution, days of great expectations, Lenin stated many times that socialism cannot be decreed from above, that a revolutionary socialist government is strong only in proportion to the consciousness of the masses, and that such a revolution can be successfully concluded "only if the majority of the population, and primarily the majority of the working people, engage in independent creative work as makers of history."[11] Lenin encouraged people to act, urging them to consider the significance of their victory and to remember "that now *you yourselves* are at the helm of state. No one will help you if you yourselves do not unite and take into *your* hands *all affairs* of the state. . . . begin right at the bottom, do not wait for anyone."[12] Excited by the prospects of 1917, Lenin was anxious to push and pull people into roles that conformed to his vision of the future. He was forced shortly to back away from that vision because his hopes were overtaken by events and by the failure of people to respond to events in a conscious and disciplined way. Nevertheless, Lenin's aspirations and expectations were clearly different from Hitler's.

Lenin's position as leader was distinctive in other ways as well; for example, he was often contradicted by colleagues and even outvoted by them on important occasions, an indignity that Hitler would never have suffered. At the same time, however, Lenin had enormous personal prestige: his declarations as an interpreter of texts and events were always phrased abstractly, but they were received as the gesture of a superior person who was perceived as particularly gifted and who could therefore make the ritual claim, "It is written, but I say. . . ."[13]

There are other exceptional individuals to think about, different kinds of characters in different cultures, who rallied, encouraged, and guided people through different crises, for example, Abraham Lincoln and Winston Churchill. The problem is that the criteria of charisma elaborated by Weber are so particular that it is hard to encompass all these individuals in any frame of reference that might be suggested by the term.[14] Nevertheless, all these different individuals (and others besides, of course) are referred to as charismatic. The concept persists, in short, partly because it addresses something real but partly, despite its weaknesses, as a paradox and a reproach to a sociological profession that would prefer not to ascribe too much significance to single individuals or to their ability seriously to affect an outcome.

The fact is, however, that we can learn more from observing the practical ability of a leader like Hitler to manipulate situational exigencies than we can learn from any of the more complex social theories organized thus far to explain his success. The Marxists in Germany at the time certainly had the better theory, compared to the Nazis, but it did not help them evaluate their situation. More to the point, an outstanding leader like Lenin, who also wanted to remain theoretically acute, to continue to believe in historical process and progress, in "the disposition of forces" as distinct from personality, missed the real significance of the role of leadership, failing to note the extent to which the medium of leadership is the message in a crisis situation and what that implied for those prepared to follow. By contrast, and however absurd in comparison Hitler's "theory" might be, his belief in the primacy of personality, his alertness to the fears and desires of people, and his acute sense of the kinds of messages important for him to deliver to different audiences enabled him to understand better than Lenin the practical political results a leader's interventions might have.

What we learn from these different observations and responses is that, no matter how coherent and consistent an ideological orientation is, even one that fosters independent judgment and objective analysis, no matter how vigorously and persistently and with what sense of justice adherents act to promote it, and no matter how well prepared they are in imagination for the resistance of those who stand to lose from the changes that they intend to effect, the need to develop and implement practical policies in response to unanticipated events not readily accommodated to ideological assumptions, the need to cope with struggles that arise when such novel policies are perceived as violating the interests, moral perspectives, and wishful expectations of various individuals and groups who had promoted the ideology in the first place, and the need in any case to face up to the sense of disappointment as the limits of change become clear all still require an extrinsic source of support, the real, physical presence of an authoritative leader over a course of time.

It is therefore important to consider another approach to this problem of leadership, one that can encompass the variety of individuals involved as well as the singular role that they played. Such leaders have appeared in times of crisis on the right, the center, and the left, and on some occasions, of course, not at all. (That is, whether they appeared on the right, the center, or the left, or whether they appeared at all, is an accidental factor.) Moreover, although they have addressed certain paramount goals, acting as the spokesmen for novel moral perspectives or for traditional but threatened ones, they have also addressed heterogeneous strivings (cognitive, moral, and wishful), rallying a variety of individuals and groups, some of whom saw themselves as rising but blocked and others as declining but deserving.

Authoritative Leaders as "Transitional Objects"

Crisis situations that threaten interests and moral standards affect the ability of perceiving, interpreting individuals to mediate between the claims of fantasy and those of the social world. These are situations in which leaders have appeared in a concrete way as "transitional objects" or in a transitional sense, providing for people an external point between fantasy and the social world, serving to encourage and support people whose interpretive capacities have been diminished, who really are less able to manage closure, synthesis, and reality testing, and hence less able to sort out what is actually happening. It is the social function of these transitional figures to reestablish for people the possibility of society as a background of safety, encouraging them to believe that they will be able again to act on familiar and cherished mandates or that they will be able to implement novel ones that had no structured, sanctioned, or legitimate past in the society (indeed, that may even have been despised and condemned) but that may now become the basis for acceptable behavior and especially for the socialization of the young.

Such figures are transitional in three senses: first, they must do for people over a course of time some of the things that people had formerly done for themselves. By narrowing and focusing attention on social problems that they declare to be soluble, by constraining and giving direction to unexpected depths of feeling, and by reorienting people to memory, enabling them to use memory as an ordering principle, to rely on the past, particularly with respect to the ways in which they had solved problems or otherwise proved themselves admirable and brave before, they forestall a retreat into purely personal concerns based on a feeling that the world has become too chaotic and threatening. Transitional figures, then, recover for people a sense of continuity and adequacy by invoking "what we were," "what we might yet become," and by convincingly explaining "how we got from there to here," fighting to preserve an interpretive capacity for people within a social space.

Obviously, the notion of transitional in this sense implies that the period of time during which these leaders were recognizably authoritative and could mobilize a following may actually have been quite limited, and, indeed, some of them did not survive the period of crisis, or were dismissed in the aftermath of one, or were elevated and celebrated as moral exemplars in the aftermath, becoming fit subjects for statues, postage stamps, and sermons, allowing the memory of a heroic period of struggle to serve as an inspiration for succeeding generations, but subject as well, if their claims and expectations appeared too excessive, to critical condemnation. Those who followed, in other words, might well have suffered from constant comparison if such figures had been allowed to retain their exalted reputations intact. Besides, these leaders were themselves politicians as well as moral exemplars, with interests and perspectives of their own that often did not appear capable of effective implementation and that were not necessarily shared by their colleagues, even through the period of crisis.

Second, these figures are transitional in the sense that they define the interests and moral perspectives that will be used by people to mediate between fantasy and the social world. These figures are therefore characterized by a language-related competence that serves to overcome a socially imposed semiotic dilemma. Insofar as anxiety, fear, sadness, anger, alarm, frustration, and other similar feelings are a response to real dangers in the world that cannot be interrupted by familiar strategies or explained by concepts that make sense under the circumstances, transitional figures may be understood as providing the right language: they are able to name the source of the problem and to specify the solution, to reassure people in cognitive as well as moral and wishful terms, to stand for or represent reality to them, offering what appears as a realistic assessment of current conditions, especially by integrating a concept of interest in their proposed solutions. That is, their ability to appeal to a heterogeneous population derives from their commitment to interests as well as from their emotional appeal, for, if they failed to make the world seem safe and the future reliable to planners, organizers, administrators, technicians, even careerists and opportunists, as well as to loyal or ecstatic followers, their ability to implement policies or to solve the problems that beset the society in the first place would be compromised.

Transitional figures, then, work to organize experience, becoming the guardians or guarantors of "structure." By finding the right language, they can constrain and direct feelings, without which their ideas would hardly appear worth struggling for; without feelings there can be no sense of loyalty or force of conviction. Marx said that theory (ideology, codified language) becomes a force when it seizes the masses, and it does, though not in the sense that Marx intended or wished to see. No one, moreover, understood this better or was more prepared to take advantage of its significance than Adolf Hitler. Hitler boasted that he could fathom the German mind, and he was certainly better able to mobilize a public than any of his competitors on the right or the left. Hitler felt that the Germans were being forced to submit passively to conditions that they could actively struggle against if they were mobilized, encouraged to believe in their worth, especially if they had concrete, visible signs of their power, the marching, uniformed columns. Hitler dwelt ceaselessly on the admirable and brave nature of the German folk, the need to reverse their wretched fortune, which was no doing of their own, the value of their traditions, which were worth preserving, the real basis of their superior entitlement, consciously and purposefully evoking a sense of unity, discipline, force, will, and the effectiveness of action against a hostile reality.

These figures are transitional in yet a third sense: they appear in society for people, ready to lead them, but they are also invented by people. They are no doubt powerful individuals, and the image they project is based on things that they have in fact done—providing through their own resolute actions the opportunity for people to take heart, filling in the gaps with whatever content is important to them, in terms of their social location and personal inclinations. These leaders were typically individuals who appeared to the public in very stark and stubborn ways as unwilling to succumb to a hostile reality and unready to submit to events that seemed frightening to others. Moreover, they very likely had also publicly and boldly anticipated, named, and declaimed against, at some risk to their own careers, if not to their lives, the sources of the current threat and thus had given another kind of demonstration by their own actions and statements that they were wise and foresightful when others were ignorant, foolish, indecisive, indifferent, or betraying, having proved able to see through mere appearances to some truth that eluded others. They were thus able to claim, on the strength of their own efforts, that fight is better than flight, that sacrifice on behalf of the preservation or initiation of a moral order must take precedence over commonsense perceptions of self-interest or notions of self-preservation, that people must temporarily suspend interest in routine concerns and take chances that under other circumstances they might never have considered taking, that actions are urgently required from ordinary people that they are capable of performing and that are necessary over the short run, perhaps even for the sake of the future of civilization itself. They have crucially left behind as part of their legacy powerful, enduring images of themselves as exemplary of personal resolve, moral conviction, revolutionary zeal, courageous rejection, stubborn resistance, tragic persistence, brazen audacity, a willingness to take risks and make sacrifices, and a confident, even defiant sense of being able to prevail against the most adverse circumstances. The names are well known—Luther, Washington, Robespierre, Lincoln, Lenin, Hitler, Mao, Churchill—as are the fabled occasions from Wittenberg to Valley Forge and Gettysburg, to the Long March and the Battle of Britain.

Nevertheless, the supportive role that transitional leaders play on the basis of their own strength of character and conviction is assessed from any number of personal and social perspectives, permitting people to construct a version of the world that they can live with in terms that they deem just and appropriate. The claim that transitional leaders play such a supportive role, serving to enhance the sense of adequacy, efficacy, and worthiness, may seem exaggerated, considering the violent and shocking activities of certain notable leaders, including Stalin, Mao, and Pol Pot. But it is important to keep in mind that Stalin and Mao at least were bitterly denounced for their destructive actions by former followers and colleagues and that the Vietnamese Communists cited Pol Pot's actions as the excuse for chasing him from power, whatever their real reasons may have been. Nikita Khrushchev condemned especially the pretense that there could have been such a superman as

Stalin, one who possessed all the extraordinary qualities that Stalin boasted of. Stalin's mocking commentary on the backwardness of the Soviet people, his pose as the first "new man," trying to embody the Communist future in his own person, elevating himself and justifying the treatment of people in whatever way he deemed necessary at the time, overstepped the transitional boundaries. Khrushchev said as much many times, emphasizing the absurd lengths to which Stalin was prepared to go in order to advance himself.[15] Stalin was determined to deprive everyone of any independent sense of space, making the social side so powerful against even the most highly placed individuals in all spheres of activity that for all intents and purposes there was no opportunity to develop alternative conceptions of how space could be used.[16] Equally interesting, though perhaps less well known, are the denunciations of Mao by the leadership of the Chinese Communist party, their bitter criticism of Mao's increasing resort to the cult of personality, of his errors in the period of the Great Leap Forward, and especially of his role in the disastrous period of the Cultural Revolution, the methods and theories of which, it was subsequently stated, should never have been applied. Indeed, Mao's Cultural Revolution came officially to be known as the "Ten Years of Calamity."[17]

Man as Meaning and as Object Seeking

One important reason for conceiving of these leaders in a transitional rather than a charismatic sense is that the former more readily encompasses the variety of leaders, providing a single standard of comparison that links them all. Another is that these transitional leaders represent only exceptional instances of the role that authoritative leadership has never ceased to play. Max Weber's notion of the "routinization of charisma," the transformation of an exceptional situation into an everyday one, particularly for the sake of economic activity, refers in part to the routinization of language, settling the criteria by which people can define the limits and forms of the social space within which they can act. But it must also in part refer to the institutionalization of leadership, not only in the bureaucratic sense that Weber addressed (the "objective necessity of adapting the order and the staff organization to the normal, everyday needs and conditions of carrying on administration"), but more precisely in a concrete, physical sense, as people continue to require in their everyday lives the real presence of a leader whom they can invest with significance, one whose virtues and strengths they can elaborate in whatever ways are important to them.[18]

In the Western tradition of social theory, the notion of modernization and the criteria that are held to distinguish modern from premodern societies involved from the start a conception of character, the ability of disciplined people to treat with the natural world as well as with sacred and secular authority, to take a critical posture with respect to both, and to develop techniques for the mastery of nature and for the replacement of any authority whose policies proved threatening to that kind of autonomous practice. Modernization in this theoretical tradition pertained to a world of self-sufficient people, capable of reasoned judgment, of independently regulating their own conduct and managing their own affairs without undue or submissive deference to the judgment of others. As one vigilant defender of liberty angrily exclaimed in response to George Washington's position on relationships to Britain and France in 1795, "When *men* are substituted for *principles,* liberty is as much outraged, as when the *Deity* is supplanted by a *priest*."[19]

On Weber's view, the main criteria of traditionalism, the privileged position of authoritative sacred figures, their control over interpretations of events in the natural world, and their insistence that things be done as they had always been done in the social world, were affected by the Protestant Reformation, however unintended all that may have been, as people initially won the right to live in accordance with their own conceptions of divine intentions, free of the mediation of clerical authority. Weber focused primarily on the conditions for the development of capitalism, on the claims for disciplined, methodical labor, the result of monastic discipline brought down into everyday life, altering the meaning and character of everyday life, emphasizing the moral value of work in a calling. But the crucial aspect of characterological demands on people in the West for self-discipline, self-control, self-observation, emotional constraint, methodical, dutiful effort, and so on involved relationships to authority, ultimately, with due concern for different contexts, on all institutional levels (religious, political, economic, familial, educational, and medical); it did not involve labor per se. Moreover, these demands are not distinctively Protestant. Rather, they are the outward behavioral signs of autonomous conscience and the capacity for autonomous practice regardless of where these appear. After all, these demands are the same ones that Lenin made on his public because they represented modernity and progress to him and he did not emerge from and was not affected by that kind of Protestant tradition. These characterological demands constituted a vital aspect of Lenin's accounting for the success and productivity of the bourgeoisie and his estimate of what it would take for the working class to master successfully and productively the natural and social worlds in their turn. In addition, this was also Freud's view of the matter in quite another sphere and location, as he insisted that people bring themselves under control with respect to the seductive lure of familial relationships if they intended to demonstrate some degree of independent judgment and effort.[20]

However, this Western and especially American emphasis on independence from authority (it was Weber's view that only in the United States had there occurred at the level of the highest office a development from charismatic acclamation of the ruler to his genuine election by the community of the ruled) always implied risk, the heightened potential for fragmentation and division, for the loss of meaning or the inability to continue to act purposefully in such a context, as both radical and conservative critics persistently pointed out.[21] The initial solution to the problem, English and American, was a commitment to property as a source of support and then subsequently, and more importantly in terms of its usefulness as a practical technique facilitating the democratization of society, to money. The pursuit and acquisition of money served, sooner rather than later, not so much as the basis for disinterested participation in government described by Bernard Bailyn, J. G. A. Pocock, and others as republican ideology or civic humanism (which was hostile to commercial enterprise on the grounds that it threatened personal independence and public virtue, without which a commonwealth of free citizens could not exist), as it did as a sign that people were able to sustain themselves as independent actors and perceiving subjects in the social world.[22] In a heterogeneous community, there were no doubt those who continued to use the republican language in the sense that was originally intended and who worried about the moral consequences of the commercialization of life. But, as character could also be construed as the essence of economic enterprise, the language of independence, autonomy, and freedom, linked to the Lockean tradition, could easily be used in the service of economic goals as well, and there were people who made it clear from the beginning that America meant business.[23]

At the same time, this emphasis on independence from authority pertained to individuals and individual accomplishment as distinct from, and even opposed to, the community at large. Communal or collective solutions appeared worrisome in the West from the beginning because they seemed to recapitulate what had existed historically when there was not only a Christian belief in providence that made singular claims with respect to salvation, man's soul, and social order, but also a structure of authority that was based on the exclusive capacity to determine the meaning and applicability of beliefs, universally inclusive with regard to souls, perhaps, but not with regard to the rights of individuals to participate in the decisions that affected their lives. This structure of authority used what it could, on behalf of either the church or the monarchical state, to destroy alternative competing beliefs and organized centers, when it could not absorb and integrate them safely. The earlier vision was a dual one, in other words, weak, impulsive, indulgent, needy, sinful man on one side, and the controlling, observant, exclusive, and hierarchical social order on the other, with no ideological or political room for the possibility of a triangular point, a perceiving, interpreting, capable, participating individual. Hence the fear and loathing of such collective solutions that persists, especially because Marxist radicals who foresaw and promised the expansion of a communal, inclusive realm of freedom ended up repeatedly reproducing another kind of dual arrangement, characterized this time as untrustworthy, self-seeking, self-promoting, greedy people on one side, and morally authoritative leadership on the other, claiming on the strength of certain texts and beliefs the exclusive right to interpret reality and make decisions about the distribution of resources for people.

Those who opposed any form of a dual vision, who declared themselves able to participate, being people of character, among the "uninfluenced and steady," as opposed to "the weak and ignorant, those susceptible of influence and of irregular passions" sought ways to protect themselves from the power of the community, primarily on the basis of property or money as rationalized by abstract principle and impersonal law, underscoring the significance of a line of thought on political authority originating with Sir Henry Maine and culminating for our purposes with Talcott Parsons.[24] According to Maine, the movement of "progressive" societies has been distinguished by the gradual dissolution of family dependency and the growth of individual obligation in its place. The tie between man and man loses its emotional character and acquires an abstract, impersonal one:

> Starting, as from one terminus of history, from a condition of society in which all the relations of Persons are summed up in the relations of Family, we seem to have steadily moved toward a phase of social order in which all these relations arise from the free agreement of individuals. In Western Europe the progress achieved in this direction has been considerable. . . . If then we employ Status . . . to signify these personal conditions [in which powers and privileges resided in the family] . . . and avoid applying the term to such conditions as are the immediate or remote result of agreement, we may say that the movement of the progressive societies has hitherto been a movement *from Status to Contract*.[25]

Status systems, then, are characterized by familial, emotionally bound types of authority, by hierarchy, privileged access, and exclusion, whereas contract systems are characterized by abstract social arrangements, by the morally evident capacity to be independent of authority, and by the enhanced possibility of access and inclusion. On this view, only those incapable of judging their own interests would remain excluded, subject to extrinsic controls.

This version of Western development influenced a number of authorities on the subject. It is obviously redolent of Jacob Burckhardt's observation that, in the Middle Ages, "man was conscious of himself only as a member of a race, people, party, family, or corporation" whereas, in the Renaissance, "man became a spiritual *individual,* and recognized himself as such."[26] But it permeates especially the work of Ferdinand Tönnies, coming down via Durkheim and Freud to Talcott Parsons, so that, in his refinement of the criteria by which we can distinguish premodern or traditional societies from modern societies, Parsons opposed such terms as *affect, ascription,* and *particularity* to *affective neutrality, merit,* and *universality.*[27] Parsons also distinguished relatively "decentralized" societies, England and Holland at an earlier time, the United States at a later time, from more highly centralized, hierarchical ones, Prussia and the Soviet Union, particularly from the standpoint of "active adaptation as distinguished from passive adjustment."[28]

The concept of modernization, the evolution of societies in these terms, has been criticized on a number of grounds (many roles in so-called modern societies are still ascriptive and bound by emotion, social development is uneven from one network of institutions and practices to another, traditional societies may well manifest universal features, in religion if in no other sphere, rationality does not have the kind of significance for objective analysis that modernization theory implies, and the reintegration of emotional expression in everyday life as promoted in the 1960s was unanticipated, effective in changing the way that people treated the world around them, and yet apparently inexplicable except in terms of "regression").[29] However, these important issues aside, the direction of change suggested by such theory is still understandable with respect to relationships to authority and with respect to the uses of money and property as a means of becoming more independent of authority and as a self-aggrandizing, morally enhancing sign of character.[30]

At the same time, this modernization process, conceived essentially as the internalization of morality, the location of agency in the self and not in mediating social agencies, the systematic encouragement of cognitive controls, enhancing thereby the capacity for decision making based on the instrumental or emotionally constrained analysis of situations and problems, never occurred in the way that Western theorists had imagined, and the paramount criterion of this judgment is the persistence of extrinsic rewards and supports and the persistence of concrete objects that serve as an indispensable source of personal and social stability. Political authority, which continues to serve as the occasion for moral and wishful constructions, is not all that remote. Moreover, to the extent that people become independent of authority, as evidently they can and do, they must rely on money and property as an alternative source of stability. Autonomous conscience, "the impartial spectator within the breast," never became as decisive for people as the modernization theorists from Maine to Parsons claimed. The ability to achieve a measure of independence from familial authority, or from religious authority, does not imply the ability to achieve a similar degree of independence in other domains. There are limits to the extent to which the family as a socializing agency can prepare people for autonomous endeavor in the wider world. Moreover, it is not a question of being "held back" in a developmental sense, of regression, weakness, or failure in Freud's terms; the social world beyond the family is a different realm of experience, much more problematic, as I have said, and the attachment to concrete objects and people at that level remains to a greater extent than conventional modernization theory accounts for.

Natalie Zemon Davis has argued, by contrast with both Maine and Burckhardt, for example, that "the exploration of self in sixteenth century France was made in conscious relation to groups to which people belonged; that in a century in which the boundary around the conceptual self and the bodily self was not always firm and closed, men and women could work out strategies for self-expression and autonomy; and . . . the greatest obstacle to self definition was not embeddedness but powerlessness and poverty."[31] In an important sense, all this is still true: the location and shape of embeddedness has changed, but the need for it, that is, for real contact with concrete objects in the environment, remains, and it is still powerlessness and poverty that affect the capacity for self-definition more than the fact of embeddedness per se.

Thus we may think of people as meaning seeking, or, as Clifford Geertz put it, "man depends upon symbols and symbol systems with a dependence so great as to be decisive for his cultural viability and, as a result, his sensitivity to even the remotest indication that they may prove unable to cope with one or another aspect of experience raises within him the gravest sort of anxiety."[32] The sociology of knowledge, Geertz went on to write, ought to be called the sociology of meaning because what is socially determined is not the nature of conception but the vehicles of conception.

This point of view is consistent with the premise that "in the beginning was the word," in the same sense that people think (a process that, as always, includes moral and wishful aspects) about eating before they actually sit down to eat. People, that is, must achieve meaning and bring order to the world in consistent ideological terms in a way that is elevated and segregated from a fundamental kind of critical examination so that the terms can command the kind of loyalty that does not give way precipitously to interest or impulse. In brief, it is the role of ideology "to render otherwise incomprehensible social situations meaningful, to so construe them as to make it possible to act purposefully within them . . . [accounting] both for the ideologies' highly figurative nature and for the intensity with which, once accepted, they are held."[33]

By the same token, however, it is not possible to think of people as meaning seeking unless they are also thought of as object seeking (in social terms). People are meaning seeking in the sense that they need to experience closure, which they can do as yet only on the basis of authoritative opinions and language provided by leaders and "experts." They are for the overwhelming part not meaning seeking in the sense that they are prepared to explore reality or develop a language of their own for interpreting it. The sources of rewards and support, in other words, remain extrinsic to a great degree, and not only for those who are incapable of judging their own interests.

Money as a Transitional Object

The utility of money in a market as a technique facilitating production and exchange has been the subject of discussion and speculation literally for ages—to choose an arbitrary point, from an observation of Publilius Syrus's that the *New York Times* uses to promote its own financial reporting ("Money alone sets all the world in motion," 42 B.C.) to John Kenneth Galbraith ("In this century the problem of getting money, though it remains considerable, has diminished. In its place has come a new uncertainty as to what money, however acquired and accumulated, will be worth").[34] There are besides a remarkable number of systematic treatises on the subject of money, especially from the seventeenth through the nineteenth centuries. But by the time that Paul Dombey peremptorily inquired of his father, "What's money?" and his father (having fleetingly considered and dismissed the elaborate technical response "involving the terms circulating-medium, currency, depreciation of currency, paper, bullion, rates of exchange, value of precious metals in the market, and so forth") replied responsibly, "Gold, and silver, and copper. Guineas, shillings, half-pence" (a reply dismissed in turn by young Paul, who was looking for something deeper, though not exactly in terms of money as a circulating medium), we are well into the distinctive world of capitalist enterprise that radical and conservative critics alike condemnèd, focusing their ire not on money as such, of course, but on those who exploited its use, especially the use of paper money, for the sake of enriching themselves at the expense of the working poor.[35]

Not surprisingly, the widespread use of paper money as a means of exchange has persisted over the longest period of time in America, just as the use and especially the pursuit of money in America—typically perceived as the result of people with no historical or cultural heritage, bereft of standards, being haphazardly thrown together—has provoked a great deal of contemptuous and hostile commentary. Thus, one of the most memorable passages from Max Weber's *The Protestant Ethic and the Spirit of Capitalism* involves Ben Franklin's teachings on the subject of money:

> Remember, that *time* is money. He that can earn ten shillings a day by his labour, and goes abroad, or sits idle, one half of that day, though he spends but sixpence during his diversion or idleness, ought not to reckon *that* the only expense; he has really spent, or rather thrown away, five shillings besides.
>
> Remember that *credit* is money. If a man lets his money lie in my hands after it is due, he gives me the interest, or so much as I can make of it during that time. This amounts to a considerable sum where a man has good and large credit, and makes good use of it.
>
> Remember, that money is of the prolific, generating nature [recalling that Martin Luther, e.g., had declared money to be sterile]. Money can beget money, and its offspring can beget more and so on.

The quoting of these lines was obviously intended to achieve an effect, especially when juxtaposed to other lines, including this one from the German author Ferdinand Kürnberger: "They make tallow out of cattle and money out of men."[36] But of course there was a great deal more still, apart even from Nathaniel Hawthorne's native observation that the proverbs in Franklin's *Poor Richard's Almanack* were all about getting money or saving it. There was William Ellery Channing's expressed disappointment with the "low, selfish, mercenary" state of Americans, Stendhal's claim that America could be summed up in the single word *dollars*, and Frances Trollope's charge that the only unity of feeling and purpose that she could find in America involved the pursuit of the dollar.[37] Tocqueville noted that, if Americans are dissatisfied with their lot, they are free to change it but that, because every man is on his own, social ties are destroyed, workers are isolated, and they end up trying "simply to gain the greatest quantity of money at the least possible cost."[38] There was also this lament of an offended priest (1834): "To New York the very focus of usury, the great emporium of North and South America, flock greedy speculators from all the extensive regions. You will see there Jews, Quakers, Tunkers, Socinians, with nominal Christians prostrate in full devotion to the idol, *Mammon;* money-changers, bankers, brokers, auctioneers of all hues, climes, and creeds on the alert to hook the simple prey; in Wall Street of that city Satan seems to have fixed his eternal abode."[39]

But there was also P. T. Barnum's lecture "The Art of Money Getting," a modest effort reminiscent of Franklin, in which Barnum claimed that money getters are the benefactors of the race (there were many no doubt who believed this: during the blizzard of 1888, some passengers trapped on stalled elevated trains in New York paid their way down on ladders supplied by on-the-spot entrepreneurs). One English visitor complained that "money is the habitual measure of all things, the only secure power, the only real distinction," echoing observations from Edgar Allan Poe's earlier critical commentary "The Philosophy of Furniture," in which Poe remarked that an American "aristocracy of dollars" had substituted for the European aristocracy of blood, making cost the sole test of the decorative merit of furnishings and the corruption of taste "a pendant of the dollar manufacture."[40] American painters made money a subject of their art (e.g., Victor Dubreuil's "Barrels of Money," of 1898, although there were many other paintings as well). Henry Duveen, the art dealer sent from England to the United States as a young man to establish the family business, was distressed by his brother's suggestion that they borrow money from their rich customers to tide them over the initial slow period. "Money," he exclaimed, "is what America is all about, and the rich will never deal with us if they suspect that we are hard pressed."*

*Of course, money was the subject of many sharp comments and commentators, including F. Scott Fitzgerald and especially the wily and insubordinate comic master Jack Benny. In one routine, Benny asked his partner (and wife), Mary Livingston, rummaging around for her makeup, what the wonderful odor was emanating from her handbag. "Money," she replied. I should also note here, by way of explanation, a recent exhibit of some sixty works of art by eleven American artists, trompe l'oeil images of currency, the oldest dating from the 1870s, through Victor Dubreuil's "Barrels of Money" (and his "Cross of Gold," 1896), to paintings by Otis Kay in the 1920s (e.g., "Money to Burn," 1927). The earliest of these artists—who were mocking the importance of money in the culture but also examining the contradictory aspects of a commerce in works of art—

By contrast with such a prosaic instance, Walt Whitman was positively grandiose in his look ahead, claiming that "the extreme business energy, and this almost maniacal appetite for wealth prevalent in the United States, are parts of amelioration and progress, indispensably needed to prepare the very results I demand. My theory includes riches, and the getting of riches, and the amplest products, power, activity, inventions, movements, etc. Upon them, as upon substrata, I raise the edifice design'd in these Vistas." Whitman saw this driven pursuit of wealth as setting the stage for the liberation of masses of people and for the development of original American personalities, especially authors and poets, "plenty of them, male and female, traversing the States, none excepted—and by native superber tableaux and growths of language, songs, operas, orations, lectures, architecture—and by a sublime and serious Religious Democracy sternly taking command, dissolving the old, sloughing off surfaces, and from its own interior and vital principles, reconstructing, democratizing society."[41]

Whitman's grand, ideal view of the matter aside, he was in a more mundane, practical way correct; money was used as a technique to democratize the society. However, it was one thing for observers of the process to imagine a self redeemed by the presence of the other, or to imagine a self renewed by contact with the primitive or the exotic, or to envision new heights of consciousness, the harmonious reconciliation of a hitherto divided self through communal association, different nineteenth-century versions of saving Romantic and revolutionary themes. But to imagine being redeemed by money and commerce, by "the great scramble," people turned thereby into a commodity, their humanity defined by the presence or absence of money, seemed too philistine, vulgar, and absurd to contemplate except as a momentary or

---

William Michael Harnett, had one of his works confiscated by the Secret Service. Harnett was warned not to produce any more lifelike pictures of money. In 1909, it became unlawful to produce any facsimile of paper money, although artists continued to do so. On the other hand, Otis Kay neither exhibited nor sold his money paintings in his lifetime. Finally, I should also mention William Gaddis's novel *JR,* which won a National Book Award in 1976, taking ironic part in the bicentennial celebrations. The first words in the novel are (absent Gaddis's spacing and punctuation, for convenience's sake), "Money . . . ? in a voice that rustled. Paper, yes. And we'd never seen it. Paper money. We never saw paper money till we came east. It looked so strange the first time we saw it. Lifeless." (See Colin Simpson, *Artful Partners: Bernard Berenson and Joseph Duveen* [New York, 1986], 22. On the subject of money in American painting, see the catalog of the Berry-Hill Galleries exhibition "Old Money: American Trompe l'Oeil Images of Currency," compiled by Bruce Chambers et al. The show ran from 11 November–17 December 1988 in New York. William Gaddis, *JR* [New York, 1976], 3.)

passing phase in an evolutionary scheme. Thus, a fellow American artist, Henry James, recoiling from the prospects, insisted on the opposite and much more widely shared opinion: "To make so much money that you won't, that you don't 'mind,' don't mind anything—that is absolutely, I think, the main American formula . . . active pecuniary gain and . . . active pecuniary gain only." James deplored "the grope of wealth" and the ability of people to accommodate any message, regardless of how lofty or moral the initial intention may have been, to this apparently insatiable drive. The structures that he saw in New York on his return to the United States (1904–5), "giants of the mere market," not only absent any history, "but with no credible possibility of time for history, and consecrated by no uses save the commercial at any cost," epitomized the despairing result of American ambition.[42]

Many social theorists in the last century and the early part of this one discussed the problem of money in this context, including Marx, Tocqueville, Weber, Freud, Tönnies, and Simmel, just to mention a number of them already referred to here. Marx's discussion of money as a measure, as a medium of exchange, and as a commodity, "The common form into which all commodities as exchange values are transformed, i.e., the universal commodity," is well known. Equally so are Weber's conception of money as the most efficient means for establishing a rational accounting system and a rationalized economy based on the exchange of goods and, from a different perspective, Freud's conception of the libidinization of money, the evidently universal exaggeration of its significance apart from its realistic utility as a medium of exchange.[43] Freud had himself been greatly affected by the lack of money, so he was not the one to deny its importance in a market society. Nevertheless, for Freud's major purposes, it made no more sense to talk about money primarily in terms of rational accounting than it did to think of the mouth as primarily the entrance to the alimentary canal.

All the specifically social theorists (not including Freud, that is) shared a range of systematic critical concerns and observations, though each emphasized a different aspect or used a different language to depict the effects on societies of money when it plays such a pivotal role. They described the devaluation of tradition, the loss or disappearance of personal relationships of all kinds, the suppression of feeling in everyday life except perhaps outside certain segregated spheres of activity (principally family and church); and they described the isolation, atomization, anomicization, the sheer indifference of people to each other and to things, a result of the enforced systematization of conduct according to rational norms, meaning that relationships could be only partial and that people could be treated no longer according to their traits and character but only according to their function. The opinions of Marx, Tocqueville, and Weber on American culture in these terms are well known and often quoted. But even so relatively distant a writer as Sir Henry Maine commented, "There has hardly ever before been a community in which the weak have been pushed so pitilessly to the wall, in which those who have succeeded have so uniformly been the strong, and in which in so short a time there has arisen so great an inequality of private fortune and domestic luxury."[44]

In addition, all the social theorists emphasized that people were involved with the pursuit and acquisition of money in the capitalist era with a degree of urgency that could not simply be explained in terms of money's utility in a system of exchange, as exemplified by Marx's reference to "the cult of money," with its "asceticism, its self-denial, its self-sacrifice," and his trenchant observation that a capitalist is a miser gone sane.[45] But they all shared the belief, too, that, if money alienates, it also emancipates. They were all no doubt familiar with the well-developed, scornful language of conservative as well as radical critics who addressed the subject ("the International of money," "king money," "rootless money," "new money," etc.). They all saw the costs of bourgeois society in these terms—but they also saw the advantages offered by it. Tönnies wrote, for example (echoing Adam Smith's observations of the effects of commercial society the century before), that the merchant, "by seeing a tangible and nevertheless abstract advantage as the real and rational purpose of his activity itself, is, in this sense, the first thinking and free human being to appear in the normal development of social life." The calculating person feels "superior and free, certain of his aims and master of his resources," though also completely indifferent to the people and things that enter into his calculations. In relation to money, "everyone is free and independent," especially of the relationships, duties, and prejudices of the traditional world.[46] Or, as Georg Simmel also put it,

> The elimination of the personal element directs the individual towards his own resources and makes him more positively aware of his liberty than would be possible with the total lack of relationships. Money is the ideal representative of such a condition since it makes possible relationships between people but leaves them personally undisturbed; it is the exact measure of material achievements, but it is very inadequate for the particular and the personal. To the discriminating consciousness, the restrictedness of objective dependencies that money provides is but the background that first

throws the resulting differentiated personality and its freedom into full relief.[47]

In fact, the most comprehensive discussion of money in these so-cial terms and among this celebrated group of writers is Georg Sim-mel's, which includes an appreciation of dynamic factors, as well as the effects of the rationalization of life, which, he observed (along with Weber), must have problematic implications for any modern social sys-tem including socialism, and of the suppression of feeling, which lib-erates people from the subjective determinations of others but also alienates them from others. Simmel discussed as well the evolution of culture as defined by the uses of money in two senses: first in the sense that an exchange economy based on money becomes more inclusive and less hierarchical (what was initially restricted to strangers or outsid-ers in the community becomes over time the shared preoccupation and interest of the entire community) and then, too, in the sense that the uses of money facilitated the internalization of culture as people became less dependent on external agents and more oriented to inner com-mands. Money in this way serves as a technique for the democratization of society.[48]

Marx had earlier acknowledged that people in capitalist societies were free to pursue their own interests—but as separate, isolated indi-viduals, and hence free merely to collide with each other. Moreover, this kind of personal independence is still limited by objective depen-dence: people are ruled by abstractions, but they are nevertheless ruled. The evolutionary process is therefore incomplete; there is yet another stage of development ahead, free individuality based on the universal development of individuals and on the subordination of their com-munal productivity to common needs. Marx found "concealed in soci-ety" the material conditions of production and the "corresponding re-lations of exchange prerequisite for a classless society," in the absence of which all revolutionary activity would be pointless.[49] But he also found, or so he claimed, the most striking results of practical develop-ment expressed in real, current social relationships, as when French so-cialist workers meet together: "Smoking, eating and drinking are no longer simply means of bringing people together. Society, associa-tion, entertainment which also has society as its aim, is sufficient for them; the brotherhood of man is no empty phrase but a reality, and the nobility of man shines forth upon us from their toil-worn bodies."[50]

Marx expected that people would make use of the knowledge ac-quired in the course of the struggle and that there would follow an internal transformation with this kind of result, the outstanding criterion of which would be the absence of any need for extrinsic supports or rewards, leadership or money. This period of industrial development opened with the unrestrained greed of individuals and states for money, but it would progress ultimately to the communal regulation of production, the end of any dependence on authoritative leaders or money, and it would prove possible finally for people "to do one thing today and another tomorrow, to hunt in the morning, fish in the afternoon, rear cattle in the evening, criticize after dinner, just as [one had] a mind, without ever becoming hunter, fisherman, shepherd, or critic."[51] Structural problems have structural solutions, objective situations reveal in a demystified world the one path that people are bound to follow, and the cult of personality or competitive greed need never enter the equation again. It pays to recall in this connection the expectations of at least some Russian radicals, encouraged by what they could infer from Marx's vision of social development and from events, and the confidence that they expressed in the early days of the revolution, concluding that neither leadership nor money (property) would ever again be a problem. Thus, one of the radical journals stated at the beginning of 1918 that "there could be a Miliukov or Kerensky epoch, but there can never be a Lenin or a Trotsky epoch. The day the revolution begins to dissolve into names, it is drawing near its close." The cult of personality, it was generally agreed, is contrary "to the whole spirit of Marxism, the spirit of scientific socialism." In 1919, the art critic, Nikolas Punin, in response to a suggestion that monuments be erected to honor the heroes of the revolution, declared that this was not really a Communist idea: there were no heroes any longer, and certainly no great heroes. The time for a heroic conception of history was gone, Punin said, never to return.[52]

Yet even Trotsky, a firm believer in the paramount role of classes that act out history's lawful mandate, had to admit that without Lenin there would have been no revolution because the other party leaders would have prevented it. This was a way of saying that in fact revolutionaries are as prone to fight the last revolution as generals are to fight the last war, and it takes an exceptional character to imagine novel solutions and impose them. If he, Trotsky, had urged the revolution forward in 1917, nothing would have happened because he lacked the authority; that anything did happen was a tribute to Lenin's singular presence.[53] This leader was clearly special, and it was important to address the confound. Thus, Lenin, or Lenin and Trotsky in the view of others, was treated as an agent of history, the leading representative of "the colossal proletarian collective," the personification of the transfer of power to the workers. "The classes, the masses, the party work through the agency of individuals; their choice of individuals demonstrates precisely the fitness of these larger forces for victory." "Proletarian class-consciousness attains its highest expression in the leaders of the organized vanguard of the working class. As personalities they are great only in the measure that they incarnate the masses. In this sense only are they giants—anonymous giants."[54]

All such evasions aside, however, this revolutionary government, like all governments regardless of ideological content, quickly revealed to all its persistent reliance on leadership, confirming in addition to the cultural hold of the past over people the insufficiency of abstract ideology to serve alone as a means of guiding and orienting collective action in a heterogeneous world. The first moral to be drawn from this is that the real physical presence of authoritative leadership continues to be an indispensable technique for maintaining a sense of the world as orderly and continuous. There are obviously people capable of taking risks, of changing themselves, and of affecting and changing their world, just as there are occasions when ideological claims have been effectively implemented apart from the dictates of authoritative leadership. But what the greatest number of people are trying to do the greater part of the time is to keep conception and perception related in ways that make sense to them. This process is facilitated by language, but it is mostly guaranteed, to the extent that social arrangements ever are, by authoritative leadership whose explanations and exhortations people can refer and defer to. With respect to Lenin and ideology, therefore, the times, the character, and his effects on the lives of people were exceptional, but the process of using leadership in a transitional way, as a technique of support, repair, and recovery in a world of multiple interests and perspectives, was not.

Political and other forms of authority remain elevated and venerated everywhere, more so than the theorists of the democratization process were able to acknowledge. The ritualization of authority cuts across all lines and exists in all cultures, to different degrees, certainly, but to significant degrees, no matter how rationalized, bureaucratized, or even democratized they may be. The recent spate of complaints about Ronald Reagan's indifferent attachment to historical truth is illustrative in this context. Garry Wills, among others, has pointed out that Reagan invents narratives that he offers to audiences as the truth, that he has claimed to be in places he never was and to have done things he never did, that he contradicts himself constantly without a hint of self-consciousness, and his references to events in American history are notoriously inaccurate.[55] Particularly egregious to historians in this last respect was Reagan's speech celebrating the centennial of the Statue of Liberty, 4 July 1986. In that speech, Reagan related how John Winthrop, standing on the tiny deck of the *Arabella*, told his audience of Quakers that the eyes of the world were on them. But, as Michael Wallace pointed out, there were no Quakers on the *Arabella*; besides, Winthrop loathed the radical Protestant sects, he did his best to ban them from Massachusetts, and, when Quakers did finally arrive in America, they were persecuted.[56]

The point is, however, that the effects of Reagan's centennial speech would not have been improved one whit if he had gotten all the facts right. The purpose of that kind of speech is to rally an audience in a moral sense, to confirm in their imagination their sense of worthiness and goodness, and to reconfirm shared ideals, not to impart information, and the more uplifting and engrossing the story, the more effective the result. What Reagan as a professional actor and politician does with such a speech is make plain what he learned best from watching other professionals like Franklin D. Roosevelt, that is, to stress and enhance the moral purpose of leadership.[57] The enlightened ideal promoted by the founders and a crucial aspect of the democratic ideology, that is, the right of the people to know, the right of educated people capable of reasoned reflection to participate in the decisions that affect them, and the obligation of a democratic government as represented by such an esteemed figure as the president to disseminate information so that rational people can participate, is part of the moral order that is being confirmed by such a speech; it is part of the story that people want to hear from the storyteller.[58] But it does not happen in practice, and it is not meant to happen. There is information that governmental agencies do collect and impart, but that is not the function of addresses to the nation by the president or other authoritative figures. Besides, not only is much vital information impossible or even just hard to get or to put together, but there are fewer people all the time to whom it can make a difference. If, as experts contend, the rate of illiteracy in the United States is anywhere from 25 to 40 percent, how could it be otherwise?[59]

This is not to say that the moral purposes of different governments have an equivalent impact on the lives of people, or that it does not matter where one lives, or that all authorities relate to their publics in the same way or affect them to the same degree. This is to say, rather, that the difference between Western societies, which have permitted and encouraged a more autonomous level of activity, and other societies has less to do with internalized morality as explained by social theorists from Maine and Durkheim to Parsons than it has to do with the continued use of authoritative figures to sustain the sense of society as a safe arena in which to pursue goals, to justify particular versions of the world, and to legitimate particular conceptions of the use of social space, even if presidents and prime ministers are not the same kinds of figures as monarchs or dictators.

The second moral to be drawn from the insufficiency of ideology as a means of guiding and orienting people in the everyday world is that the extent to which people were able historically to change the form of authoritative control, to distance themselves from it and develop a more autonomous existence, depended on their ability to substitute money and property as concrete or transitional objects of support.[60] The aspiration, need, and in many cases compulsion to get money and to strive mightily to acquire more of it, derided and condemned by any number of observers and critics, was not in the final analysis a matter of the cultural poverty of bourgeois societies but the condition on which most people could manage any level of autonomous practice at all, whatever terms might be used by different individuals and groups to justify it. One proof of this is the resort to market mechanisms in leader-centered societies when the leadership wishes their citizens to become more productive and committed. Urging citizens to engage the market and to become more independent of authority has thus far required such societies also to legitimate personal gain, in a word, money. Money and property were and are the signs of a capacity for independent activity and the condition on which such activity occurs. To be sure, the need to use money and property in this transitional way implies both the possibility for and a limitation on the extent of independent activity—the source of this limitation being the inability as yet to separate such activity from fantasies on one side (of strength, mastery, singularity, exceptional worthiness, desirability, of having other, more, different, better people and things than one already has) and from fears of the power of the social world on the other.

To put it another way, it is not the idea of duty prowling around in our lives like the ghost of dead religious beliefs that accounts for the sense of cultural unease in capitalist societies, as Weber declared; it is rather the tension described earlier, between the opposed and contradictory aspirations among individuals and groups for greater freedom from authority and for greater dependence on it, that prowls around, as money and property continue to serve as a compromise solution in changing circumstances, keeping the two desires in some kind of balance.[61] It must be emphasized in this context that Joseph Schumpeter's belief that the capitalist process "takes the life out of the idea of property," that the transition in the capitalist era from real property in land or in a factory to more abstract forms of property in money and stock is bound to relax the owners' grip, loosen the sense of moral urgency and the will to fight to protect such property so that in the end no one will care what happens and the subsequent transition to socialism will occur all the more easily, misses the significance of money to people precisely as a transitional object that is connected more to different forms of political or cultural authority than it is to different forms of property. (Henry Adams was perhaps not on the mark but closer to it when he wrote in 1902 that "new power was disintegrating society, and setting independent centres of force to work, until money had all it could do to hold the machine together. No one could represent it faithfully as a whole.")[62]

Thus, authority never devolves to the "administration of things" because people must continue to invest it with qualities that it does not intrinsically possess as a means of bolstering their sense of adequacy, continuity, and safety. Similarly, money never devolves to a means of exchange promoting the progressive rationalization of culture because it must also be similarly invested. Marx had already wondered why people put more faith in things than in each other, why they could not accept the premise that, because productivity occurs in a communal context, there is no real need to separate or elevate themselves or distinguish themselves in terms of their particular effort. But the problem was that society was not becoming more simplified as Marx expected; it was becoming more complicated, as exemplified in the heterogeneity problem, and the aspirations of people to pursue their own interests, to work, take care of their families, and so on, were threatened and compromised in ways that Marx had not anticipated.[63] On the other hand, this critique is not peculiarly applicable to Marx, for all the other theorists whose constructs undergirded social theory in the twentieth century suffered similarly for related reasons: equality never turned out to be the problem that Tocqueville thought it would, integration never worked out in the manner that Durkheim hoped it would, and the rationalization process never developed in the way or to the extent that Weber feared it would.

In any event, there are basically two alternative social forms in the world, distinguished either by the primacy of authoritative leadership, secular or religious, claiming more or less exclusive rights to the interpretation of reality, promoting political passivity, subordination, and dependence, or by the primacy of money, which makes possible a more independent level of activity, though at the risk of allowing even vastly inequitable manipulations of the market at the expense of the greatest number of people, who, largely bereft of resources, are left exposed and vulnerable. It is possible in this world to substitute one social form for the other: certain Soviet or East and Central European artists, for example, have repudiated the principle of bureaucratic control of their careers and come West to test their skills in the marketplace; by contrast, many bourgeois individuals have repudiated the right to pursue a self-interested course of action, subordinating themselves to the dictates of authoritative leadership, whether constituted as party or church. But no social order anywhere has ever attempted to continue in the absence of both.

This is not to say, however, that all social practice is exhausted by these two possibilities. To begin with, as I noted earlier, there are occasions when ideological orientations have proved sufficient to account for social change. Granting eighteen-year-olds the right to vote permitted a greater separation from authority for a segment of the population without implying or obligating any special dependence on money or property to make it effective. This step, which has proven to be significant, did not involve, as steps taken contemporaneously on gender issues did, a struggle for independent access to money and property as a means of separating from familial and other forms of authority. But, even beyond such an instance, market relationships, including relationships to authority and money, appear as heterogeneous in practice as any other, in terms of nationality (the French view of money and property is quite different from the American, obviously) and also in terms of class, gender, and age.

What can be said, and all that I mean to say, is that historically the ability to sustain the separation from the authority of monarchy and church depended less on abstract internalized morality than on the widespread acceptance and availability of a different kind of concrete object that could be used transitionally in the sense I have described.* In short, the argument is meant to stand without becoming schematic or rigid, without subordinating the significance of every kind of event to the two alternatives, authority and money, and without implying that all separations from authority and all forms of reliance on money as a social technique resemble each other or must invariably be treated in the same way.

---

*It cannot be emphasized too strongly that money and property are not the only things that play such a role in a heterogeneous world, though they have played the most important role in practice. There are also books, e.g., and, while it would be extremely difficult to diminish the role of money, property, and authority in "the life of the mind," this issue is one of primacies, and people have been able to distance themselves from money and property on one side and from authority on the other in this context. Weapons too, in certain societies, play a transitional role as the attachment to them is clearly greater than the need for self-defense would indicate.

The Appeal of Wishful Solutions:
Structure and Community

The problems presented by heterogeneity, and by the world of transitional phenomena and objects, emerged from the history of the West and can be interpretively assessed in a comprehensive way only insofar as this history continues to be integrated in the assessment. There are two concepts in particular, however, that have hampered our ability to understand historically the relationships implied by these problems.[64] One is structuralism variously construed, the attempt to bypass the surface clutter in the expectation of discovering an underlying "deep" or "essential" reality. Structuralists of all stripes delineate an unobservable or unconscious realm of activity that determines and unifies the variety at the surface. Scientific knowledge on this view can be inferred not from observable data but only from and by virtue of a theoretical knowledge of this deeper reality. Structuralists do build not on the subjective reporting of people but rather on imaginative conceptual leaps that repudiate the notion of the conscious or subjective intentionality of actors, denying them any autonomous capacities. Of the two worlds, the observer's and the subject's, structuralisms of every sort depend exclusively on the observer's world.[65] Thus, Jacques Lacan has stated that individuals who have attained a capacity for symbolization are freed from one kind of imprisonment (unmediated sensory experience) only to enter a new kind of imprisonment, the preexisting world of symbols that determines their thoughts even as they believe themselves to be self-determining. As Marx also stated earlier, in other, social terms (which Ernst Bloch referred to as Marx's "cold stream"), "It is not a question of what this or that proletarian, or even the whole proletariat, at the moment *regards* as its aim. It is a question of *what the proletariat is,* and what, in accordance with this *being,* it will historically be compelled to do."[66]

Of course, there are still other forms of structuralism, but, whatever the form, structuralists remain indifferent to the unique features of history, and they cannot account for changing contents over time. That is, structuralists can attempt to explain retrospectively any content that appears in terms of their own constructs, but they cannot anticipate the surface forms that contents take, nor can they really manage retrospective interpretations without some kind of inferential leap.* Still, struc-

---

*"Levi-Strauss likes to claim that he has shown 'wonderful symmetries,' 'perfect homologies,' or 'complete inversions' in myths, but it would be fairer to say that . . . if his descriptions of them are often 'wonderful,' the relations he describes are not. 'Perfect symmetries' are truly achieved only by ignoring some of the data and by re-describing the

turalist arguments continue to be attractive in all forms, as durable and persistent as poison ivy, and still other ones will no doubt appear.

The second concept, then, is community, elaborated typically, though not exclusively, in other terms. Paul Ricoeur, for example, referred to the utopian function of culture, which is based in human imagination and which "has a prospective and explorative function in regard to the inherent possibilities of man. It is, par excellence, the instituting and constituting of what is humanly possible. In imagining his possibilities, man acts as a prophet of his own existence."[67] Ernst Bloch, that strange disciple of Marx, referred to this utopian viewpoint as it occurs in Marx as the "warm stream," which supplements the mechanistic "cold stream" and is indispensable to it; he referred to it also as "the good New," "anticipatory consciousness," the "Not-Yet-Become," the still unachieved "Homeland," and a lot else besides in the same vein.[68] All freedom movements, writes Bloch, are guided by utopian aspirations, especially radical movements oriented toward a concept of community.

It does seem that earlier references to extrinsic sources of reward and support and attachments to transitional objects and phenomena imply the possibility for further social development, an expanded sphere of autonomous practice, an expansion of the space between the private and the public worlds that people can use to develop autonomous capacities. This possibility has historically been the primary subject of utopian imagination, epitomized in one vision or another of the harmonious community. The most recent popular expression of the desire or wish for community is the work of Robert Bellah and his colleagues, *Habits of the Heart*.[69] The classic expression, the one that has proved most effective in mobilizing people for political action, is Marx's, the promise that the bourgeois mode of production would be the last antagonistic mode, that the contradictions within capitalism must lead to a resolution beyond conflict, the key being the socialization of the means of production and the reproduction of cooperative relationships that are understood to follow necessarily from that.

However, the idea that cooperative modes of production would foster cooperative relationships on all other levels, that the democratization of economic structures must lead to the democratization of all structures in a world finally removed from the alienating experiences of authority and money, that removing the economy from the sphere of

---

rest in terms of carefully selected abstract synechdoches" (Dan Sperber, *Le savoir des anthropologues* [Paris, 1982], 112. Clifford Geertz, "The Cerebral Savage: On the Work of Claude Levi-Strauss," in *The Interpretation of Cultures* [New York, 1973], 345–59).

competition would eliminate self seeking, class advantage, and class struggle, a single interest superseding conflicting interests, permitting the emergence of a single perspective, as the way is cleared for objective assessments of the environment, all this was based on an imaginatively constructed but for all practical purposes nonexistent social psychology. Given historical and contemporary experience with all the common social factors (productive processes, political and familial relationships, religious commitments, and so on), it is necessary to conclude that the variety of social locations important to people became and persisted historically as so many occasions for the expression of subjective intentions and aspirations, as multiple and competing interests and perspectives became in turn the paramount consequence of the history. The particular ideological contents, claims for autonomy and inclusion, and the various morally animated repudiations of these claims, all of which occurred in the context of multiple locations, compel subjective expression and heterogeneous response, revealing that space is defined and used differently by different people at the same time and over time, the result of an active process of construction abetted by the vagaries of need, the deviousness of language, and the assessments of reality that are developed within the different locations (of which class is only one). In short, all social arrangements, including those based on the socialization of the means of production, give rise to multiple interests and perspectives and to heterogeneous groups and factions.

The only sign of the harmonious community, then, is the fantasy of community that has been consciously exploited not only in the lucubrations of a writer like Ernst Bloch but on at least one crucial occasion in practice as well, in the efforts of the one political activist who felt with some justification empowered by his community and enabled by his own sense of providential mission to do it, Adolf Hitler, as expressed on a number of occasions but especially in his speech to members of the Nazi Party at Nuremberg, 13 September 1936: "How deeply we feel once more in this hour the miracle that has brought us together! Once you heard the voice of a man, and it spoke to your hearts . . . and you followed that voice. . . . Now that we meet here, we are all filled with the wonder of this gathering. Not every one of you can see me and I do not see each one of you. But I feel you and you feel me! . . . Now we are together, we are with him and he is with us, and now we are Germany!" [70]

The practical problems for history, social theory, and political practice are subjectivity and the heterogeneous interests and perspectives that follow from it, as well as the discontinuities. But in a larger sense these are only the signs of a still more crucial problem, that is, how to define and use and in any case keep open the space that people need in order to sustain their capacity for creating meaning out of the chaotic flow of events and experience. The Western societies redefined the concept of space, opening it to a greater degree than it had ever been opened before, but the very autonomy and inclusion that were promoted then created difficulties that made further development along the same route problematic. Subjectivity, heterogeneity, and discontinuities became the specific source of these difficulties because of the need to maintain a coherent sense of how social relationships are organized or how society works, which is also why structuralist ideas and the ideas of community that Marx and others promoted are both so logical in their appearance and so inconceivable in their hermetic perfection.

Thus it happens in the wake of events in the twentieth century that the most appropriate language for conceiving such a prospective community is no longer the rigorous theoretical language that Marx preferred, of historical stages and process, evolutionary development, class struggle, means and modes of production, material reality, real, concrete social relationships, false consciousness, social forces, and the like; rather, it is the language of a fantast like Bloch, who thought of himself as a Marxist, the mystified language of the "Not Yet Conscious," the "Can Be," the "Optimum," the "Become," the "mediated Novum," the "Concrete Forward Dream," the "Always Promised Land," the "Will toward Utopia," etc.[71] This is confirmed implicitly by the inability of Robert Bellah and his colleagues to address in their book the idea of community prospectively in sociological terms or in any terms other than those of moral encouragement.

Concluding Remarks on the Definition and Pursuit of the Problem

Erich Fromm wrote that he had learned from two masters, Marx and Freud, but that Marx was the more important because he discussed society and social relationships seriously and systematically as the only arena in which man's problematic condition can be addressed. However, Marx really had very little useful to say about the mental or dynamic side of things, which is nevertheless part of the problem, to which there can be no solution without a workable conception of how the two spheres are related. The fact that psychoanalysis failed as rigorous social theory or as a technique of uncontaminated communication that could provide in its own terms a way of relating them does not make the problem go away. The problem, specifically, how we got from the high expectations and grand possibilities of the enlightened eighteenth century, from the notions of expanded spheres of freedom, reason, and inclusive practices, from the organizational efforts to establish an arena for and the moral legitimacy of such practices, to the disastrous consequences of the ongoing struggle, the great calamities of the twentieth century, is a real one and merits continued effort, however difficult the task, considering the problems of subjectivity, heterogeneity, and discontinuities already discussed, and however slight the prospects admittedly are right now for understanding it.

On the other hand, continued attention to the problem requires a research strategy appropriate to the contents, which include what psychoanalysts tried mistakenly to stake out exclusively as the problem or, to avoid deflecting attention unnecessarily, as psychoanalysis is presently trapped in problems of its own, what artists have always recognized as included among the contents of the problem, the terms of which Henry James lucidly addressed in his *Notebooks* as "the terrible law of the artists . . . the law by which everything is grist to his mill—the law, in short, of the acceptance of all experience, of all suffering, of *all* life, of *all* suggestion and sensation and illumination." James emphasized in a manner that compels attention the desire to live "*in* the world of creation," to achieve inspiration by "a depth and continuity of attention and meditation," to feel "the multitudinous presence of all human situations and pictures . . . all passions, all combinations" (including, in one place in his *Notebooks,* "discouragements and lapses, depressions and darknesses," and, in another place, "depression, melancholy, remorse and shame"), to sit tight and see the things that float by, trying to catch those things that are important, to overcome his fear of letting himself go and getting into all the different worlds that people inhabit.[72] This vision or version of art approximates a conception of the problem because it acknowledges all the sources of struggle, including both mind and the social world, as artistic discipline itself requires a degree of control over and independence from both mind and world, some willingness to imagine the dangers that exist for people in both spheres, some capacity for making productive use of the inevitable tension between the two, and a language with which to express it all.

There are without a doubt any number of works of art that similarly recreate in the most interesting way aspects of the private world, tensions between private and public worlds, and techniques to mediate between the two, to instruct a heterogeneous audience in life's requirements. In *Middlemarch,* to cite an example from one such work already referred to, George Eliot proposed interestingly—long before Harold Lasswell made the same point also referred to earlier—that "our passions do not live apart in locked chambers, but, dressed in their small wardrobe of notions bring their provisions to a common table." However, the most powerful work of art in which all our terms and themes appear (private and public worlds, heterogeneous interests and perspectives, authoritative leadership, money, social conflict, and prospective community) is Herman Melville's *Moby-Dick*. Melville, the perceiving, interpreting artist, more alert than others to all the sources of struggle, explored the turmoil both of mind and of the social world.[73] The voyage of the *Pequod*, after all, was intended by the owners of the vessel and the sailors to be a profit-making venture, as all such whaling voyages were.[74] The realistic if dangerous goal of earning a living at sea by killing and rendering whales was "usurped" by the monomaniacal Ahab, who was intent on his own private aim, the pursuit and destruction of the white whale.[75] Ahab had the clear perception that the sailors were vulnerable to the appeals of authority, especially, in this shipboard community, because of the customs, traditions, and usages of the sea, that their feelings could be roused and that they could be turned from their mundane, workaday purposes to his own.[76]

Ahab understood further that so many different individuals must be provided with an interim motive consistent with their own purposes, for they did not have the reason and therefore the stamina to persist in the pursuit of his; and that motive was money.[77] Besides, as Ahab realized, once he turned away from the proper purpose of the voyage, the sailors were no longer morally obligated to follow him. Especially the chief mate, Starbuck, constantly invoking the true and original purpose of the voyage, might rebel against his leadership "unless some ordinary, prudential circumstantial influences were brought to bear upon him."[78] But Ahab also imagined that he could collapse and exploit the divided individuality of the sailors and unify them around his single-minded, if mad, purpose, which he did:

> They were one man, not thirty. For as the one ship that held them all; though it was put together of all contrasting things—oak, and maple, and pine wood; iron, and pitch, and hemp—yet all these ran into each other in the one concrete hull, which shot on its way, both balanced and directed by the long central keel; even so, all the individualities of the crew, this man's valor, that man's fear; guilt and guiltlessness, all varieties were welded into oneness, and were all directed to that fatal goal which Ahab their one lord and keel did point to.[79]

This was one depiction and imagined use of community, compelled by the power of Ahab, the realized destructive power of social order against people. But there was another depiction of community that was expressed and remained as a fantasy, Ishmael's fantasy, as he engaged in the shipboard task, "the sweet and unctuous duty" of squeezing the coagulated lumps of whale sperm back into fluid:

> Squeeze! squeeze! squeeze! all the morning long; I squeezed that sperm till I myself almost melted into it; I squeezed that sperm till a strange sort of insanity came over me; and I found myself unwittingly squeezing my co-laborers' hands in it, mistaking their hands for the gentle globules. Such an abounding, affectionate, friendly, loving feeling did this avocation beget; that at last I was continually squeezing their hands, and looking up into their eyes sentimentally; as much as to say,—Oh! my dear fellow beings, why should we longer cherish any social acerbities, or know the slightest ill-humor or envy! Come; let us squeeze hands all round; nay, let us squeeze ourselves into each other; let us squeeze ourselves into the very milk and sperm of kindness.[80]

But Ishmael turned away from his fantasy—as he was able subsequently to examine the significance of Ahab's—not in a spirit of alarm, anxiety, or shame or fearful either of the idea of merging with others. Rather, Ishmael concluded, on the basis of "many prolonged, repeated experiences," that man must reject the radical conceit of "universal felicity," lowering or at least shifting "his conceit of attainable felicity; not placing it anywhere in the intellect or the fancy; but in the wife, the heart, the bed, the table, the saddle, the fire-side, the country."[81] There are, in short, real intimations of merger, fantasy intimations, but it is a mistake—which people nevertheless make—to "insist upon the universal application of a temporary feeling or opinion." The important issue is to maintain one's "separate identity," to persist as a perceiving, interpreting individual, acting as a triangular point between two extremes, the power of fantasy and the power of the social world. It is necessary to recognize that there is an accessible fantasy world in which everything, especially everything to do with love and hate, works out perfectly as all resistance is mastered, but that one cannot linger there, much less act on its premises. It is also necessary to recognize that subordination to the dictates of authoritative leadership harbors dangers for one's identity—the notion that Ishmael started out with, that authority is a fact of life and one can easily live with being ordered about on board ship because not only does one get paid for the labor but sailors know how to stake out a space even against formidable captains, this notion proved false.

It is necessary to recognize finally as well that the ability of people in any circumstance to sustain themselves still depends on their continued attachment to familiar people and to the things and routines of everyday life. The problems of mind and society, of multiple interests and perspectives emerging from multiple tasks and locations, and of divided minds, emerging from interior reflections, especially as a way of evading the necessity for continuing the struggles imposed by everyday life, weaken them and make them vulnerable to fantasy and authority. But familiar, ordinary attachments to people, things, and routines can afford them a measure of protection by allowing them some distance from both. In the light of Leo Marx's brilliant examination of Melville's expression of pastoral strivings, it should be noted that Melville's emphasis must be placed on the attachment to familiar, ordinary people and things as an indispensable technique of stability in a world of mental and social conflict, not on the image of "rural tranquillity" as such, because this was the crucial insight, and one that remained valid even after this rural world had decisively passed.*[82]

That is, the relationship to people and things as Melville depicted it is still a vital technique of stability in a world still riven by conflict. For the kind of middle-class commercial society that Melville derided but that achieved a sturdy dominance was at no point without its deep conflicts, at its lowest points distinguished by its failure to allow people to manage relationships to other people and things without great turmoil, and at every point largely indifferent—in a strange way, considering the shared religious tradition—to the fate of its citizens. But, however ably or luckily the rulers of this society have managed domestic and overseas conflicts in the past, the most recent challenge to its continued dominance, the persistent, systemic inability to pursue and use novel technologies in order to remain competitive in world markets, raises serious questions precisely at the level of relatedness. The novel technologies emerging from the most recent developments in the ongoing industrial expansion do not require labor in the form associated with earlier developments; on the contrary, the amount of labor that these technologies require diminishes as the skill level increases so that they have the capacity actually to release people from the necessity of labor as formerly understood.

It is not clear that the responsible elites can respond to this situation (which necessitates in the first place breaking the moral and ideological connection between income and work) or that they have not

---

*It is useful to recall here that earlier Tocqueville too had observed that in democratic societies people strive continually, though not for any lofty goals, and that life is generally spent in eagerly acquiring small objects.

in fact become for the first time an obstacle to increased technological development as a way of protecting their own interests.[83] Moreover, if competitive politics is the technique for integrating multiple and competing interests and perspectives in democratized societies and money remains the key resource, the basis for access to things in the sense that Melville explored, and to decision-making processes that foster or inhibit relationships in a heterogeneous world, then it is important in any event to reconsider how this resource is acquired and distributed. People who fail to acquire this resource in amounts sufficient to enable them to act in markets or, worse, who are cut off from markets because the economy is insufficient to absorb the numbers, or because access is arranged in favor of privileged elites, or because of various other kinds of exclusionary practices, such people are likely to exhibit behavior characteristic of life at the poles, where one of the two sides, fantasy or the social world, has gotten the upper hand. Such behavior, moreover, clearly takes escapist, violent, or apathetic forms, when it does not involve a search for the consolations of authoritative leadership. This is why powerlessness and poverty are still the principal issues: the kind of accounting that occurs in the political marketplace, the comparison to others especially in terms of the availability of money as a resource, the capacity to acquire and spend resources in all the various markets, the subjective assessment of the reasons for the lack of resources, none of this occurs in a vacuum or in a situation independent of heterogeneous standpoints, examples, and techniques of struggle. If the study of history has any lessons left to teach anyone, the variety of likely effects on people of the sense of powerlessness and poverty over a course of time must surely be one of them.

The discussion of Melville's *Moby-Dick* brings us full circle in a sense, back to our starting point, the novelists' critique of history and theory and the assertion that, because of their intuitive capacity and their capacity for language, they can interpret and explain the significance of events in a way that the others cannot. Indeed, there is probably not anywhere a better proof of this assertion or a better representation of the struggle that people must wage on two sides, mind and society, than Melville's novel, which, with its discussions of realistic, moral, and wishful strivings, its attention to detail and philosophical speculation, its capacity to encompass simultaneously the intricate details of a particular tale along with a high degree of generality and complexity, is a paramount example of what novelists are asserting and complaining about. Historians and theorists cannot accomplish this, or so it is said: if they focus on a particular instance in complex detail, they lose the generality, the larger interpretive point, and, if they focus on generality, they lose the complexity of detail. Historians and theorists therefore are always reductionist: in order to explain instances, they must either evade the issue of process or simplify the issue by abstracting, excluding, and distorting. Apart from the vagaries of language, which also serve to separate them from the reality that they are trying to engage, they have never really grasped the significance of historical change as manifest especially in heterogeneity, diversity, and discontinuity.[84] Their concepts of historical development, the different interpretive schemes that they have provided people with, are fictions, and, as Saul Bellow has said, the next one that they provide will also be a fiction. Historians talk about "the roots of this, the cause of the other, the source of events, the history, the structure, the reasons why."[85] While they do have an effect, it is not the one intended. Hence Norman Mailer's belief that only great fiction counts because only fiction still believes that one mind can see it whole.[86]

Melville did in fact see a great deal, and more than most. Take, for example, the juxtaposition that occurs in *Moby-Dick* within the first four pages, in a chapter entitled "Loomings," of money, hostile and benign fantasies, autonomy, subordination and dependence both "physical and metaphysical," the fact of authority in the lives of people everywhere (and the authority of sea captains), not to mention the dreary meanness of petty commercial life for ordinary people who rush down to the water at every opportunity, as Melville describes it, dreaming of escape.[87] Take also Melville's account of multiple perspectives and his sense that people construe for themselves the significance of things in terms of their own interests and perspectives, which makes Ahab's mastery of the crew all the more significant and Melville's treatment of that kind of authority all the more prescient. For who now could miss the political relevance of Ahab's perception of his own behavior, "All my means are sane, my motive and my object mad?"[88]

Melville's fascinating and complex views of the social world as expressed in *Moby-Dick* are obviously worthy of the high esteem in which they are held. But are novelists and critics then right when they assert that this kind of truth is all that is possible and that historians and theorists cannot do nearly as well in any event? Or, more to the point, must they be right? Can historians and theorists manage with reference to historical data, that is, with reference to subjectivity, heterogeneity, and discontinuity, to describe the experiences of people who tried to control the situations that they encountered with a similar degree of generality and complexity in a way that is not just an observer's invention, a moral claim, a wishful gesture, or a fiction, as Bellow has put it, serving political and ideological purposes? On just this point, William H. Sewell, Jr., has written, quite recently in fact, that,

> if capitalist development is uneven in the sense I have been arguing . . . that is, if it produces not an increasingly solid and uniform proletarian continent but a continually changing archipelago of variegated working class categories . . . then the appropriate explanatory strategy for labor historians is not to look for evidence of proletarianization behind every surge of working-class political radicalism but to ask how and why workers with widely varying economic trajectories and work-place experiences could successfully be constituted as political insurgents.[89]

Can historians and theorists generate a conception of the social world that addresses the question raised by this statement in an integrative way, one that encompasses both mind and society on a level other than the trivial or the random and that is distinguishable from a fictional account? There is no definite answer, of course, but the powerful critique that has been leveled against history and theory has raised a different kind of question, one that requires different strategies as well.[90] The question raised by Sewell's statement, which is justified by evidence and experience after all, simply renders unacceptable certain approaches and proposed solutions the plausibility of which had hitherto been more or less taken for granted, suggesting the possibility of other ones. Thus, while the process of reexamination of historical events based on this kind of question may be just beginning, it is nevertheless a promising one, and it will be interesting to see how theory and practice are affected by it.

Notes

Introduction

1. Hayden White quoted in Frederika Randall, "Why Scholars Become Storytellers," *New York Times Book Review* (hereafter cited as *NYTBR*), 29 January 1984, 31. I will rely heavily on the contents that have appeared in this journal of opinion, particularly because of its exceptional reach and because of what the repeated appearance of this kind of content implies in a sociological sense. On this subject, see Lewis Coser et al., *Books: The Culture and Commerce of Publishing* (New York, 1982), 317. See also Hayden White, "The Politics of Interpretation: Discipline and De-Sublimation," in *The Politics of Interpretation,* ed. W. J. T. Mitchell (Chicago, 1983), 136–37.

2. Cynthia Ozick, "The Muse, Postmodern and Homeless," *NYTBR,* 18 January 1987, 9.

3. Robert Musil, *The Man Without Qualities,* trans. Eithne Wilkins and Ernst Kaiser (New York, 1980), 34.

4. Ibid., 59; see also 17, 24–25, 30, 70, 72, 85. Peter Schneider, "The Light at the End of the Novel," *NYTBR,* 26 July 1987, 23.

5. Carl L. Becker, "Everyman His Own Historian," in *Everyman His Own Historian* (Chicago, 1966), 252, 245, 248, 252–53.

6. Carl L. Becker, *The Eve of the Revolution: A Chronicle of the Breach with England* (New Haven, Conn., 1921), vii–viii.

7. Carl L. Becker, "The Spirit of '76," in *Everyman His Own Historian,* 47.

8. Carl L. Becker, *The Heavenly City of the Eighteenth Century Philosophers* (New Haven, Conn., 1961).

9. Cushing Strout, *The Pragmatic Revolt in American History: Carl Becker and Charles Beard* (Ithaca, N.Y., 1966), 41. J. H. Hexter, *On Historians: Reappraisals of Some of the Makers of Modern History* (Cambridge, Mass., 1979), 39–41.

10. By "the simplest levels" I mean the ability to forecast the number of automobile fatalities on a particular holiday given an estimated number of cars

on the road or the ability to say that people representing certain types of economic interests are likely to favor tariffs and that people representing other types of economic interests are likely to oppose tariffs.

11. Charles E. Lindblom and David K. Cohen, *Usable Knowledge: Social Science and Social Problem Solving* (New Haven, Conn., 1979), 14–17. In addition, in 1980 there appeared a special issue of *Public Interest* entitled "The Crisis in Economic Theory." On this topic, see also Leonard Silk reporting on the national meetings of economists in the *New York Times,* 1 January 1982, 36; and Lester G. Thurow, *Dangerous Currents: The State of Economics* (New York, 1983). Lewis Coser referred to the crisis in sociology in his presidential address to the American Sociological Association in 1975, quoted in Mary F. Rogers, *Sociology, Ethnomethodology and Experience* (New York, 1983), 12. On psychology, see David Joravsky, "Body, Mind, Machine," *New York Review of Books* 29 (21 October 1982): 46–47; or Robert Kanigel, "Storing Yesterday," *Johns Hopkins Magazine* (June 1981), 31.

12. Lawrence Stone, "History and the Social Sciences in the Twentieth Century," and "The Revival of Narrative: Reflections on a New Old History," in *The Past and the Present* (Boston, Mass., 1981), 3–44 (esp. 20), and 74–98. Gordon S. Wood, in his review of Robert Middelkauf's *The Glorious Cause* (New York, 1982), argued that for a historian to write a narrative history, emphasizing or selecting one unique series of events rather than any other possible one, he must assume "some connecting plot in the events, that they are going somewhere; he has given them 'a teleological meaning. . . .' Such teleological narrative history cannot be truly scientific; it is simply story telling, not essentially different from fiction" ("Star Spangled History," *New York Review of Books* 29 [12 August 1982]: 8–9). C. Vann Woodward followed Wood's review almost immediately with a defense of narrative history ("A Short History of American History," *NYTBR,*15 August 1982, 3, 14). This was followed by a letter from Eric H. Monkkonen to the editor of the *NYTBR* (5 September 1982, 21) that accused Woodward of "representing the worst in the recent wave of anti-intellectual Luddism" and by another letter on the subject (Thomas Hines, 3 October 1982, 31). Wood's review was addressed further by Jackson Lears, John P. Diggins, and Cushing Strout (*New York Review of Books,* 29 [16 December 1982]: 58–59). See also Jonathan Yardley, "The Narrowing World of the Historian," *AHA Perspectives* 20, no. 6 (September 1982): 21–22; Hayden White, "The Question of Narrative in Contemporary Historical Theory," *History and Theory* 23, no. 1 (1984): 1–33; and Gordon S. Wood, "Intellectual History and the Social Sciences," in *New Directions in American Intellectual History,* ed. John Higham and Paul K. Conkin (Baltimore, 1979), 27–41, esp. 30–31. On the issue of "thick" (analytic) as opposed to "thin" (straight-line) narrative strategies, see Allan Megill and Donald N. McCloskey, eds., *The Rhetoric of the Human Sciences: Language and Argument in Scholarship and Public Affairs* (Madison, Wis., 1987), 231–32.

13. For the counterargument in terms of "good progress" and "significant achievements," see, respectively, Randall Collins, *Three Sociological Traditions* (New York, 1985), vii; and Robert N. Bellah et al., *Habits of the Heart:*

ife (New York, 1986), 298. On
, Randall Collins, ed., *Sociological*
study of emotion, see n. 77 in

cal position entails, Donald N.
lernism," particularly as it affects
nt of White's that "what it is able
the scientist's and especially the
personal convictions" (*The Rhet-*
. The relativism that is implied in
ues of scholarship. The concern is
one standpoint from another by
to say that one system of social
n terms of moral preferences, no
biting the subjective strivings of
d safely apart from the dictates of
it matter that I cannot discuss fur-
f it turns up in the context of the
h authoritative leaders in the past
r and have been able to rally people
of conflict and disorder, there is no
terms or to predict outcomes: it is
lapt to the kind of radical relativism
rceive the world as chaotic because
row or closed conception of social
nce Stone in these terms (ibid., 48).
have nevertheless wished to remain
rescue it from the many contradic-
(class, class conflict) by amplifying
of imperialism and moving on suc-
logy as opposed to class, hegemony,
moral economy, the unconscious and hence socially uncontaminated sources of
rebellion, structural necessities, ideal speech acts, etc. But the network was not
rescuable except in moral terms by any of these manipulations and does not
appear rescuable by any subsequent ones.

16. Fred Weinstein and Gerald M. Platt, *The Wish to Be Free* (Berkeley,
Calif., 1969), and *Psychoanalytic Sociology* (Baltimore, 1973).

17. For example, Anthony D. Smith, *The Concept of Social Change: A
Critique of the Functionalist Theory of Social Change* (London, 1980).

18. We had argued that situations of loss involving superordinate and
subordinate relationships led to concerted action based on aggressive strivings.
But loss can occur or be experienced in other ways, among equals, e.g., so that
maintaining the notion of aggressive strivings against authoritative figures as a
source of social change made much less sense. (Weinstein and Platt, *The Wish
to Be Free*, 33–35). There were other problems as well, which will be clarified
in the text.

19. There is a notion of interpretation as a problem as it appears in the phenomenological-hermeneutic tradition. I am not referring to the notion of interpretation in that sense here. Rather, I am referring to the less grandiose sense of interpretation as historians typically use the term when referring to their attempts to explain the significance of what they are writing or talking about. On the hermeneutic issue, see, e.g., Richard E. Palmer, *Hermeneutics: Interpretation Theory in Schleiermacher, Dilthey, Heidegger and Gadamer* (Evanston, Ill., 1969). The quotation is from Emile Durkheim, *Professional Ethics and Civic Morals,* trans. Cornelia Brookfield (Westport, Conn., 1983), 99. See also Peter McHugh, *Defining the Situation: The Organization of Meaning in Social Interaction* (New York, 1968), 7–55; and Peter L. Berger and Thomas Luckmann, *The Social Construction of Reality: A Treatise in the Sociology of Knowledge* (New York, 1967).

20. Of course, professional social scientists have departed from the founders in a technical or technological sense, but they are still connected to them in an interpretive sense. No matter how numerate, statistical, or technologically proficient professional social scientists get, they still have to make interpretive statements about people's motives, intentions, and reasons in order to make sense of their data in any larger way, and the chances are that they have done so in terms provided by the founders, whatever the variations may be. I refer to Marx, Tocqueville, Weber, Durkheim, Georg Simmel, Freud, and some notable but still relatively few others.

21. Clifford Geertz, "Ideology as a Cultural System," in *The Interpretation of Cultures* (New York, 1973), 218. One of the problems with the concept of ideology is getting a discriminable definition of it. According to Geertz, ideology occurs and appears suasive when received culture fails. My own view of ideology is different, as I will explain in chap. 3 below.

22. A discussion of Winnicott's transitional concepts, along with the relevant bibliography, occurs in chap. 3 below.

23. Anthony Giddens discusses the facilitating and constraining aspects of social order in *The Constitution of Society: Outline of the Theory of Structuration* (Berkeley, Calif., 1984), 169–206. See also his *Central Problems in Social Theory: Action, Structure, and Contradiction in Social Analysis* (Berkeley, Calif., 1979). Giddens's conception of the problem is a very strong one, but I prefer nevertheless the transitional language for the reasons given, the terms of which are further extensively amplified in the chapters below.

24. The list, in other words, is meant to be illustrative, not exhaustive. Leadership, money, and property have persistently been central to historical and social conflicts, as conditions or objects of integration, just as the factors of heterogeneity and discontinuity constitute conditions of disintegration. There are other integrative objects, of course, including flag and country on one level and especially family and gender on another.

Chapter One

1. Hayden White, *Tropics of Discourse: Essays in Cultural Criticism* (Baltimore, 1985), 31–35. Michael Gorra, "The Sun Never Sets on the English

Novel," *NYTBR*, 19 July 1987, 24. On the value of history as distinct from historians, see Gore Vidal's letter to the editors, *New York Review of Books* 35 (28 April 1988): 56–58.

2. Gorra, "The Sun Never Sets on the English Novel," 24. John Banville, "Physics and Fiction: Order from Chaos," *NYTBR*, 21 April 1985, 41, 42.

3. Gorra, "The Sun Never Sets on the English Novel," 24–25.

4. The first quotation is of E. L. Doctorow in Bruce Weber, "The Myth Maker," *New York Times Magazine*, 20 October 1985, 26. The second quotation is from Mario Vargas Llosa, "Thugs Who Know Their Greek," *NYTBR*, 7 September 1986, 7. In this review of Rubem Fonseca's *High Art*, Vargas Llosa stated that "true literature is again going out on the street to load up on adventures." Carlos Fuentes, in his review of Augusto Roa Bastos's *I the Supreme* (*NYTBR*, 6 April 1986, 1, 32–34), raised a different issue, how to compete with history, how to create characters richer, crazier, more imaginative than those offered by history.

5. John Lukacs, review of *God's Fifth Column*, by William Gerhardie, *NYTBR*, 29 November 1981, 9.

6. In an attempt to find a language to describe novels that blend reality and fantasy, "a problem that's plagued reviewers at least since E. L. Doctorow's 'Ragtime,'" Cyra McFadden has suggested, in addition to *faction* (fact and fiction), *mystory* (myth and history) and *yearnalism*, for what really happened and what the author wishes had happened because it makes a better story ("Love among the Orange Roofs," *NYTBR*, 15 March 1987, 13). Norman Mailer has discussed his particular intentions in writing *The Executioner's Song* in an "objective" style (Michiko Kakutani, "Mailer Talking," *NYTBR*, 5 June 1982, 39–40).

The quotation is of E. L. Doctorow in Bruce Weber, "The Myth Maker," 78. Wilfred Sheed points out that *The Executioner's Song* is called fiction, though it is about real people, while Bob Woodward and Scott Armstrong's *The Brethren* is called nonfiction even though it is partly based on conjecture. In *The Basement,* which is based on a true incident, Kate Millet wrote that she "invented" her character, though the publisher described the book as nonfiction (Michiko Kakutani, "Do Facts and Fiction Mix?" *NYTBR*, 27 January 1980, 3, 28–29). Kakutani notes that, "in *Hustling,* her study of prostitution, Gail Sheehy constructed composite characters from various individuals she had interviewed. In her 'interpretive biography,' *Closing Time: The True Story of the 'Goodbar' Murder,* Lacey Fosburgh allowed that she had 'created scenes or dialogue I think it is reasonable and fair to assume could have taken place, perhaps even did.' Mr. Woodward and Mr. Armstrong note in the preface [to *The Brethren*] that they 'attributed thoughts, feelings, conclusions, predispositions and motivations to each of the justices'" (ibid., 28–29). Moreover, journalists too are augmenting their work in this way. Tom Wolfe, who invented the phrase *new journalism,* claims not only that journalism can examine behavior, as it has always done, but that it can also explain motivation, by "giving the reader the feeling of being inside the character's mind and experiencing the emotional reality of the scene as he experienced it" (ibid., 29). See also the reviews by Pete Hamill of *Cold Storage*, by Wendell Rawls, Jr. (*NYTBR*, 24 February

1980, 13), and of *Who Killed Karen Silkwood,* by Howard Kohn (*NYTBR,* 13 December 1981, 34). In the latter review, Hamill, himself a journalist, referred to those "accursed 'non-fiction novels,' unbelievable as history, unacceptable as fiction." Hamill objected to Kohn's reconstruction of Karen Silkwood's inner thoughts, about which he could not have known. See also, e.g., Theodore Draper's critique of Strobe Talbott's *Deadly Gambits, NYTBR,* 9 December 1984, 3, 32–34.

7. Norman Mailer claimed that he did his best to make *The Executioner's Song* a factually accurate account, and Truman Capote stated that *In Cold Blood* is based on all the techniques of fictional art, though the book is also "immaculately factual" (Kakutani, "Do Facts and Fiction Mix?" 28). On the other hand, the novelist Donald Windham, an estranged friend of Capote's, has claimed that the two main characters in Capote's book were dead before the book appeared and that "the only living authority for the factualness of much of the narrative was Truman himself. It was a perfect setup for his kind of invention" (see John Howland, Jr., review of *Lost Friendships: A Memoir of Truman Capote, Tennessee Williams and Others,* by Donald Windham (New York, 1987), *Newsday,* 10 March 1987, pt. 2, 9. See the discussion in Kakutani, "Do Facts and Fiction Mix?" of, e.g., Gore Vidal's *Burr* and Rhoda Lerman's *Eleanor.* Lerman stated elsewhere (Herbert Mitgang, "Fiction Factions," *NYTBR,* 29 April 1979, 54) that she had done three years of research on Eleanor Roosevelt at Hyde Park but felt that she could not use what she knew except in a novel. See also James Lardner, "The Endangered Quotation Mark," *NYTBR,* 15 January 1984, 12.

8. Doctorow's statement appeared in Kakutani, "Do Facts and Fiction Mix?" 28–29. See also Cushing Strout, "The Antihistorical Novel," in *The Veracious Imagination: Essays on American History, Literature and Biography* (Middletown, Conn., 1985), 183–98.

9. David Leavitt, review of *World's Fair,* by E. L. Doctorow, *NYTBR,* 10 November 1985, 3.

10. The first quotation is of Justin Kaplan, "In Pursuit of the Ultimate Fiction," *NYTBR,* 19 April 1987, 24. The second is of Shirley Christian, "The Revolution Seizes the Pen," *NYTBR,* 27 January 1985, 24. The third is of Kaplan, "In Pursuit of the Ultimate Fiction." "Historians know they're not objective. Why should fiction writers be denied the composition of history?" (E. L. Doctorow quoted in Weber, "The Myth Maker," 42).

11. Michiko Kakutani, review of *The Real Life of Alejandro Mayta,* by Mario Vargas Llosa, *New York Times,* 8 January 1986, sec. C, 21.

12. Erica Jong, "The Life We Live and the Life We Write," *NYTBR,* 10 February 1985, 26. See also the comments on Harry B. Henderson's estimate of the ability of novelists to blend fact and fiction successfully in Thomas Fleming, "Inventing Our Probable Past," *NYTBR,* 6 July 1986, 20.

13. A remark made in passing by Yasmine Gooneratne, quoted in a review by Steven R. Weisman of her *Relative Merits: A Personal Memoir of the Bandaranaike Family of Sri Lanka, NYTBR,* 21 September 1986, 43. Perry Meisel noted that a work of fiction could be a historiographic achievement ("Young Wittgenstein," *NYTBR,* 11 October 1987, 18).

14. Nicola Chiaromonte, *The Paradox of History* (Philadelphia, 1985), xxi.

15. Hayden White, review of *The Paradox Of History,* by Nicola Chiaromonte, *NYTBR,* 22 September 1985, 7.

16. The first quotation is of Cynthia Ozick, "The Muse, Postmodern and Homeless," 9. (See also the remarks of Philip Roth in William H. Gass, "Deciding to Do the Impossible," *NYTBR,* 24 January 1987, 24.) The second is of George Levine, "Darwin and the Evolution of Fiction," *NYTBR,* 5 October 1986, 61.

17. The two quotations on independence from factual fidelity and mythopoeic history are from George Garrett, "Young Fenians in Love and History," *NYTBR,* 3 January 1988, 26. Garrett writes, "Mythopoeic historical fiction, though it may often prove to be faithful to the facts, is primarily concerned with other things, and whatever else it may be, is comfortably contemporary in its professed values, its vices and virtues." The other quotes in that section are from Michiko Kakutani, "Books of the Times," *New York Times,* 7 January 1987, sec. C, 24, quoting here Robert Coover.

18. The different statements appear, respectively, in Mitgang, "Fiction Factions," 54 (quoting the novelist Rhoda Lerman); Walter Lord, "Can't Anybody Here Fight This War?" *NYTBR,* 13 September 1987, 9; and Jay Cantor, "Don't Cry for Him," *NYTBR,* 22 May 1988, 16. J. M. Coetzee stated in his review of *Waiting: The Whites of South Africa,* by Vincent Crapanzano (*NYTBR,* 14 April 1985, 28), that "historical explanations, and in particular historical explanations of the self, no longer have much hold" on South African youths or their contemporaries around the world.

19. Hannah Arendt, *On Revolution* (New York, 1969), 82–85.

20. George Steiner wrote that Stendahl, Conrad, and Manzoni "brought to immediate enactment in the lives of essentially private, ordinary men and women the turbulence, the corrupting claims, the seductions of ideological and class conflicts. They made graphic, as no political history or theory can, the 'totalitarian' quality in all modern bureaucratic nation states" ("Language under Surveillance: The Writer and the State," *NYTBR,* 12 January 1986, 36). The second quotation is from William S. McFeely, "One Nation, Perilously Divisible," *NYTBR,* 23 August 1987, 6. C. Vann Woodward has suggested other reasons for this claim, including "probably the fragmentation of history by professionals, their retreat into specializations, their abandonment of the narrative style" ("Gilding Lincoln's Lily," *New York Review of Books* 34 [24 September 1987], 23).

21. Saul Bellow did not say why this was the case (see Michiko Kakutani's interview with Bellow, *NYTBR,* 13 December 1981, 28–30). Offering his own novel *Freedom* (New York, 1987) as serious history, William Safire has also claimed that "you can get at the truth in a novel without the hangups of a historian" (see the review by Don E. Fehrenbacher of Safire's novel, *American Historical Review* 94, no. 2 [1989]: 523–24.

22. These statements appeared, respectively, in a book advertisement—a very unkind blow—*NYTBR,* 4 November 1984, 8; Mary Lee Settle, "Recapturing the Past in Fiction," *NYTBR,* 12 February 1984, 36, where her argu-

ment emphasizes the secondary and perhaps even trivial role of historians as against novelists; and Douglas Unger quoted in *NYTBR*, 5 February 1984, 8. On Mary Lee Settle, see also the review of her novel *The Scapegoat* by E. L. Doctorow, and Roger Shattuck's interview with her, in *NYTBR*, 26 October 1980, 1, 40–42, 43–45. For a list of authors in addition to Mary Lee Settle who insist on as much historical authenticity and accuracy as possible in these terms, see Garrett, "Young Fenians in Love and History," 26.

23. Nadine Gordimer quoted in *New York Times*, 14 January 1986, sec. C, 12.

24. Fleming, "Inventing Our Probable Past," 20. Fleming also wrote that "good historical novelists can reshape the skewed map of the American past in the public mind."

25. Schneider, "The Light at the End of the Novel," 23. Stout, "The Antihistorical Novel," 183–85.

26. John Patrick Diggins has pointed out, e.g., that Henry Adams was the first great historian to grasp the impossibility of writing history, a result of the fact that "neither his narrative form nor even his 'scientific' attempt to establish sequential connections yielded causal understanding." Henry James added that, because of this circumstance, the novelist must succeed to the sacred office of the historian (John Patrick Diggins, letter to the editor, *New York Review of Books* 29 [16 December 1982]: 58–59.

27. Norman Mailer quoted in "How Is Fiction Doing? A Symposium," *NYTBR*, 14 December 1980, 3. On the subject, Mailer has also said that history has become more novelistic than the novel (ibid.).

28. The first quotation is from Woodward, "Gilding Lincoln's Lily," 23; the second is from Harold Bloom, "The Central Man," *New York Review of Books* 31 (19 July 1984): 5. Other critics have been much less kind, including especially one cited by Woodward, Richard N. Current, "Fiction as History: A Review Essay," *Journal of Southern History* 52 (February 1986): 78–82; but see also Gabor S. Britt, "Looking for Lincoln in the 1980's," *NYTBR*, 8 February 1987, 35; and Justin Kaplan, "A Fat and Hungry Nation," *NYTBR*, 14 June 1987, 1, 42.

29. Kenneth Lynn, *NYTBR*, 23 September 1984, 3.

30. On Robert Coover, see Michiko Kakutani, "The Dark Side of Virtue," *New York Times*, 22 August 1987, 14; on Graham Greene, see Kathryn Morton, "The Story Telling Animal," *NYTBR*, 23 December 1984, 2; on Robert Critchfield, see Hugh Nissenson, *NYTBR*, 23 March 1986, 1, 51; on Mario Vargas Llosa, see Suzanne Jill Levine (from a summary of her earlier review of *Conversations in the Cathedral*), *NYTBR*, 4 November 1984, 42; on Carlos Fuentes, see Earl Shorris, *NYTBR*, 27 October 1985, 1, 47; and on Augusto Roa Bastos, see Carlos Fuentes's review of *I the Supreme*, *NYTBR*, 6 April 1986, 33. I might also note the promotional reference to William Safire's *Freedom* as "a significant work of history—a breakthrough book that uses fiction to reveal the truth about the sources of our freedom" (*NYTBR*, 30 August 1987, 17). On the Thomas Flanagan references, see Garrett, "Young Fenians in Love and History," 26, 27.

31. Morton, "The Story Telling Animal," 2.

32. The first quotation is of E. L. Doctorow, in Weber, "The Myth Maker," 42; the second is of William Styron, in Fleming, "Inventing Our Probable Past," 20.

33. On this statement of Hemingway's, see Raymond Carver, "Coming of Age, Going to Pieces," *NYTBR*, 17 November 1985, 3.

34. We should keep in mind that two of the things that novelists are always ready to write enthusiastically about are themselves and each other. It is really difficult to believe their own claims for insight and knowledge.

35. White, *Tropics of Discourse*, 125.

36. Banville, "Physics and Fiction," 41, 42.

37. For an indication of how crude the argument over turf can get, see the exchange of letters among Harold Holzer, Richard N. Current, and Gore Vidal, "Vidal's 'Lincoln': An Exchange," *New York Review of Books* 35 (18 August 1988): 66–69.

38. Baruch Hochman, "Doomsday as Gang Bang, or Dodging the Reality of the Holocaust," *Tikkun* 2, no. 1 (1987): 103–7.

39. Thomas was also able to observe that the life that people experienced at the time, the history that they were a part of, was beyond even Freud's considerable powers to anticipate, understand, or explain. The novelist's treatment of psychoanalysis as a failed cultural enterprise is another old story, of course. See, e.g., Erica Jong, *Fear of Flying* (New York, 1974), 143–44 (or the entire section, 121–44). The main issue here is whether novelists treat psychoanalysis scornfully or as a gallant but doomed intellectual effort. The figure of Freud appeared once in E. L. Doctorow's *Ragtime* ([New York, 1976], 39–44); Doctorow offered a version of Freud's trip to America to deliver the Clark lectures. D. M. Thomas began his fictionalized account of Central European history by offering another version of Freud's trip to America to deliver the Clark lectures (*The White Hotel* [New York, 1980], 3–6). It should be noted that Thomas has a critical sense of what psychoanalysis or psychoanalytic therapy is about, which informs his purposes as a novelist. See his review of *A Secret Symmetry: Sabina Spielrein between Jung and Freud,* by Aldo Carotenuto, *New York Review of Books* 28 (13 May 1982): 3, 6.

40. The quotation is from Sigmund Freud, "Constructions in Analysis," in *The Standard Edition of the Complete Psychological Works of Sigmund Freud,* ed. James Strachey, 24 vols. (London, 1953–74), 23:265–66 (hereafter cited as *Standard Edition* by volume and page number). On Freud's inferential leaps, see Michael Franz Basch, "Theory Formation in Chapter VII: A Critique," *Journal of the American Psychoanalytic Association* (hereafter cited as *JAPA*) 24, no. 1 (1976): 88. For Thomas's portrayal of the case history, see *The White Hotel,* 89–144; see also the "correspondence" between Freud and his patient, 181–200.

41. Psychoanalysts for obvious reasons are not always disposed to discuss these problems, but it would be naive to pretend that they are not aware of them. See Donald Spence, "Clinical Interpretation: Some Comments on the Nature of Evidence," in *Psychoanalysis and Contemporary Science,* ed. Theodore

Shapiro, vol. 5 (New York, 1978), 367–88, where all the points mentioned are discussed. See also Stanley Leavy, *The Psychoanalytic Dialogue* (New Haven, Conn., 1980), 14; and Heinz Kohut, "The Two Analyses of Mr. Z," *International Journal of Psycho-analysis* (hereafter cited as *IJPA*) 60, no. 3 (1979): 7–8. Kohut has also stated that there is no basis for deciding on the validity of interpretations among opposed points of view, specifically, Kleinian, ego psychological, or Kohutian. This suggests that the cure, whatever *cure* refers to, is in the relationship to the therapist, not in the therapist's interpretations. See Robert S. Wallerstein, "One Psychoanalysis or Many?" *IJPA* 69, no. 1 (1988): 13–14.

42. Bruno Bettelheim, *Freud and Man's Soul* (New York, 1984), 31–32, 41, 44. See also *New Yorker,* 1 March 1982, 52–93, where a substantial portion of this work was also published.

43. Darius Ornston, "Strachey's Influence: A Preliminary Report," *IJPA* 63, no. 2 (1982): 409–26, and "Freud's Conception Is Different from Strachey's, " *JAPA* 33, no. 2 (1985): 379–412, esp. 389. Patrick J. Mahoney, "Freud and His Writing," *JAPA* 32, no. 4 (1984): 847–64. The possible need for a revised *Standard Edition* was publicized in *IJPA* 65, no. 2 (1984): 214; and Malcolm Pines, "Guest Editorial," *IJPA* 66, no. 1 (1985): 1. Strachey's work, however, has also been defended. See Emmett Wilson, "Did Strachey Invent Freud?" *International Review of Psychoanalysis* 14, no. 3 (1987): 299–315.

44. Bettelheim, *Freud and Man's Soul,* viii.

45. Ibid., 5.

46. The quotation is from the work of another veteran psychoanalyst, Edward Glover, "Examination of the Klein System of Child Psychology," *Psychoanalytic Study of the Child* 1 (1945): 85. See also the discussion of aggression in Heinz Hartmann, Ernst Kris, and Rudolph M. Loewenstein, "Notes on a Theory of Aggression," *Psychoanalytic Study of the Child* 3–4 (1949): 9–36.

47. Malcolm Pines, "Guest Editorial," 1.

48. On the historical background of the choice of languauge in the *Standard Edition* and of Freud's own role in the translation of his work, see Riccardo Steiner, "A World-Wide International Trademark of Genuineness," *International Review of Psychoanalysis* 14, no. 1 (1987): 33–102.

49. Roy Schafer, "Action: Its Place in Psychoanalytic Interpretation and Theory," *Annual of Psychoanalysis* 1 (1973): 161. Schafer himself provides a brief but strong bibliography critical of Freud's positivist inclinations, including Paul Ricoeur's *Freud and Philosophy* (New Haven, Conn., 1971). Schafer has also written an appreciation of Heinz Hartmann's contribution useful to look at in this context ("An Overview of Heinz Hartmann's Contributions to Psychoanalysis," *IJPA* 51 [1970]: 279–97). Bettelheim claimed that the early Freud was positivist in the sense indicated by Schafer but that humanistic influences dominated the later work. This argument would be hard to sustain.

50. It is a taken-for-granted view in the psychoanalytic literature that psychoanalysis was intended by Freud as a natural science. Freud said that it was and that it had to be. See James G. Blight, "Psychoanalysis vs. Hermeneutics," *Psychoanalysis and Contemporary Thought* 4, no. 2 (1981): 151; Merton

Gill, "The Point of View of Psychoanalysis," *Psychoanalysis and Contemporary Thought* 6, no. 4 (1983): 523–51, esp. 533–35; Adolf Grünbaum, "Testing Psychoanalytic Theory, Pts. 1, 2," *Psychoanalysis and Contemporary Thought* 5, nos. 2, 3 (1982): 172, 311–14 (esp. 312). See also Stanley A. Leavy, "Speaking in Tongues," *Psychoanalytic Quarterly* 52, no. 1 (1983): 35.

51. Bettelheim makes the routine claim that those who emphasize the scientific side of Freud's work "possibly" seek to distance themselves from the emotional import of it. At the same time, Bettelheim notes that Anna Freud was involved with the production of the *Standard Edition,* and she was certainly involved with the *Psychoanalytic Study of the Child.* See Bettelheim's remarks in *Freud and Man's Soul,* 32, 7, 15.

52. Geertz, *The Interpretation of Cultures,* 5, 44, 345–59, 362–63.

53. Bettelheim, *Freud and Man's Soul,* 43.

54. Robert Paul, "Did the Primal Crime Take Place?" *Ethos* 4, no. 3 (1976): 311–52. Paul explained that Freud did not use the Lamarckian idea in *Totem and Taboo,* although critics routinely claim that he did. Freud did use it shortly thereafter, however, as noted below.

55. On historical development, see Weinstein and Platt, *Psychoanalytic Sociology;* on language, see John Forrester, *Language and the Origins of Psychoanalysis* (New York, 1980).

56. Sigmund Freud, *The Psychopathology of Everyday Life,* in *Standard Edition,* 6:259.

57. Quoted in Paul, "Did the Primal Crime Take Place?" 319–20.

58. Sigmund Freud, *Civilization and Its Discontents,* in *Standard Edition,* 21:130–31.

59. Henry Edelheit, "On the Biology of Language," in *Psychiatry and the Humanities,* ed. Joseph H. Smith, vol. 3, (New Haven, Conn., 1978), 62.

60. Sigmund Freud, *An Outline of Psychoanalysis,* in *Standard Edition,* 23:188.

61. Jean G. Schimek, "A Critical Re-examination of Freud's Concept of Unconscious Mental Representation," *International Review of Psychoanalysis* 2 (1975): 173. Daniel Rancour-Laferriere, "Sociobiology and Psychoanalysis," *Psychoanalysis and Contemporary Thought* 4, no. 4 (1981): 439.

62. Oliver Sacks quoted in *NPAP News and Reviews* 1 (Winter 1987): 4.

63. "Scientific Proceedings, Panel Reports," *JAPA* 33, no. 1 (1985): 170.

64. Warren S. Poland, "The Analyst's Words," *Psychoanalytic Quarterly* 55, no. 2 (1986): 258.

65. Charles Brenner, "Some Observations on Depression, on Nosology, on Affects, and on Mourning," *Journal of Geriatric Psychiatry* 7, no. 1 (1974): 10.

66. Theresa Benedek quoted in O. H. D. Bloomfield, "Psychoanalytic Supervision," *International Review of Psychoanalysis* 12, no. 4 (1985): 405.

67. Marshall Edelson, *Hypothesis and Evidence in Psychoanalysis* (Chicago, 1984), 136–37. See also, e.g., Harold P. Blum, "The Position and Value of Extra-Transference Interpretation," *JAPA* 31, no. 3 (1983): 590.

68. See, however, Lillian B. Rubin, *Quiet Rage: Bernie Goetz in a Time of Madness* (New York, 1986). Rubin explained the behavior of Goetz ("the subway gunman") in psychoanalytic terms, although she never interviewed her subject; she acquired knowledge of his childhood experiences through interviews with his sisters. This is a bizarre procedure for a psychoanalyst or a psychoanalytic text.

69. Bettelheim, *Freud and Man's Soul,* 47–48.

70. On multiple meanings of myths and symbols, see Mary Douglas, "The Meaning of Myth," in *The Structural Study of Myth and Totemism,* ed. Edmund Leach (London, 1967), 49–69.

71. See the exchange between John Bowlby, "Grief and Mourning in Infancy and Early Childhood," and Anna Freud, "Discussion of Dr. John Bowlby's Paper," *Psychoanalytic Study of the Child* 15 (1960): 9–52, and 53–62.

72. On psychoanalysis as meaning seeking, see Jacob A. Arlow and Arnold Rothstein, "Interpretation: Toward a Contemporary Interpretation of the Term" (panel report), *JAPA* 31, no. 1 (1983): 237; Arnold Goldberg, "The Scientific Status of Empathy," *Annual of Psychoanalysis* 11 (1983): 159; Richard V. Kaufman, "Oedipal Object Relations and Morality," *Annual of Psychoanalysis* 11 (1983): 245. See also, of course, Ricoeur, *Freud and Philosophy;* and Geertz, "Ideology as a Cultural System," 193–233.

73. On British object relations theorists, see Howard A. Bacal, "British Object-Relations Theorists and Self-Psychology: Some Critical Reflections," *IJPA* 68, no. 1 (1987): 81–89. On the problem of object relations in general (including British versions), see Jay R. Greenberg and Stephen A. Mitchell, *Object Relations in Psychoanalytic Theory* (Cambridge, Mass., 1983).

74. David Will, "Psychoanalysis and Philosophy of Science," *International Review of Psychoanalysis* 13, no. 3 (1986): 166.

75. On Freud's 1914 standards for psychoanalysis, see *On the History of the Psychoanalytic Movement,* in *Standard Edition,* 14:16. Also, on Freud's different definitions of what qualifies as psychoanalysis, see Arnold M. Cooper, "Psychoanalysis at One Hundred," *JAPA* 32, no. 2 (1984): 253–54. The quote is from Arnold Goldberg, "Translation between Psychoanalytic Theories," *Annual of Psychoanalysis* 12/13 (1985): 129–30.

76. Joseph Sandler, "Unconscious Wishes and Human Relationships," *Journal of Contemporary Psychoanalysis* 3, no. 2 (1981): 188. Arnold H. Modell, "Affects and the Complementarity of Biologic and Historical Meaning," *Annual of Psychoanalysis* 6 (1978): 168. Robert R. Holt, "Drive or Wish? A Reconsideration of the Psychoanalytic Theory of Motivation," in *Psychology versus Metapsychology: Psychoanalytic Essays in Memory of George S. Klein,* ed. Merton M. Gill and Philip S. Holzman, *Psychological Issues Monograph* no. 36, vol. 9, no. 4 (1976): 194.

77. Vann Spruell, "Narcissism: Theories of Treatment," *JAPA* 22, no. 2 (1974): 273. Guntrip quoted in Will, "Psychoanalysis and the Philosophy of Science," 165.

78. On these four standpoints, see, respectively, Heinz Kohut, *The Analysis of the Self* (New York, 1971) and *The Restoration of the Self* (New York,

1977); Linda Joan Kaplan, "The Concept of Family Romance," *Psychoanalytic Review* 61, no. 2 (1974): 171; Arnold H. Modell, "Self Preservation and the Preservation of the Self," *Annual of Psychoanalysis* 12/13 (1985): 70, 80, and, on D. W. Winnicott, 77. Modell also states that "there is no uniformity of opinion within psychoanalysis" (82). Modell's response to the problem of fragmentation or diversity is to attempt a synthesis of several of these standpoints by way of reintegrating the discipline, while Arnold Goldberg's response is that it does not matter, for this is the situation at the moment and the terms are not translatable ("Translation between Psychoanalytic Theories"). Modell also refers here (75–76) to Kohut's questioning of the centrality of the Oedipus complex.

79. On the work of Winnicott, see the essays in Simon A. Grolnick and Leonard Barkin, eds., *Between Reality and Fantasy: Transitional Objects and Phenomena* (New York, 1979). I do not mean to suggest that Kaplan's work or Modell's is the equivalent in scope or stature of Kohut's or Winnicott's, only that they present yet other interesting, competing points of view. The last major discussion is Max Schur, *The Id and the Regulatory Principles of Mental Functioning* (New York, 1966). See also Michael E. Shulman, "On the Problem of the Id in Psychoanalytic Theory," *IJPA* 68, no. 2 (1987): 161–73. On the other aspects, see Darius Ornston, letter to the editor, *JAPA* 34, no. 2 (1987): 491.

80. Slowly but surely psychoanalysts are themselves coming to this same conclusion. See Wallerstein, "One Psychoanalysis or Many?" Wallerstein (along with Joseph Sandler) believes that psychoanalysts ought to strive for "a unitary clinical theory that is empirically testable" because the larger metapsychological inferences are in the realm of intellectual commitments and moral values. There is thus far and for the long term no valid basis for choosing one theoretical standpoint over another (see 15–17). The same is then true for a strictly psychoanalytic psychohistory. This still leaves room for psychobiography perhaps, but only for elite figures, given any kind of reasonable standard, and this raises ideological problems of another sort.

81. Sigmund Freud, *Group Psychology and the Analysis of the Ego*, in *Standard Edition*, 18·69. On phylogenetic assumptions, e.g., see Herbert Marcuse, *Eros and Civilization* (New York, 1962), 50–51.

82. Current research indicates that children experience family life differently, that there are different "microenvironments" in a household; in families, the differences among siblings are greater than the similarities. In a sense, psychoanalysts always knew this, and they would not try to predict the outcome of life for two children in the same family. See Daniel Goleman's report in the *New York Times*, 28 July 1987, sec. C, 1, 5.

83. The long quotation is from Clifford Geertz, *Works and Lives: The Anthropologist as Author* (Stanford, Calif., 1988), 144; see also, e.g., 135–38 and compare these pages with 5, 43, 362–63 of Geertz's *The Interpretation of Cultures*. The short quotation on "diverse phenomena" is from ibid., 44. I did not include the problem of self-conception or identity, but identity in these terms should be conceived of as situational and people as having multiple life histories. Among other things, as the self is constituted in relation to others

and to changing situations, it is hard to imagine the self being something constant over time. On the question of life histories, see Roy Schafer, *The Analytic Attitude* (New York, 1983), 204–11.

84. George Kennan, "History, Literature and the Road to Peterhof," *NYTBR*, 29 June 1986, 42. See also Fleming, "Inventing Our Probable Past."

85. Stone is quoted in Randall, "Why Scholars Become Storytellers."

86. William Bennet, review of *Fit for America*, by Harvey Green, *NYTBR*, 23 March 1986, 32.

87. Leon Litwak, review of *The Crucible of Race*, by Joel Williamson, *NYTBR*, 16 September 1984, 12.

88. Andrzej Walicki, *A History of Russian Thought from the Enlightenment to Marxism*, trans. Hilda Andrews-Rusiecka (Stanford, Calif., 1979), 20.

89. Karl Marx, *The Eighteenth Brumaire of Louis Bonaparte* (New York, 1968), 16, 47.

90. See Frederic Jameson, review of *The Family Idiot: Gustave Flaubert, 1821–1856*, by Jean-Paul Sartre, *NYTBR*, 27 December 1981, 5.

91. Michael Haines, *Fertility and Occupation: Population Patterns in Industrialization* (New York, 1979), 244–49. Konrad H. Jarausch has stated that "theoretical agnosticism tends toward numerical antiquarianism," but it is more appropriate to state that agnosticism in the matter of subjective intentions leads to numerical (as well as to narrative) antiquarianism ("Quantitative History in Transition," *AHA Perspectives* 20, no. 6 [September 1982]: 16). Lawrence Stone has also commented on this dilemma of quantitative history ("History and the Social Sciences in the Twentieth Century," 36–39). Stone has been criticized in turn by Charles Tilly for his comments (*As Sociology Meets History* [New York, 1981], 36–37).

92. Edmund S. Morgan, "Heaven Can't Wait," *New York Review of Books* 31 (31 May 1984): 33.

93. Michel Foucault, *The Order of Things* (London, 1970), 364, 374.

94. Jacques Barzun, *Clio and the Doctors: Psycho-History, Quanto-History and History* (Chicago, 1974), 60, 69, 146; David Stannard, *Shrinking History: On Freud and the Failure of Psychohistory* (New York, 1980), 121. Freud's standard for psychoanalysis in 1914 (*On the History of the Psychoanalytic Movement*, 16) included transference and resistance, implying unconscious mental contents and conflicts. By this standard, Barzun's and Stannard's conclusions are psychoanalytic. Frank Kermode has written that, "if a narrative emerges, possessing the virtues of plausibility, causal connection, and closure, it may well provide a measure of satisfaction; but these after all are the virtues of fiction, and fiction that completely satisfies such conventional requirements can be suspected of mendacity" ("What Nathalie Knew," *New York Review of Books* 31 [25 October 1984]: 49). See also Lawrence Stone, review of *The Puritan Way of Death*, by David Stannard, *New York Review of Books* (12 October 1978): 44.

Frederick Crews has also written of psychoanalysis as "a pseudoscience trafficking in dogma." The resiliency of psychoanalysis, he states, "lies not in intellectual virtues possessed by the theory but in the nature of its appeal to its adherents, most of whom have undergone an unnerving and cathartic experience of thought reform that has no counterpart outside the realms of religious and political indoctrination. Indeed . . . psychoanalysis shows every sign of being not just a method and a psychology but also a faith, with all that this implies about psychic immunity from rationally based criticism." In form, this is a highly abstract, theoretical statement that bypasses the surface variety and the consciously expressed belief to the contrary of a large number of people, locating a shared and contradictory belief underneath. It is a statement—and we do not have much choice in the use of languauge because the kind of non-psychoanalytic social-psychology that ought to undergird and justify it does not exist—that involves unconscious dynamic mental activity, transference, repression, and identification. If we had to describe the process by which all this mental activity occurs—people who persist in calling themselves scientists but whose thought is not correctible by rational argument, who mistake faith for science, who resolutely fail to acknowledge the requirements of scientific endeavor that consciously they understand and claim to adhere to and who reinforce the error, acting as "facilitators" for each other—we would not be as remote from Freud's expired conception of mass psychology as Crews would like to be. On the other hand, if there is no intention of addressing the issue of process, then the statement about content is relevant only in the terms described by Hayden White and not different in fact from the dogmatic statements that Freudians are declared to make. According to Crews, the crucial criterion with respect to psychoanalysis is falsifiability. If I could figure out how Crews's own statement could be put to the same test, I would think a lot more of the critique than I do. (Frederick Crews, "Beyond Sulloway's Freud: Psychoanalysis Minus the Myth of the Hero," in *Skeptical Engagements* [New York, 1986], 89.)

95. Gore Vidal, letter to the editors, *New York Review of Books* 35 (28 April 1988): 56.

96. In John Gardner's novel *Freddy's Book* (New York, 1980), one of the characters mutters, "Pseudohistory," while another relates, "I blinked, not sure whether it was a joke or a slip of the tongue, and tentatively corrected him, my tone ironic: 'Psychohistory'" (31). See also Britt, "Looking for Lincoln in the 1980's."

97. Historians sometimes do not even bother with a middle term; they just make assertions. On the subject of a "middle term," see Geertz, *The Interpretation of Cultures*, 207.

98. See, e.g., the chapter "The Phenomenology of Peter L. Berger," in *Cultural Analysis*, by Robert Wuthnow et al. (New York, 1986), 21–76.

99. There was an incident following the Statue of Liberty centennial celebration in New York in which a deranged individual, just released from the mental ward of a New York hospital, attacked passengers on the Staten Island ferry, killing and wounding a number of them. In this context, with questions raised about what psychiatrists and hospital administrators could have been thinking about when they released this individual, it was reported in the *New York Times* that psychiatrists do not yet have a measure that will allow them to predict who will or will not be violent that is even crudely accurate (Daniel

Goleman, "Tough Call for Psychiatrists: Deciding Who Is Dangerous," 13 July 1986, 18). It has also been publicly reported, e.g., that "quantitative measurements of criminal behavior are notoriously imprecise." Professional observers are skeptical of efforts "to predict criminality or to intervene in child development." (Earl Lane, "Predicting Lives of Crime," *Long Island Newsday*, 4 June 1985, 11.)

100. These two contradictory statements appeared in the same article, Daniel Goleman, "The Roots of Terrorism Are Found in Brutality of Shattered Childhood," *New York Times*, 2 September 1986, sec. C, 1, 8. There are of course disclaimers that appear in this type of article; i.e., "no generalization will fit every terrorist." But what reader will try to fathom the complexities suggested by that statement, especially when it is also stated, without qualification, explanation, and especially without reference to the statement of the psychiatrists mentioned in n. 99 above, that "the loss of traditions that give meaning to life leaves people prey to extreme ideologies" or that "the hallmark of the fanatic's ideology is an apocalyptic vision that divides the world into good and evil," and so on. For one newspaper commentary on another of these issues, successful career women leaving the work force to be at home with their children, see Brenda Lane Richardson, "Professional Women Do Go Home Again," *New York Times*, 20 April 1988, sec. C, 1, 10.

101. On why women are psychotherapy's best customers, see Katha Pollitt, *New York Times*, 9 January 1986, sec. C, 2. On the American fascination with Sherlock Holmes, see Karl E. Meyer, *New York Times*, 5 January 1986, Arts and Leisure section, 1, 19. On athletes and drugs, see "Why Athletes Turn to Drugs?" *New York Times*, 30 August 1987, sec. 5, 8; on why people want to be scared silly, see *Long Island Newsday*, 15 October 1987, pt. 2, 5. On fan violence at soccer matches, see Clive Toy, "Why Soccer Serves as a Vehicle for Fan Violence," *New York Times*, 2 June 1985, Sports section, 2. Lionel Tiger suggested that the Cabbage Patch doll craze seemed "like a grotesque symptom of a profound historical shift in the meaning and rate of childbearing" (*NYTBR*, 26 February 1984, 13). On the family conflict over who gets to use the television remote control, a problem that seems to arise "when more than one member of the family needs to feel secure," see "Relationships," *New York Times*, 17 November 1986, sec. B, 10. A Soviet commentator offered an explanation of the popularity of Rubik's cube—it had to do with America's loss of control around the globe leading to a compensatory need to master the cube— but I have lost the reference. On the other hand, on Soviet views of fan violence at soccer matches, see Flora Lewis, *New York Times*, 9 June 1985, 19. See also Ira Berkow, "The Abundance of Skullduggery in Baseball," *New York Times*, 23 August 1987, Sports section, 3; and Neil G. Bennett and David E. Bloom, "Why Fewer American Women Marry," *New York Times*, 13 December 1986, 27. Seymour Martin Lipset, "Why Youth Revolt," *New York Times*, 24 May 1989, sec. A, 31.

102. This quotation is from the *New York Times*, 14 March 1983, Sports section, 2.

103. On the Oreo Cookie, see William R. Greer, "Oreo at 75, the

World's Favorite Cookie," *New York Times,* 4 June 1986, sec. C, 6. Greer is quoting here Harold J. Kassarjian, a consumer psychologist at the University of California, Los Angeles, the editor of the *Journal of Consumer Research.* The reference in the second quotation is to revived interest in the liberal arts (Edward B. Fiske, "Liberal Arts, Long in Decline, Are Reviving around the Nation," *New York Times,* 9 November 1986, 1, 34). The individual quoted is Joseph D. Duffey, chancellor of the University of Massachusetts. On computerized games, see Eric Schmitt, "L. I. Photon Soldiers Zap Foes for Free," *New York Times,* 31 August 1987, sec. B, 3.

104. Erich Fromm, *Man for Himself* (New York, 1947); T. W. Adorno et al., *The Authoritarian Personality* (New York, 1950); Erik H. Erikson, *Childhood and Society* (New York, 1950); David Riesman, *The Lonely Crowd* (New York, 1950); Marcuse, *Eros and Civilization;* Kenneth Keniston, *The Uncommitted: Alienated Youth in American Society* (New York, 1960), *Young Radicals: Notes on Committed Youth* (New York, 1968), and *Youth and Dissent: The Rise of a New Opposition* (New York, 1971); Charles A. Reich, *The Greening of America* (New York, 1970); Christopher Lasch, *The Culture of Narcissism* (New York, 1979).

105. Keniston, *The Uncommitted,* 8–9 and *Young Radicals,* 17–18. The shift in Keniston's subject matter between 1960 and 1968 is revealed in the subtitles of his books. Keniston is always careful to explain the sources of his data, particularly the background of the people he is dealing with and their numbers. *The Uncommitted* is actually based on interviews with thirty-six Harvard students, twelve of whom are described as normal and twelve more as mildly alienated, leaving twelve as "deeply disaffected." Similar numbers are given in *Young Radicals (The Uncommitted, 14; Young Radicals,* 11, 14). The question is, however, whether readers took these numbers into account when they used these texts. On this, see, e.g., Saul Friedländer, *History and Psychoanalysis,* trans. Susan Suleiman (New York, 1978), 111. The quotation from Reich's *The Greening of America* is on 234, but see also 223, 225–34. The quotation from Lasch's *The Culture of Narcissism* is on 82, but see also 23, 89.

106. Marcuse, *Eros and Civilization,* 162 64. The problem of narcissism was by then emerging as a theme in psychoanalysis generally. See Annie Reich, *Annie Reich: Psychoanalytic Contributions* (New York, 1973).

107. Henry Malcolm, *Generation of Narcissus* (Boston, 1971), 144–45, 153–54. For Lasch's emphasis on secondary narcissism as distinct from Marcuse's emphasis on primary narcissism, see Lasch, *The Culture of Narcissism,* 79.

108. Consider the youthful support for George McGovern in 1972 (Michael Novak referred to the McGovern rally at Madison Square Garden during the presidential campaign of that year as a celebration of "the resurrection of our youth culture") and the admiration and support of similarly youthful individuals for the character and politics of Ronald Reagan in 1980 and after or, for that matter, the more recent claim, which also runs counter to the taken-for-granted logic of psychoanalysis and the social sciences, that "the 'me decade' has come to an end and people are increasingly receptive to calls for cooperation, compassion and even a degree of sacrifice" (Michael Novak, *Choosing Our*

King [New York, 1974], 225, 228). Robert S. McElvaine, "The Kennedy Complex," *New York Times,* 27 September 1987, sec. E, 23. On Robert Bellah's aspirations for community and that of his coauthors (*Habits of the Heart*), see Gerald M. Platt and Rhys H. Williams, "Religion, Ideology and Electoral Politics," *Society* (July/August 1988): 38–45.

109. Gordon S. Wood, *The Creation of the American Republic* (New York, 1969), 389. Wood refers often to the discontinuity (449, 472, 524, 594, 606) and heterogeneity (esp. 484, 491–92) of the American Revolution.

110. Eugen Weber, cited on the editorial page of the *Long Island Newsday,* 4 July 1986, 58. It was difficult to pass up the emancipatory significance of the date.

111. On this same Independence Day, 4 July 1986, there appeared in the *New York Times* (sec. C, 23) a review by Herbert Mitgang of *Why the South Lost the Civil War,* by Richard Beringer et al., wherein it was explained how, during the Civil War, the Confederate leadership altered their conception of fundamental war aims. But this was better explained by C. Vann Woodward in a review that appeared the same week in the *New York Review of Books,* "Gone with the Wind," 33 (17 July 1986): 3–6.

112. George Levine, "Darwin and the Evolution of Fiction," *NYTBR,* 5 October 1986, 61.

113. G. W. F. Hegel, *Philosophy of Right,* trans. T. M. Knox (Oxford, 1958), 84, 280, 286. Jacob Burckhardt, *The Civilization of the Renaissance in Italy,* trans. S. G. C. Middlemore (Oxford, 1945), pt. 2, p. 81.

114. Philip Rieff, *The Triumph of the Therapeutic* (1966) (Chicago, 1987), x.

115. The data on therapy appeared in Morton Hunt, "Navigating the Therapy Maze," *New York Times Magazine,* 30 August 1987, 28. Recent entries in the therapeutic field include such things as forum, insight, actualizations, Silva mind control, and lifespring. But interest in new forms of metaphysical religion, mediums, the occult, reincarnation, psychic healing, satanism, and "spirit guides" must also be included. See the report by Robert Lindsey, "Spiritual Concepts Drawing a Different Breed of Adherent," *New York Times,* 29 September 1986, sec. A, 1, and sec. B, 12. Mark Landler, "Selling Practical Enlightenment," New York Times, 13 March 1988, sec. E, 7.

Chapter Two

1. Jean-Jacques Rousseau, *The First and Second Discourses,* ed. Roger D. Masters, trans. Roger D. Masters and Judith R. Masters (New York, 1964), "Discourse on the Sciences and Arts," 51, and "Discourse on the Origin and Foundations of Inequality," 141, 150–61, 172–73, 176–77. See also Michael Ignatieff, "John Millar and Individualism," in *Wealth and Virtue: The Shaping of Political Economy in the Scottish Enlightenment,* ed. Istvan Hont and Michael Ignatieff (Cambridge, 1983), 340; William Charlton et al., *The Christian Response to Industrial Capitalism* (London, 1986), 31.

2. Alexis de Tocqueville, *The Old Regime and the French Revolution,* trans. Stuart Gilbert (New York, 1955), 107.

3. Rousseau began his inquiry in *The Social Contract* (trans. Willmoore Kendall [Chicago, 1954]) by considering the possibility of an integrative principle, taking first the family, explaining that, once the child no longer needs the parents, the natural bond is dissolved and that if they continue together it is out of choice so that even the family is kept together by agreement and not by natural necessity (1–4).

4. Louis-Antoine Saint-Just, *Oeuvres Complètes,* ed. Charles Vellay, 2 vols. (Paris, 1908), 2:228–41, 272–77, 305–32, esp. 329–32, 376–87, 477, 483–84. The French on all sides remained sensitive to the problem of factions, i.e., multiple interests and multiple perspectives. See, e.g., Alexandre Keller, *Bonaparte et le coup d'état,* vol. 5 of *Correspondance, bulletins et ordres du jour de Napoléon,* 5 vols (Paris, n.d.), 60–63.

5. Tocqueville, *The Old Regime and the French Revolution,* 136–37, 94.

6. Georg Simmel quoted by Tom Bottomore and David Frisby in the introduction to their translation of Simmel's *The Philosophy of Money* (London, 1978), 25.

7. Alexis de Tocqueville, *Democracy in America,* trans. Henry Steele Commager, 2 vols. (New York, 1947) 2:273, 280, 292.

8. Friedrich Schiller, *Essays Aesthetical and Philosophical* (London, 1910), letter 6, 37–44. Rieff, *The Triumph of the Therapeutic.*

9. Quoted in Jürgen Habermas, *Knowledge and Human Interest,* trans. Jeremy J. Schapiro (Boston, 1971), 297–98; see all the references to Nietzsche (290–300), which are interesting in terms of the argument presented here. But see also Dominick LaCapra, "Habermas and the Grounding of Critical Theory," *History and Theory* 16, no. 3 (1977): 251.

10. Max Weber, *The Methodology of the Social Sciences,* ed. and trans. Edward A. Shils and Henry A. Finch (New York, 1949), 81. Jürgen Kocka, "The Social Sciences between Dogmatism and Decisionism: A Comparison of Karl Marx and Max Weber," in *A Weber-Marx Dialogue,* ed. Robert J. Antonio and Ronald M. Glassman (Lawrence, Kans., 1985), 140–41, 145–46, 154. This is the best available discussion of Weber's views on culture and theory.

11. George Eliot, *Middlemarch, vol. 12 of The Writings of George Eliot,* 25 vols. (Boston, 1908), 244–45.

12. Herman Melville, *The Confidence-Man: His Masquerade,* vol. 12 of *The Works of Herman Melville: The Standard Edition,* 16 vols. (New York, 1963), 8–9. Nathaniel Hawthorne ("A Peaceable Man"), "Chiefly about War Matters," *Atlantic Monthly* (July 1862): 59–60 (quoted also in Thomas Beer, *Hanna,* [New York, 1929], 49–50). This reference was provided to me by August Alfieri, a graduate student in history at the State University of New York, Stony Brook. For yet another list, see chap. 4 below.

13. Tocqueville, *Democracy in America,* 1:151, 235; 2:280–81, 285, 292.

14. Hans Gerth and C. Wright Mills, eds. and trans., *From Max Weber: Essays in Sociology* (New York, 1948), 310.

15. Durkheim, *Professional Ethics and Civil Morals,* 94. Henry Adams, *The Education of Henry Adams,* ed. Ernest Samuels (Boston, 1974), 457, 460–61.

16. George P. Landow, *Images of Crisis: Literary Iconology, 1750 to the*

Present (London, 1982). Walter E. Houghton, *The Victorian Frame of Mind* (New Haven, Conn., 1957), "Anxiety," 54–92. Stephen G. Brush, *The Temperature of History: Phases of Science and Culture in the Nineteenth Century* (New York, 1978), 61, 65, 67, 73, 103–5, 111, 123–27; Robert A. Nye, *Crime, Madness, and Politics in Modern France* (Princeton, N.J., 1984), 121–26, and "Sociology and Degeneration: The Irony of Progress," in *Degeneration: The Dark Side of Progress,* ed. J. Edward Chamberlin and Sander L. Gilman (New York, 1985), 49–71. See also George Mosse's introduction to Max Nordau's *Degeneration* (New York, 1968), xv–xxxiv. For the language of shipwreck etc., see Landow, *Images of Crisis,* 104–5, 110, 115, 121.

17. Jean-Jacques Rousseau, *Emile,* trans. Barbara Foxley (London, 1957), 320; see also 164, 295, 300, 352, 373, 418, 431–32. Bronislaw Baczko, "Rousseau and Social Marginality," *Daedalus* 107, no. 3 (1978): 35. On Herzen, see Edward Acton, *Alexander Herzen and the Role of the Intellectual Revolutionary* (London, 1979), 169. On Henry James, see Leon Edel and Lyall H. Powers, eds., *The Complete Notebooks of Henry James* (New York, 1987), 217–18, 126. The London references are 1881 and 1895, the New York reference dating from his return to the United States in 1905. Henry James, *The American Scene,* with an introduction by Leon Edel (Bloomington, Ind., 1968), 121; see generally James's comments on 84–85, 116–21, 131–39, 201.

18. Beatrice Webb quoted in Houghton, *The Victorian Frame of Mind,* 79. Arnold is quoted in Landow, *Images of Crisis,* 105. On the theme of transcendental homelessness, see Wuthnow et al., *Cultural Analysis,* 67; Richard Sennett, *The Uses of Disorder: Personal Identity and City Life* (New York, 1970), xv. Joseph Conrad, *Victory* (New York, 1932), 3. Lukacs is quoted in Bottomore and Frisby's introduction to Simmel, *The Philosophy of Money,* 17. For Henry Adams on New York, see *The Education of Henry Adams,* 499. Adolf Hitler, *Mein Kampf,* trans. Ralph Mannheim (Boston, 1971), 21–25, 30, 37, 41, 52. Sigmund Freud, *"Civilized" Sexual Morality and Modern Nervous Illness,* in *Standard Edition,* 9: 183–85. On the notion of "urban degeneration" and the changing attitude toward the city historically, see Gareth Stedman Jones, *Outcast London: A Study of the Relationship between Classes in Victorian Society* (Oxford, 1971), 127–31, 281–89. Of course, see also Robert Musil's *The Man Without Qualities,* 3–4.

19. Tocqueville, *Democracy in America,* 1:111–12, 2:310–14, 319–23, 329–32. Of course, others also saw life as remediable in these terms, notably John Stuart Mill (see Bernard Semmel, *John Stuart Mill and the Pursuit of Virtue* [New Haven, Conn., 1984], 156–88).

20. Max Weber, *Economy and Society,* ed. Guenther Roth and Claus Wittich, 2 vols. (Berkeley, Calif., 1978), 2:1399–1419.

21. Ferdinand Tönnies, *Community and Society,* trans. Charles P. Loomis (New York, 1963), 34–35, 37–42, 50, 65, 77.

22. Howard Selsam et al., *The Dynamics of Social Change* (New York, 1975), 69–81. See, e.g., the discussion in Philip Abrams, *Historical Sociology* (Ithaca, N.Y., 1982), 33–70.

23. Philip J. Kain writes of this phrase of Marx's that "we must decide

how to understand this statement" ("Marx's Dialectic Method," *History and Theory* 20 [1981]: 301). But why after 120 years do we still have to decide that?

24. The Nazis intended to legitimate the expression of emotion in everyday life, but this integration of emotion achieved a higher degree of legitimacy in Western societies in the 1960s. There was also a "blood and soil" element of Nazi ideology that was not itself a unitary thing. On the left, Franz Fanon advised revolutionaries to stay out of cities because of the anonymous quality of human contacts there (Sennett, *The Uses of Disorder,* xv).

25. T. S. Eliot's comments appear in the first of three lectures delivered by him at the University of Virginia in 1933. The lectures were subsequently published as *After Strange Gods* (New York, 1934); the quotation appears on 20. On Ezra Pound, see Robert Casillo, *The Genealogy of Demons: Anti-Semitism, Fascism, and the Myths of Ezra Pound* (Evanston, Ill., 1988), passim. On George Santayana, see John McCormick, *George Santayana: A Biography* (New York, 1987), 359–61, 364–67. Alain Robbe-Grillet related in his memoirs (*Le Miroir Qui Revient* [Paris, 1984], 116–21, 15), how his parents believed that Jews threatened to destroy the old Europe and that the Nazis would protect Europeans from this fate. Henry Adams wrote (in an essay characteristically entitled "Chaos"—after the word *education, chaos* is probably the word that recurs most often in *The Education of Henry Adams*) that, had he not been born in 1838 in the shadow of the Boston State House and brought up in the early Victorian period, he too would have adjusted himself to new conditions and made his court at the residence of the Prince of Wales, "in partnership with the American woman and the Jew banker" (*The Education of Henry Adams,* 285). On the subject of chaos, incidentally, see the headnote chosen by T. S. Eliot for *After Strange Gods.*

26. On this language of Robespierre's and its significance, see Weinstein and Platt, *The Wish to Be Free,* 108–36; Carol Blum, *Rousseau and the Republic of Virtue* (Ithaca, N.Y., 1986), 153–68, 216–59.

27. V. I. Lenin, "The Tasks of the Proletariat in Our Revolution," and "What's to be Done?" in *Collected Works,* 44 vols. (London, 1961–70), 24: 88, and 5:514n.

28. Hitler, *Mein Kampf,* 30, 51, 65.

29. Joseph de Maistre wrote, e.g., "Once let everyone rely on his individual reason in religion, and you will see immediately the rise of anarchy of belief or the annihilation of religious sovereignty. Likewise, if each man makes himself the judge of the principles of government you will see immediately the rise of civil anarchy or the annihilation of political sovereignty" (*The Works of Joseph de Maistre,* trans. Jack Lively [New York, 1965], 108).

30. Ibid., 108–9.

31. The phrase is Gordon Wood's (*The Creation of the American Republic,* 492). Wood has numerous references to the heterogeneity problem in American society (see, e.g., 484, 491–92).

32. Thomas Paine quoted in Eric Foner, "Tom Paine's Republic: Radical Ideology and Social Change," in *The American Revolution: Explorations in the*

History of Radicalism, ed. Alfred F. Young (Dekalb, Ill., 1976), 208; referred to also in Wood, *The Creation of the American Republic,* 230 (see also 236); and Melvin Yazawa, *From Colonies to Commonwealth: Familial Ideology and the Beginnings of the American Republic* (Baltimore, 1985), 117.

33. *The Federalist,* ed. Henry Cabot Lodge (New York, 1892), no. 10 (James Madison), 54.

34. Webster quoted in Michael Kammen, *A Season of Youth: The American Revolution and the Historical Imagination* (New York, 1978), 43. William R. Taylor, *Cavalier and Yankee: The Old South and American National Character* (New York, 1969), 30.

35. *The Federalist,* no. 10 (James Madison), 53.

36. Weinstein and Platt, *The Wish to Be Free,* 201–6, 213–16. Richard Buel, Jr., *Securing the Revolution: Ideology in American Politics, 1789–1815* (Ithaca, N.Y., 1972), 101.

37. Tocqueville, *Democracy in America,* 2:313.

38. V. I. Lenin, "The International and Domestic Situation of the Soviet Republic," "How to Organize Competition?" "Integrated Economic Plan," "Better Fewer, but Better," and "Purging the Party," in *Collected Works,* 33:214, 223; 26:412; 32:141–45; 33:487–90; and 33:39–40.

39. Maurice Brinton, *The Bolsheviks and Workers' Control, 1917–1921* (London, 1970), 85. Brinton writes of Bolshevism as "a monstrous aberration, the last garb donned by a bourgeois ideology . . . the last attempt of bourgeois society to reassert its ordained division into leaders and led." On Lenin as the philosopher of a bourgeois revolution, see also Karl Korsch, *Marxism and Philosophy* (London, 1970); and Serge Bricanier, *Pannakoek and the Workers' Councils,* trans. Malachy Carroll (St. Louis, 1978). It was an old criticism, but it had a particular poignancy in the late 1960s and 1970s. On this, see also Frederic J. Fleron, Jr., and Lou Jean Fleron, "Administration Theory as Repressive Political Theory: The Communist Experience," *Newsletter on Comparative Studies of Communism* 6, no. 1 (November 1972): 20, 28.

40. V. I. Lenin, "To Italian, French and German Communists," in *Collected Works,* 30:54–55.

41. V. I. Lenin, "Tenth Congress of the R.C.P. (B.)," in ibid., 32:169, 177.

42. V. I. Lenin, "A Letter to a Comrade on Our Organizational Tasks," in ibid., 6:248.

43. V. I. Lenin, "The Conditions for Admitting New Members to the Party," in ibid., 33:257.

44. T. H. Rigby, *Lenin's Government: Sovnarkom, 1917–1922* (London, 1979), 207–38.

45. At the thirteenth Party congress, Leon Trotsky delivered the most famous statement in the vein of self-effacement: "In the last instance the party is always right, because it is the only historic instrument which the working class possesses for the solution of its fundamental tasks. . . . One can only be right with the party and through the party because history has not created any other way for the realization of what is right." It is difficult to write about Trotsky in this period and not refer to this statement (see Robert V. Daniels,

The Conscience of the Revolution [Cambridge, Mass., 1960], 240; Baruch Knei-Paz, *The Social and Political Thought of Leon Trotsky* [Oxford, 1978], 379). On the last-ditch effort, see V. I. Lenin, "Letter to the Congress," in *Collected Works,* 36:593–96.

46. J. V. Stalin, "Once More on the Social Democratic Deviation in Our Party," in *Works,* 13 vols. (Moscow, 1948–55), 9:63. Stalin actually referred here to a "fractional bacchanalia" (I. V. Stalin, *Sochineniia,* 13 vols. [Moscow, 1946–51], 9:60). In this speech, Stalin charged that the opposition wanted to form another party, and he challenged them to do it. Stalin constantly returned to the related themes of bourgeois democracy, of multiple parties, and of turning the Communist party into a "discussion club" or a "parliament of opinions." See, e.g., J. V. Stalin, "Political Report of the Central Committee to the Sixteenth Congress of the C.P.S.U. (B.)," in *Works,* 12:366–67.

47. The quotation is from Jan Kavan, "Iron Curtains in East Europe Are Corroding," *Long Island Newsday,* 10 February 1988, 73. This point of view has in fact been elaborated in many places.

48. Durkheim, *Professional Ethics and Civic Morals,* 63. See also Tocqueville, *Democracy in America,* 1:111–12, 2:310–14, 319–23, 329–32, especially these last pages for the main implications of this strategy. Still another strategy for coping with the heterogeneity problem appeared in the context of the South African dictatorship, a plan to federalize the South African republic or reshape it into a cantonal system. See Frances Kendall and Leon Louw, *After Apartheid: The Solution for South Africa* (San Francisco, 1987).

49. Adorno et al., *The Authoritarian Personality.* Seymour Martin Lipset, *Political Man: The Social Base of Politics* (New York, 1963), 114–37.

50. Erich Fromm, *Escape from Freedom* (New York, 1964), 236, 221.

51. Adorno et al., *The Authoritarian Personality,* 753, 759, 762–66.

52. Shulamit Volkov, "Antisemitism as a Cultural Code: Reflections on the History and Historiography of Antisemitism in Imperial Germany," *Leo Baeck Yearbook* 23 (1978): 25–46. See also John Boyer, *Political Radicalism in Late Imperial Vienna: Origins of the Christian Social Movement, 1848–1897* (Chicago, 1981). With respect to Vienna, Boyer points out that there were so many conflicting images of Jews employed there that anti-semitism cannot be thought of as a unified standpoint.

53. Edward A. Shils, "Authoritarianism: 'Right' and 'Left,'" in *Studies in the Scope and Method of "The Authoritarian Personality,"* ed. Richard Christie and Marie Jahoda (Glencoe, Ill., 1954), 28. Apart from any immediate political considerations of a left-right sort, Adorno et al. could not have included an interpretation of the Soviet experience in their work because the psychosocial theory that they employed, which was based on familial socialization in particular conditions, did not apply to that experience, so, rather than strengthening their argument by addressing this example, they would have compromised it.

54. Gerald M. Platt, "Thoughts on a Theory of Collective Action: Language, Affect, and Ideology in Revolution," in *New Directions in Psychohistory,* ed. Mel Albin (Lexington, Mass., 1980), 75. See, e.g., Lipset, *Political Man,* 95, 148, n. 29.

55. In one famous instance, the Nazis polled 13,765,781 votes (37.4

percent of the total) in July 1932 and 11,737,000 (33.1 percent of the total) in the elections of November 1932. This shift was related at the time to an economic upturn in Germany. The point is that a shift in commitment of some two million voters over such a short period of time in a crisis situation cannot be adequately explained on the basis of class or of any other similar category. Feelings about adequacy and continuity seem more relevant (Weinstein, *Dynamics of Nazism*, 50n, 53–57).

56. See the important paper by Gerald M. Platt, "The Psychoanalytic Sociology of Collective Behavior: Material Interests, Cultural Factors and Emotional Responses," in *Advances in Psychoanalytic Sociology*, ed. Jerome Rabow, Gerald M. Platt, and Marion S. Goldman (Malabar, Fla., 1986), 215–37.

57. Tocqueville, *Democracy in America*, 2:377–82.

58. Tocqueville, *The Old Regime and the French Revolution*, 179, 175–76.

59. Ibid., 138–39, 144, 146–47.

60. Ibid., 121, 124–25, 133–34, 187.

61. Ibid., 135, 121, 124, 204.

62. Ibid., 122, 173, 187, 205, 207.

63. Max Weber, *Economy and Society*, 2:921.

64. I am following here distinctions elaborated by Platt, "The Psychoanalytic Sociology of Collective Behavior," 226.

65. Selsam et al., *The Dynamics of Social Change*, 76–77.

66. On Durkheim and Weber, see, e.g., Abrams, *Historical Sociology*, 23–34, 73–107.

67. If, as Weber argued, all knowledge is perspectival and, at the same time, the subjective significance of action must be specified, then the result, as observers will interpret the significance of action from their own perspectives of different segments of a population, is the multiplication of entities.

68. The term *latent function* is of course Robert Merton's, but see especially in these terms something like Perry Anderson, *Lineages of the Absolutist State* (London, 1974). An argument for the synthesis or integration of social and cultural dimensions has also been made, the two being related "not in any reductionist or causally a priori order but as mutually influencing aspects of behavior" (Wuthnow et al., *Cultural Analysis*, 256).

69. The quotation pertaining to different forecasts from the same data is from Robert D. Hershey, Jr., "Reading the Economic Future," *New York Times*, 7 March 1988. sec. D, 1. The other quotations and points of discussion are from James Gleick, "When Chaos Rules the Market," *New York Times*, 22 November 1987, Business section, 1, 8. Gleick has written extensively on chaos theory (*Chaos: The Making of a New Science* [New York, 1987]), the point of which is to deal with erratic behavior "that appears to be random but is not. The essence of their approach [i.e., scientists interested in chaos theory] is a search for underlying patterns of a kind that have been discovered in a wide variety of seemingly random systems" (1). Chaos theorists, in other words, imagine order to be ingrained in apparent disorder. Whether any of this has

any applicability to historical concerns remains to be seen. On the dynamic effects of the stock market crash and the reflections that it has prompted, see also Louis Uchitelle, "The Uncertain Legacy of the Crash," *New York Times,* 3 April 1988, Business section, 1, 6.

70. Tocqueville, *The Old Regime and the French Revolution,* 164. Tocqueville also wrote in his *Recollections* (ed. J. P. Mayer and A. P. Kerr, trans. George Lawrence [Garden City, N.Y., 1970], 62) that he detested absolute systems that represent all historical events as derived from some great first cause and irreversibly linked so that people are banished in effect from the history that they experience.

71. Robert Owen quoted in Noel W. Thompson, *The People's Science: The Popular Political Economy of Exploitation and Crisis, 1816–1834* (Cambridge, 1984), 202.

72. Moses Hess, "Über das Geldwesen," in *Philosophischen und sozialistischen Schriften, 1837–1850,* ed. Auguste Cornu and Wolfgang Mönke (Berlin, 1961), 346. The Marx reference is to the preface to *A Contribution to the Critique of Political Economy,* in Selsam et al., *The Dynamics of Social Change,* 53.

73. Marcuse, *Eros and Civilization,* 82.

74. The phrase *local knowledge* is Clifford Geertz's (*Local Knowledge: Further Essays in Interpretive Anthropology* [New York, 1983]). Donald Barthelme's line is cited by John Barth, "A Few Words about Minimalism," *NYTBR,* 28 December 1986, 3. Barth notes that the line is from Barthelme's novel *Snow White* (New York, 1984). I read the novel but could not find the line. Still, it could easily be there, and, in any case, it is an appropriate thought for the occasion. See also Roland Barthes, *The Grain of the Voice,* trans. Linda Coverdale (New York, 1985), 276–77.

75. Weinstein and Platt, *The Wish to Be Free,* 33–35.

76. See the asterisked note on pp. 68–69 above.

77. For the emphasis on feelings in psychoanalysis as distinct from drives and as having occurred rather recently, see Sandler, "Unconscious Wishes and Human Relationships"; Modell, "Affects and the Complementarity of Biologic and Historical Meaning"; Michael Franz Basch, "The Concept of Affect: A Reexamination," *JAPA,* vol. 24, no. 4 (1976); Frank M. Lachmann and Robert D. Stolorow, "The Developmental Significance of Affective States," *Annual of Psychoanalysis,* vol. 8 (1980); W. W. Meissner, "Can Psychoanalysis Find Its Self?" *JAPA,* vol. 34, no. 2 (1987); Sidney J. Blatt and Rebecca Smith Bahrends, "Internalization, Separation-Individuation, and the Nature of Therapeutic Action," *IJPA,* vol. 68, no. 2 (1987); and Adam Limentani, "Presidential Address: Variations on Some Freudian Themes," *IJPA* 67, no. 2 (1986): 237–39. In history, see Peter N. Stearns and Carol Z. Stearns, "Emotionology: Clarifying the History of Emotions and Emotional Standards," *American Historical Review* 90, no. 4 (October 1985): 813–36. Stearns and Stearns have also written a book on the subject (Carol Z. Stearns and Peter N. Stearns, *Anger: The Struggle for Emotional Control in America's History* [Chicago, 1986]). In sociology, see Randall Collins, "Is 1980s Sociology in the Doldrums?" *American Journal of Sociology* 91, no. 6 (May 1986): 1348–49. Collins's answer is no, and

one of the reasons is the sociological study of the emotions, which he claims is promising. It is also interesting that the traits typifying "the neurotic person" are given for lay consumption as "chronic anxiety, long periods of sadness and pessimism, unremitting tension, incessant hostility" (Daniel Goleman, "Study Affirms Link of Personality to Illness," *New York Times*, 29 January 1988, sec. C, 1).

Chapter Three

1. For what is still an excellent summary statement on the variety and uses of this kind of language, see Benjamin Nelson, "Cultural Cues and Directive Systems," in *On the Roads to Modernity: Conscience, Science and Civilizations*, ed. Toby Huff (Totowa, N.J., 1981), 17–33.

2. Berger and Luckmann, *The Social Construction of Reality*, 92–128, esp. 102–3.

3. Bertolt Brecht quoted in Peter Jelavich, "Popular Dimensions of Modernist Elite Culture," in *Modern European Intellectual History: Reappraisals and New Perspectives*, ed. Dominick LaCapra and Steven L. Kaplan (Ithaca, N.Y., 1982), 247. Michel Foucault, *Language, Counter-Memory, Practice* (New York, 1977), 207–8.

4. "Christine, a full member of the Communist Party of the Phillipines at the age of 20, is a 'mass organizer.' . . . She introduces farmers to the concepts of feudalism, imperialism and bureaucratic capitalism" (Seth Mydans, "In Truce Filipino Rebels Press a Political War," *New York Times*, 18 January 1987, sec. 1, 1).

5. The Brazilian pedagogical theorist Paolo Freire would deny this, and he has done much to try to reverse this. See, e.g., his *Pedagogy of the Oppressed*, trans. Myra Bergman Ramos (New York, 1972).

6. Egon Bittner, "Radicalism and the Organization of Radical Movements," *American Sociological Review* 28, no. 6 (1963): 928–40.

7. Raymond Williams, *Marxism and Literature* (London, 1978), 55. I have changed the order in which Williams listed these several definitions of ideology.

8. On the subject of false consciousness, see, most recently, the interchange between John Ashworth, "The Relationship between Capitalism and Humanitarianism," and Thomas L. Haskell, "Convention and Hegemonic Interest in the Debate over Antislavery: A Reply to Davis and Ashworth," *American Historical Review* 92, no. 4 (October 1987): 815, and 861.

9. The unacceptable logic of Marx's treatment of ideology as false consciousness is discussed by Walter Carlsnaes, *The Concept of Ideology and Political Analysis* (Westport, Conn., 1981), 59–63.

10. On the distinction between Marx's use of ideology and Lenin's, see ibid., 23–88, 101–59, esp. 111.

11. For a variety of other views on the subject, see John B. Thompson, *Studies in the Theory of Ideology* (Berkeley, Calif., 1984), 73–147. For Clifford

Geertz's particular conception of ideology, see his "Ideology as a Cultural System," 193–233, esp. 218–19.

12. See Schafer, *The Analytic Attitude,* 88.

13. Nietzsche quoted in Habermas, *Knowledge and Human Interest,* 296; see also LaCapra, "Habermas and the Grounding of Critical Theory."

14. The quoted statement is that of Adam Ferguson, in Thomas Bender, *New York Intellect* (New York, 1987), 4. Rousseau, *Emile,* 159–65, 414. See also Allan Bloom, "The Education of Democratic Man," *Daedalus* 107, no. 3 (1978): 138–39.

15. Carlsnaes, *The Concept of Ideology and Political Analysis,* 110–11, 128, 138. Abraham Ascher, *Pavel Axelrod and the Development of Menshevism* (Cambridge, Mass., 1972), 198–99.

16. Marx, *The Eighteenth Brumaire of Louis Bonaparte,* 15, 47.

17. Karl Marx and Friedrich Engels, *The Manifesto of the Communist Party,* trans. Samuel Moore, in *Karl Marx: The Essential Writings,* ed. Frederic L. Bender, 251 (New York, 1972).

18. Weinstein and Platt, *The Wish to Be Free,* 203.

19. Eugene D. Genovese, *The Political Economy of Slavery* (New York, 1967), 208.

20. Roy Schafer, "The Loving and Beloved Superego," *Psychoanalytic Study of the Child* 15 (1960): 163–88.

21. See, e.g., Emile Durkheim, *The Elementary Forms of Religious Life,* trans. Joseph Ward Swain (New York, 1965), 29–30, 238–40, and 239, n. 6.

22. Peter Winch, *The Idea of a Social Science and Its Relation to Philosophy* (London, 1958), 111–20. See also the discussion and references in Jürgen Habermas, *The Theory of Communicative Action,* trans. Thomas McCarthy, 2 vols. (Boston, 1984), 1:53–55.

23. See the discussion in Carlsnaes, *The Concept of Ideology and Political Analysis,* 59–63.

24. Geertz, "Ideology as a Cultural System," 194–95.

25. As Louis Althusser put it for his own contradictory purposes, "There is no practice except by and in ideology; there is no ideology except by the subject and for subjects." The point is that ideology is always a matter of "base," not "superstructure." On Althusser in this context, see Thompson, *Studies in the Theory of Ideology,* 90–96.

26. Talcott Parsons, *Personality and Social Structure* (Glencoe, Ill., 1951), 19. Mary Douglas, *Purity and Danger: An Analysis of the Concepts of Pollution and Taboo* (Binghamton, N.Y., 1980), 129–39. Lawrence Kohlberg, *The Psychology of Moral Development: The Nature and Validity of Moral Stages* (San Francisco, 1984). Richard B. Weiner, *Cultural Marxism and Political Sociology* (Beverly Hills, Calif., 1981).

27. For fantasy's early disparagement, see James Miller, *Rousseau: Dreamer of Democracy* (New Haven, Conn., 1984), 9. On its identification with psychoanalysis or psychohistory, see the interesting paper by Neil J. Smelser, "Collective Myths and Fantasies," in *Advances in Psychoanalytic Sociology,* ed. Rabow, Platt, and Goldman, 316–28.

28. "Violent fantasy" appears in Haskell, "Convention and Hegemonic Interest in the Debate over Antislavery," 850 (the context in which this phrase appears is not self-evident, and the reader is invited to examine the text); "collective fantasy" in Geertz, *Local Knowledge,* 40, 47; "fantasies of ritual" in Leon Edel, introducution to *The Complete Notebooks of Henry James,* ed. Edel and Powers, xiii; "the erotic, fantastic components" in Joan W. Scott, "Gender: A Useful Category of Historical Analysis," *American Historical Review* 91, no. 5 (December 1986): 1060 (the reference is to Jessica Benjamin, "Master and Slave: The Fantasy of Erotic Domination," in *Powers of Desire: The Politics of Sexuality,* ed. Ann Snitow, Christine Stansell, and Sharon Thompson (New York, 1983), 280–99. Rousseau's "fantasy" in Frank E. Manuel, "A Dream of Eupsychia," *Daedalus* 107, no. 3 (1978): 2; the capitalists "engaged in . . . the exchange of fantasies" or gambling on wish fulfillments in J. G. A. Pocock, *Virtue, Commerce, and History* (New York, 1985), 98–100, 112; "creatures of fantasy" in Nicholas Phillipson, "Adam Smith as Civic Moralist," in *Wealth and Virtue,* ed. Hont and Ignatieff, 189; "the prevalent fantasy of electoral sway" in Mark Crispin Miller, "Suckers for Elections," *NYTBR,* 8 February 1987, 32; and "women's different fantasies" in Christine Froula, "So Many Female Rivals," *NYTBR,* 7 February 1988, 13. See also, e.g., Daniel Goleman, "For Some People, Half of Day Is Spent in Fantasy," *New York Times,* 15 December 1987, sec. C, 1–2. The word or concept is used most extensively, e.g., in Jerrold Seigel, *Bohemian Paris: Culture, Politics, and the Boundaries of Bourgeois Life, 1830–1930* (New York, 1987). Sometimes, too, the word *dream* is used, as in "a dream of 'cultural wholeness'" (Daniel R. Browder, "Review of Books," *American Historical Review* 91, no. 5 [December 1986]: 1244). See also Taylor, *Cavalier and Yankee,* 16, 21; Leo Marx, *The Machine in the Garden* (New York, 1964), 6.

29. Don Locke, *A Fantasy of Reason: The Life and Thought of William Godwin* (London, 1980), 8. The idea or concept of fantasy is discussed systematically (though not in psychoanalytic terms) by John L. Caughey, *Imaginary Social Worlds: A Cultural Approach* (Lincoln, Nebr., 1984), 157–96.

30. Georg Lukacs, *History and Class Consciousness,* trans. Rodney Livingstone (Cambridge, Mass., 1971), 27 (translation altered for the sake of readability).

31. "On many occasions there would come a . . . moment when the mind liberated itself from the body and went off independently into the most incredible flights of fantasy. This detachment of the mental faculties from the miseries of the flesh may have its parallels in drug-taking or religious trances, but for us it was an involuntary act of self-preservation that protected some of us from going stark, staring ravers, leaving us just mildly demented" (quoted in Bill Mauldin, review of *To the Kwai—and Back: War Drawings, 1939–1945,* by Ronald Searle, *NYTBR,* 10 August 1986, 10).

32. Ernst Bloch, *The Principle of Hope,* trans. Neville Plaice, Stephen Plaice, and Paul Knight, 2 vols. (Cambridge, Mass., 1986), 1:6–7, 11–13.

33. Ibid., 10. The use of the phrase *dream-construct* is arbitrary, mostly a matter of keeping the language consistent, as Lenin at this point changed his

language (V. I. Lenin, "Chto delat'?" in *Sochineniia,* 4th ed., 39 vols. [Moscow, 1951–60], 5:476). See also Lenin, "What's to Be Done?" 510. The editors here refer to fantasy (fantasies), although their own use of language is not consistent (see n. 41 below).

34. V. I. Lenin, "Philosophical Notebooks," in *Collected Works,* 38:372–73.

35. Leon Trotsky, *The New Course,* translated with an introduction by Max Shachtman (Ann Arbor, Mich. 1965), 55.

36. V. I. Lenin, "Eighth Party Congress of the R.C.P. (B.)," in *Collected Works,* 29:152.

37. V. I. Lenin, "Our Revolution," in ibid., 33:480.

38. Lenin, "How to Organize Competition," 413.

39. Ibid.

40. V. I. Lenin, "Seventh Congress of the R.C.P. (B.)," in *Collected Works,* 27:129–30.

41. V. I. Lenin, "Desiatyi s'ezd RKP(b)," in *Sochineniia,* 32:193, and "Tenth Congress of the R.C.P. (B.)," in *Collected Works,* 32:216–17. The problem referred to in n. 33 above recurs here in a very unfavorable way. It should be noted not only that did Lenin not pursue the negative prospect but that he went on to say that—in spite of the kinds of errors he was already familiar with—there is nothing wrong in such fantasizing for without it no one would have dared to conceive of revolution in a country like Russia. Lenin and Freud had pretty much the same sense of the matter: without fantasy thinking, there would be no movement. Both believed that there was no risk in the process because it is controlled by a commitment to rigorous objectivity and relentless criticism. There are some things wrong with this position, however; for one, they take their own mastery of intentions and situations far too much for granted. But, more important, their point of view is based on the belief that the audience that they address simply takes what they say in the spirit that they mean to convey. But what if the audience misperceives that spirit, or takes what they say too concretely, or misses the significance of metaphoric expression, or has goals, needs, and even agendas for which they have not calculated?

42. Leszek Kolakowski, *Main Currents of Marxism,* 3 vols. (New York, 1982), 3:523, 524.

43. For an explicitly conservative reference, see Marjorie Brierly, "'Hardy Perennials' and Psychoanalysis," *IJPA* 50 (1969): 450. For liberal and radical references, see respectively, Erikson, *Childhood and Society;* and Marcuse, *Eros and Civilization.* Jay Cantor, in a review of *The Peron Novel,* by Tomás Eloy Martinez ("Don't Cry for Him"), refers to this phenomenon specifically, quoting "Peron" as follows: "The reason I've been a leading figure in history time and time again is precisely because I have contradicted myself."

44. The concept of fantasy has been amplified in many directions since Freud's initial explanation of it. The familiar and by now anachronistic structural theory compelled amplification. For example, Joseph Sandler and others have pointed out that the "force" behind wishful strivings need not be an instinctual drive but can just as readily be the need to avoid painful experience,

to preserve a sense of safety and well-being, defined in terms of continuity, self-esteem, a sense of adequacy, and so forth (Joseph Sandler, "Dreams, Unconscious Fantasies and 'Identity of Perception,'" *International Review of Psychoanalysis* 3, no. 1 [1976]: 36). But many others, including Melanie Klein, D. W. Winnicott, and Heinz Hartmann, have also elaborated the concept in different ways. For a brief overview, see Greenberg and Mitchell, *Object Relations in Psychoanalytic Theory.* Hartmann, for one, has explained that fantasy thinking enables one to approach problems from a different perspective, imagining solutions that would not have resulted from more logical, disciplined thought (ibid., 240).

45. Jerome Neu, "Fantasy and Memory: The Aetiological Role of Thoughts According to Freud," *IJPA* 54, no. 4 (1973): 383–97.

46. Jean-Jacques Rousseau, *Émile ou de l'éducation* (Paris, 1961), 64. Rousseau claimed here that realistic thinking is limited but that fantasy thinking is not, the other point of view.

47. Fantasy thinking, indispensable to creative activity, is also permitted in the privileged confines of the therapist's office. But it may be worth one's life to try and act on fantasy in the everyday world. In fact, the strategy of psychoanalytic therapy is to remove the individual, as much as any social arrangement can allow, from the sense of time and of the outside world, permitting or facilitating the process of fantasy thinking. These premises guided the action in Bernardo Bertolucci's *The Last Tango in Paris* (1972).

48. I have relied here on Jean G. Schimek, "The Interpretation of the Past: Childhood Trauma, Psychical Reality and Historical Truth," *JAPA* 23, (1975): 854–55, and "A Critical Re-examination of Freud's Concept of Unconscious Mental Representation." On the contentless quality of drives, see Allan Compton, "The Current Status of the Psychoanalytic Theory of Instinctual Drives," *Psychoanalytic Quarterly* 52, no. 3 (1983): 365.

49. Sigmund Freud, *Totem and Taboo,* in *Standard Edition,* 13:159–60.

50. Ibid., 160.

51. See the discussion in Neu, "Fantasy and Memory," 383–84.

52. Josef Breuer and Sigmund Freud, *Studies on Hysteria,* in *Standard Edition,* 2:176–78, 69–70n.

53. This story was told by Frank J. Sulloway, *Freud, Biologist of the Mind* (New York, 1983), 199–204, 259–61, 385–90; for the short version of it, see Stephen Jay Gould, "Freud's Phylogenetic Fantasy," *Natural History* 12 (1987): 10–19. See Freud, *Totem and Taboo,* 158, and *From the History of an Infantile Neurosis,* in *Standard Edition,* 18:97.

54. See n. 54, chap. 1, and the text at that note.

55. Karl Marx, *Early Writings,* ed. and trans. T. B. Bottomore, with a foreword by Erich Fromm (New York, 1964), xiii.

56. Leon Trotsky, *Literature and Revolution* (New York, 1957), 254–56.

57. Marx, *Early Writings,* 155; on the subject of private property and Communism, see 153–67. On the reference to *A Contribution to the Critique of Political Economy* (the bourgeois mode of production is the last antagonistic mode), see Bender, ed., *Karl Marx,* 162–63.

58. Freud, *The Psychopathology of Everyday Life*, 258–59.

59. See, e.g., Thompson, *Studies in the Theory of Ideology*, 137.

60. Sigmund Freud, "Heredity and the Neuroses," in *Standard Edition*, 3:153.

61. Freud, "Inhibitions, Symptoms and Anxiety," 150; Basch, "The Concept of Affect: A Re-examination," 759, 775; Lachmann and Stolorow, "The Developmental Significance of Affective States," 215; Modell, "Affects and the Complementarity of Biologic and Historical Meaning," 168; Meissner, "Can Psychoanalysis Find Its Self?" 393. In addition, as late as 1987 we still find references to countertransference as a "neglected topic" and to "the relatively sparse discussion of counter-transference," although the situation is not nearly as one sided as it used to be (Blatt and Bahrends, "Internalization, Separation-Individuation, and the Nature of Therapeutic Action," 282). According to Blatt and Bahrends, it was not until 1984 that "the term countertransference ever appeared in the title of a program at the meetings of the American Psychoanalytic Association." See also Limentani, "Presidential Address: Variations on Some Freudian Themes."

62. Riccardo Steiner, "The Controversial Discussions," *International Review of Psychoanalysis* 12, no. 1 (1985): 41.

63. Robert B. Reich, "The New 'Competitiveness' Fad," *New York Times*, 14 January 1987, sec. A, 27 (Reich discussed four different definitions of *competitiveness*). Mark A. Uhlig, "Milk Industry in New York Is in Upheaval," *New York Times*, 3 August 1987, sec. A, 1; sec. B, 5 (dairy industry spokespeople claimed that competition only produces chaos in the marketplace, i.e., in their marketplace). William Roberts, "Farm Prospects Better, but Worries Increase," *New York Times*, 14 January 1987, sec. A, 12. William Robbins, "After a Year of Subsidized Gains, Signs of New Hope," *New York Times*, 14 February 1988, sec. 4, 4. Milt Freudenheim, "A.M.A. Board Studies Ways to Curb Supply of Physicians," *New York Times*, 14 June 1986, sec. A, 1.

64. See, e.g., James P. McCollom, *The Continental Affair: The Rise and Fall of the Continental Illinois Bank* (New York, 1987).

65. Freudenheim, "A.M.A. Board Studies Ways to Curb Supply of Physicians," 15. Jonathan Rose, "Who Said We Have too Many Doctors?" *New York Times*, 29 June 1986, sec. 3, 2. However, the Justice Department later, in 1988, under Richard Thornburgh, did say that price fixing among doctors and dentists would be investigated. See Milton Freudenheim, "Doctors' Concern: Fixing Prices and Price Fixing," *New York Times*, 18 December 1988, sec. 4, 7.

66. On Winnicott and religion, see W. W. Meissner, *Psychoanalysis and Religious Experience* (New Haven, Conn., 1984), 164–79; on art and literary criticism, see Rosemary Dinnage, "A Bit of Light," in *Between Reality and Fantasy: Transitional Objects and Phenomena*, ed. Simon A. Grolnick and Leonard Barkin (New York, 1979), 366. Dinnage argues that imaginative powers were misrepresented by classical psychoanalysis, especially with reference to the ability to produce art. She is not the first to have promoted this argument. On sociology, see Aaron David Gresson III, "Transitional Metaphors and the Political Psychology of Identity Maintenance," in *Cognition, Symbolism and Meta-*

phor, ed. Robert E. Haskell (Norwood, N.J., 1987). See also, e.g., Christopher Lasch, *The Minimal Self: Psychic Survival in Troubled Times* (New York, 1984), 193–95.

67. See Winnicott's classic paper "Transitional Objects and Transitional Phenomena: A Study of the First Not-Me Possession," *IJPA* 34 (1953): 1–25. See also his *The Maturation Process and the Facilitating Environment* (New York, 1965), and *Playing and Reality* (New York, 1971).

68. Charles Rycroft, *Psychoanalysis and Beyond,* edited with an introduction by Peter Fuller (Chicago, 1986), 20, 141–42. For a different view of Winnicott, see F. Robert Rodman, ed., *The Spontaneous Gesture: Selected Letters of D. W. Winnicott* (Cambridge, Mass., 1987).

69. According to Rycroft, Winnicott was "a meliorist, believing in the efficacy of maternal love in leading man towards faith, hope and charity," leading him to a degree of blindness "to things masculine and sexual" (*Psychoanalysis and Beyond,* 120, 142).

70. Oliver Sacks linked Winnicott's work to that of L. S. Vygotsky on language as a transitional object. See Sacks's review "What's It Like to Be a Child," *NYTBR,* 24 May 1987, 21. L. S. Vygotsky, *Thought and Language,* ed. and trans. Eugenia Hanfmann and Gertrude Vakar (Cambridge, Mass., 1962).

71. Berger and Luckmann, *The Social Construction of Reality.*

72. Sir Henry Sumner Maine, *Popular Government* (London, 1885), 61. Weinstein and Platt, *Psychoanalytic Sociology,* 102–6.

73. Gerald M. Platt has generously allowed me to adapt these (modified) paragraphs on speakers and audience from an as-yet unpublished paper of his, also on the subject of ideology, a subject on which we have different views.

74. P. N. Medvedev/Mikhail Bakhtin, *The Formal Method in Literary Scholarship: A Critical Introduction to Sociological Poetics,* trans. Albert J. Wehrle (Baltimore, 1978), 14.

75. Geertz, "Ideology as a Cultural System," 216, 217–18.

76. Ibid., 216. See also Victor Turner, "Social Dramas and Stories about Them," in *On Narrative,* ed. W. J. T. Mitchell (Chicago, 1981), 152.

77. Frances Fitzgerald, "Reporter at Large," *New Yorker,* 28 July 1986, 61.

78. William M. Reddy, *Money and Liberty in Modern Europe: A Critique of Historical Understanding* (New York, 1987), esp. 74. Reddy has written recently as well that money is used as a liberating technique, but his viewpoint is vastly different from the one presented here.

Chapter Four

1. Liz Harris, "Holy Days, Pt. 1," *New Yorker,* 16 September 1985, 42. The Hasidic movement is described here as centered on its leaders, who are noted as much for their charisma as for their piety and scholarliness, even though the leadership is traditionally passed on "from generation to generation, in dynastic fashion." For Hollywood's definition of charisma, see Aljean

Harmatz, "Crossing the Line to Stardom," *New York Times,* 7 June 1987, Arts and Leisure section, 42.

2. The idea of clothing as charismatic appeared in the supplement to the *Daily Hampshire Gazette,* 16 September 1985, 9.

3. In two books on the subject of charismatic leadership published in the same year, one author stated that the British "may not be susceptible to charismatic affect" and that Winston Churchill was not a charismatic leader, while the second stated by contrast that "Churchill possessed the gift of natural charisma." See the review by A. J. Wilson, *American Historical Review* 90, no. 3 (June 1985): 651.

4. Talcott Parsons discussed "charismatic movements" in terms of the psychological insecurities that arise "where established routines, expectations and symbols are broken up or are under attack" (introduction to Max Weber, *The Theory of Social and Economic Organization,* ed. Talcott Parsons [New York, 1964], 71). Clifford Geertz explains the other view in "Centers, Kings, and Charisma: Symbolics of Power," in *Local Knowledge,* 121–46.

5. See Anthony Giddens, "Jürgen Habermas," in *The Return of Grand Theory in the Human Sciences,* ed. Quentin Skinner (Cambridge, 1985), 121–40, esp. 131.

6. One crucial criterion of this conclusion is the extent to which integrative rather than rebellious behavior is expected. The therapeutic situation does not by definition obligate integrative as opposed to rebellious behavior, but it is safe to say that the majority of psychoanalysts, perhaps the overwhelming number, would consider that they had done their job correctly if things worked out that way. But, in addition to the fact that insight, rather than being self-generated, is guided in terms of received cultural conceptions of autonomy, measured in part by the ability to find the analyst and in part also by the ability to pay the fees, there is also the fact that psychoanalysis is on principle interminable, and there are reasons for that that involve authority. In an earlier work (Weinstein and Platt, *The Wish to Be Free,* 138), Gerald Platt and I referred to an observation of Heinz Hartmann's on the increased insight into mental processes that occurs as one means of coping with turbulent, disruptive conditions. I would emphasize now that this has not yet occurred anywhere except in the presence of an authoritative figure.

7. Michel Foucault, "The Subject and Power," in *Michel Foucault: Beyond Structuralism and Hermeneutics,* ed. Hubert L. Dreyfus and Paul Rabinow (Chicago, 1982), 208–26.

8. Weber, *Economy and Society,* 1:241–42, 2:1112–13.

9. Norman H. Baynes, ed., *The Speeches of Adolf Hitler, April 1922–August 1939,* 2 vols (New York, 1969), 1:321 (translation revised).

10. Hitler, *Mein Kampf,* 42, 107, 249, 342, 351, 355, 377, 471 ("mysterious powers"), 478, 532.

11. V. I. Lenin, "The Immediate Tasks of the Soviet Government," in *Collected Works,* 27:241.

12. V. I. Lenin, "To the Population," in ibid., 26:297.

13. Weber, *Economy and Society,* 1:243, 2:1115.

14. See the interesting paper by John Camic, "Charisma: Its Varieties, Preconditions, and Consequences," in *Advances in Psychoanalytic Sociology,* ed. Rabow, Platt, and Goldman, 238–76.

15. Nikita Khrushchev, *Texte integral du rapport secret de M. Khrouchtchev* (Paris, 1956), 57, 60, 62, 65–67, 73, 75–76, 80, 92.

16. I have not included Hitler in this context because he never got the chance to attack his own public in the same way as these others did, though he would no doubt have welcomed the chance, having given ample evidence with his attack on the terminally ill, the insane, and crippled people.

17. *Resolution on CPC History 1949–1981)* (Beijing, 1981), 27–36.

18. Weber, *Economy and Society,* 1:252.

19. Quoted in Buel, *Securing the Revolution,* 108. See also, e.g., John Locke, "Error," in *The Life of John Locke with Extracts from his Correspondence, Journals and Common-place Books,* by Lord King, 2 vols. (London, 1830), 2:75–76.

20. Sudhir Kakar, an Indian psychoanalyst trained in the United States, has commented on the difficulty of his task in India in just these terms: "The purpose of psychoanalysis is to free a person to make some choices. . . . You are trying to help a patient become autonomous. That goes completely against the cultural grain of India, where the emphasis has always been on one's obligations to family or community" (Steven R. Weisman, "Indian Analyst Turns Freudian Eye on His Compatriots," *New York Times,* 20 January 1988, sec. C, 1).

21. Weber, *Economy and Society,* 2:1127–28.

22. See the special issue of *American Quarterly* (vol. 37, no. 4 [1985]) devoted largely to "Republicanism in the History and Historiography of the United States," particularly the paper by the special editor, Joyce Appleby, "Republicanism and Ideology," 461–73.

23. J. R. Pole, *Foundations of American Independence, 1763–1815* (Indianapolis, 1972), 125. Pole quotes the Reverend John Murray in a sermon of 1783 attacking "the love of money," which "by whatever means obtained, rages universally."

24. The language is that of William Beers of Connecticut, 1791, quoted in Buel, *Securing the Revolution,* 101.

25. Henry Sumner Maine, *Ancient Law* (Gloucester, Mass., 1970), 163–64.

26. Burckhardt, *The Civilization of the Renaissance in Italy,* pt. 2, p. 81.

27. George Feaver, *From Status to Contract: A Biography of Sir Henry Maine, 1822–1888* (London, 1969), 58. A good short introducution to the typological tradition that distinguishes premodern or traditional from modern societies in terms of character, internalized morality, emotional constraint, independence from political and other forms of authority, and the like is John C. McKinney and Charles P. Loomis, "The Application of Gemeinschaft and Gesellschaft as Related to Other Typologies," in Tönnies, *Community and Society,* 12–25. This introduction includes a brief discussion of Parsons's "Pattern Variables of Action Orientation." The authors mention here a fifth "pattern vari-

able," "collectivity orientation/Self-Orientation," that was later dropped by Parsons in order to avoid condemning socialist systems to a premodern status by definition (and to make his scheme more symmetrical).

28. Talcott Parsons, "Comparative Studies and Evolutionary Change," in *Comparative Methods in Sociology,* ed. Ivan Vallier (Berkeley, Calif., 1971), 116–17. Tocqueville, *Democracy in America,* 1:243.

29. These different aspects of criticism, with the exception of the reintegration of affect in everyday life, are discussed in Anthony D. Smith, *The Concept of Social Change: A Critique of the Functionalist Theory of Social Change* (London, 1973), 61, 67. See also, e.g., Buel, *Securing the Revolution,* 75.

30. Weinstein and Platt, *The Wish to Be Free,* 197–203.

31. Natalie Zemon Davis, "Boundaries and the Sense of Self in Sixteenth Century France," in *Reconstructing Individualism,* ed. Thomas Heller et al. (Stanford, Calif., 1986), 53.

32. Clifford Geertz, "Religion as a Cultural System," in *The Interpretation of Cultures,* 99.

33. Geertz, "Ideology as a Cultural System," 220. See also Nelson, "Cultural Cues and Directive Systems."

34. From an ad run often by the *New York Times,* e.g., 5 June 1988, sec. 4, 28. On Publilius Syrus, see N. G. L. Hammond and H. H. Scullard, eds., *Oxford Classical Dictionary,* 2d ed. (Oxford, 1970), 899. John Kenneth Galbraith, *Money: Whence It Came, Where It Went* (Boston, 1975), 2.

35. Charles Dickens, *Dombey and Son,* ed. Alan Horsman (London, 1974), 93–94. See also, e.g., A. E. Monroe, *Monetary Theory before Adam Smith* (New York, 1966); or Noel W. Thompson, *The People's Science: The Popular Political Economy of Exploitation and Crisis, 1816–1834* (Cambridge, 1984).

36. Max Weber, *The Protestant Ethic and the Spirit of Capitalism,* trans. Talcott Parsons (New York, 1958), 48–49, 50–51.

37. For Stendhal, see Frederic Ewen, *Heroic Imagination: The Creative Genius of Europe from Waterloo (1815) to the Revolution of 1848* (Secaucus, N.J., 1984), 438. For Channing, see Robert H. Wiebe, *The Opening of American Society* (New York, 1984), 289. For Trollope, see Neil Harris, *Humbug: The Art of P. T. Barnum* (Boston, 1973), 71.

38. Tocqueville, *Democracy in America,* 2:270, 273.

39. Benjamin Nelson, *The Idea of Usury: From Tribal Brotherhood to Universal Otherhood,* 2d ed. (Chicago, 1969), 127n.

40. Harris, *Humbug,* 155–56. On the English visitor, see Gunther Barth, *City People: The Rise of Modern City Culture in Nineteenth Century America* (New York, 1980), 20. On the stalled trains, see *New York Times,* 12 March 1988, sec. B, 1. Edgar Allan Poe, "The Philosophy of Furniture," in *The Complete Works of Edgar Allan Poe,* 12 vols. (Boston, 1902), 10:101–2, 106. The visitor's comment is from 1864; Poe's essay originally appeared in 1840.

41. Walt Whitman, *Democratic Vistas* (New York, 1949), 51, 10–11, 61, 66–67. John C. Cawelti, *Apostles of the Self-Made Man: Changing Concepts of Success in America* (Chicago, 1968), 81–82.

42. James, *The American Scene,* xiv–xv, 11, 76–77, 80, 83, 94, 159–61,

164, 192. Mary Kupiec Cayton, "The Making of an American Prophet: Emerson, His Audiences, and the Rise of the Culture Industry in Nineteenth Century America," *American Historical Review* 92, no. 3 (June 1987):614–15, 619.

43. Karl Marx, *Grundrisse: Foundations of the Critique of Political Economy,* trans. Martin Nicolaus (Harmondsworth, 1973), 115–238, "The Chapter on Money," esp. 202, 216, 223. Weber, *Economy and Society,* 1:75–84, 166–79. Sigmund Freud, "Character and Anal Erotism," in *Standard Edition,* 9:173–75, and "On Transformations of Instinct as Exemplified in Anal Erotism," in ibid., 17:128, 131.

44. Maine, *Popular Government,* 51.

45. Marx, *Grundrisse,* 232–33. See also Marx, *Early Writings,* 169–73, 189–94.

46. Tönnies, *Community and Society,* 74, 81, 94, 124–25.

47. Simmel, *The Philosophy of Money,* 303.

48. Ibid., 150–51, 225–27, 237–39, 296. For the bureaucratic perils of modern industrial organization, whether capitalist or socialist, see Alvin Gouldner, *Against Fragmentation: The Origins of Marxism and the Sociology of Intellectuals* (New York, 1985), 83. On an exchange economy becoming less hierarchical, see also Marx, *Grundrisse,* 204.

49. Marx, *Grundrisse,* 158–59.

50. Marx, *Early Writings,* 176.

51. Marx, *Grundrisse,* 225. Karl Marx and Friedrich Engels, *The German Ideology,* ed. C. J. Arthur (New York, 1978), 53.

52. Nils A. Nilsson, "Spring 1918: The Arts and the Commissars," in *Art, Society, Revolution: Russia, 1917–1921,* ed. Nils A. Nilsson (Uppsala, 1979), 42–43, 48.

53. Leon Trotsky, *History of the Russian Revolution,* trans. Max Eastman, 3 vols. (Ann Arbor, Mich., 1960), 1:329–30.

54. Victor Serge, *Year One of the Revolution,* ed. and trans. Peter Sedgwick (Chicago, 1972), 60–61.

55. Garry Wills, *Reagan's America: Innocents at Home* (New York, 1987).

56. Michael Wallace, "Reagan and History," *Tikkun* 2, no. 1 (1987): 16–17.

57. Reagan declared to the American Bar Association in 1983 that "one of my dreams is to help Americans rise above pessimism by renewing their belief in themselves" (ibid., 15).

58. Buel, *Securing the Revolution,* 122, 107.

59. E. D. Hirsch, Jr., *Cultural Literacy: What Every American Needs to Know* (Boston, 1987), 1–2. Hirsch indicated that only two-thirds of the public is literate and that "even among those the average level is too low and should be raised."

60. It pays to review Habermas's uses of Nietzsche in this context—see *Knowledge and Human Interests,* 290–300.

61. Weber, *The Protestant Ethic and the Spirit of Capitalism,* 182.

62. Joseph A. Schumpeter, *Capitalism, Socialism and Democracy* (New York, 1975), 141–42. Adams, *The Education of Henry Adams,* 419.

63. Marx, *Grundrisse,* 161–62.

64. I have not included the terms offered by the conventional professional social sciences because they are much more empirical and hence self-correcting.

65. Gerald M. Platt, "Structuralism," in *The Encyclopedic Dictionary of Psychology,* ed. R. Harre and R. Lamb (Oxford, 1983).

66. Karl Marx and Friedrich Engels, *The Holy Family, or Critique of Critical Criticism: Against Bruno Bauer and Company* (Moscow, 1975), 44–45. Bloch, *The Principle of Hope,* 205. Hence also Louis Althusser's claim that the real protagonists of history are the social relations of production etc. (Louis Althusser and Etienne Balibar, *Reading Capital,* trans. B. Brewster [London, 1970], 180). See also, e.g., Nicos Poulantzas, *Classes in Contemporary Capitalism,* trans. D. Fernbach (London, 1975).

67. Paul Ricoeur, *History and Truth* (Evanston, Ill., 1965), 213, 126–28.

68. Bloch, *The Principle of Hope,* 1:4–10, and passim.

69. Bellah et al., *Habits of the Heart,* e.g., 270–71.

70. J. P. Stern, *Hitler: The Führer and the People* (Hassocks, 1975), 90. Max Domarus, *Hitler Reden und Proklemationen, 1932–1945,* 2 vols. (Würzburg, 1962), 1:641; see also 570, Hitler's speech of 30 January 1936, where he declared, "I have founded this SA. . . . I have led you for the last fourteen years. I have learned to know you. I know that everything you are, you have become through me; everything I am, I am only because of you." See also Baynes, ed., *The Speeches of Adolf Hitler,* 207. Stern's text is the most useful for our purposes because he underscores all the biblical references and connections in the speech quoted.

71. Bloch, *The Principle of Hope,* 1:4–10, and passim.

72. Edel and Powers, eds., *The Compete Notebooks of Henry James,* 30, 61–62, 78, 190.

73. See the summary discussion in Edwin Haviland Miller, *Melville* (New York, 1975), 192–203.

74. Herman Melville, *Moby-Dick,* ed. Harrison Hayford and Hershel Parker (New York, 1967), 71, 99, 162. "They were bent on profitable cruises, the profit to be counted down in dollars from the mint."

75. Ibid., 184, 160–61, where Melville refers to Ahab as mad, crazy, and monomaniacal and Ahab states, famously, "All my means are sane, my motive and my object mad."

76. Ibid., 129, 131, 141–43, 147. "'Twas not so hard a task," Ahab says.

77. Ibid., 183–84. "They may scorn cash now; but let some months go by, and no perspective promise of it to them, and then this same quiescent cash all at once mutinying in them, this same cash would soon cashier Ahab."

78. Ibid.

79. Ibid., 455. For Melville's version of multiple perspectives, see 360–62.

80. Ibid., 348–49. These remarkable passages are often quoted. See Marx, *The Machine in the Garden,* 304–5; or Rowland A. Sherrill, *The Prophetic Melville: Experience, Transcendence, and Tragedy* (Athens, Ga., 1979), 156.

81. On "attainable felicity," see Melville, *Moby-Dick,* 349. See also Mel-

ville's letter to Nathaniel Hawthorne, 1 [?] June 1851, in *The Portable Melville*, ed. Jan Leyda (New York, 1975), 433–34, where all this is discussed.

82. On "separate identities," see Melville, *Moby-Dick*, 349. On Ishmael's rationalizations of relationships to authority, pay, and evasion, see ibid., 15. On the image of "rural tranquillity," see Marx, *The Machine in the Garden*, 305. In relation to the issue raised by Marx, technology and the pastoral ideal, see John F. Kasson, *Civilizing the Machine: Technology and Republican Values in America, 1776–1900* (New York, 1977).

83. The existence of a labor shortage now and for the future is being publicized, and there likely is such a shortage—at the local burger joint, the supermarket and discount outlet checkout stands—of domestic help of various sorts and so on. These jobs, which pay minimum or close to minimum wages, for the greatest part have no fringe benefits and especially no medical coverage.

84. See White, *Tropics of Discourse*, 1–23, and passim.

85. Saul Bellow, *Mr. Sammler's Planet* (New York, 1970)—the quotation is from 3, the reference to explanatory constructions as fictions 19.

86. On Norman Mailer, see n. 27, chap. 1, and the accompanying text.

87. Melville, *Moby-Dick*, 12–15.

88. Ibid., 360–61; and n.75 above.

89. See William H. Sewell, Jr., "Uneven Development, the Autonomy of Politics, and the Dockworkers of Nineteenth Century Marseille," *American Historical Review* 93, no. 3 (June 1988): 637. On the theoretical significance of these several questions, see Platt, "The Psychoanalytic Sociology of Collective Behavior," 232–35.

90. See also, e.g., Joan W. Scott, "Deconstructing Equality-versus-Difference: or, the Uses of Poststructuralist Theory for Feminism," *Feminist Studies* 14, no. 1 (Spring 1988): 33–50.

Index